P.O.V.

LIVING

THE GUY'S GUIDE TO GETTING AHEAD, GETTING IT RIGHT, AND GETTING BY WITH STYLE

LARGE

RANDALL LANE AND THE EDITORS OF P.O.V.

HarperPerennial
A Division of HarperCollinsPublishers

P.O.V. LIVING LARGE. Copyright © 1998 by Randall Lane and the editors of *P.O.V.* magazine. All rights reserved. Printed in the United States of America. No part of this book may be used or reproduced in any manner whatsoever without written permission except in the case of brief quotations embodied in critical articles and reviews. For information address HarperCollins*Publishers*, Inc., 10 East 53rd Street, New York, New York 10022.

HarperCollins books may be purchased for educational, business, or sales promotional use. For information, please write to: Special Markets Department, HarperCollins Publishers, Inc., 10 East 53rd Street, New York, New York 10022.

FIRST EDITION

Design by Charles Kreloff

ISBN 0–06–273521–7

Library of Congress Cataloging-in-Publication Data
Lane, Randall.
  P.O.V. living large : the guy's guide to getting ahead, getting it right, and getting it often / by Randall Lane and the editors of P.O.V. — 1st ed.
        p.   cm.
  ISBN 0–06–273521–7 (pbk.)
  1. Single men—Life skills guides. 2. Bachelors—Life skills guides. I. P.O.V. (New York, N.Y.) II. Title.
  HQ800.3.L36 1998   98–21260
  646.7'0086'52—dc21   CIP

98 99 00 01 02 ◆/RRD 10 9 8 7 6 5 4 3

CONTENTS

**GILLETTE
SENSOR EXCEL:**
The finest shaving blade known to man.

STEAK, MEDIUM RARE:

Or, at most, medium. A true carnivore enjoys the taste of meat.

TWO CREDIT CARDS: Do you really need more?

ZIPPO LIGHTER:
Even if you don't
smoke, it's a
classy accessory.

PAYING ON THE FIRST DATE:

As rudimentary as opening a door.

ACKNOWLEDGMENTS

Any book is a collabrative effort, this one more than most. Much of this material was based upon or inspired by articles that appeared in *P.O.V.* magazine. Special credit belongs to Adam Kleiner who was instrumental in seeing this project to fruition. *P.O.V.* editors Michael Callahan, Larry Smith, Edward Sussman, Ty Wenger and Cheryl Della Pietra all shaped the stories that help shape the book. And numerous *P.O.V.* writers delivered pieces that contibrute to the backbone of *Living Large*. Among the noteworthy: Tony Alessandra, Chuck Arehart, Amy Beim, Nicole Beland, Zev Borow, Vicki Botnick, Micheal Bradley, Bill Brent, Adam Buckley Cohen, Chris Cronis, Marla Cukor, Mubarak S. Dahir, Brian Dawson, Sherise Dorf, Ted Doyle, Malachy Duffy, Jeff Edelstein, Rachel Elson, Cheryl Family, Michael Finkel, Chris Franchino, Laura Fraser, David Futrelle, Anthony Giglio, Chris Hamel, Lou Harry, Jay Heinrichs, Woody Hochswender, Allan Hoffman, Kevin Hogan, Darren Kani, Chuck Kapelke, Jenny Kellner, Jonas Kleiner, Michael Learmonth, Jon Lesser, Rebecca Lewin, James Lowell, Philippe Mao, Rudy Maxa, Tom McGrath, Patrick O'Donnell, Larry Olmsted, Andrew Page, Faye Penn, Carlos A. Rosas, Chris Rubin, John Rubino, Alison Schecter, Regina Schrambling, Alan Sepinwall, Jenn Shreve, Robin Sidel, Michelle Silver, Richard Sine, Peter Spiegel, Morey Stettner, Andrew Strickman, Bert Sugar, David Templeton, Julie Tilsner,

THANK YOU NOTES:

Because courtesy never goes out of style.

Salvatore Tuzzeo, Jim Waltzer and Brad Wieners. Drew Massey, Allison Hemming, Chris Sugden and Jay Goldberg were the people behind the people, providing crucial support for the project. And our editor at HarperCollins, Jay Papasan, kept on our ass, and made sure the train ran on time.

INTRODUCTION

I was once hurled this most creative of insults: "You're such a . . . guy."

To which I had a prompt response: "Thank you."

A guy is different from a man (that's your dad) or a boy (that's your nephew). Your Guy Period is that brief window between college and lifelong commitment, a time heavy on adventurousness and disposable income, low on know-how. The stakes are considerable: Fail at guydom, and you're just another overgrown frat boy or Peter Pan complex waiting to happen. But if you can pull it off, if you can be the consummate guy—fun, daring, smart, creative and stylish— the world is yours for the taking. It's a state of being we call Living Large.

Alas, mastering the art of being a guy is a tricky proposition. There are enough choices in every aspect of our lives to boggle our booze-addled brains. Our career options are unlimited. Go corporate, gaining knowledge and stock options, or take advantage of technology, start a company and starve while waiting for the big payoff? Investing our hard-earned jack presents even more opportunities: thousands of stocks and mutual funds, or still fancier and riskier investments—anything but the interest-bearing checking account.

At night, we can choose from 20 different cuts of steak, order a bottle of wine from any one of 40 countries, and drive one of 60

A FIRM HANDSHAKE: It let's everyone know you mean business.

automobiles marketed to us. Weekends and vacations make the whole world available. And then there's women. From the first date (dinner or hike) to the last (when should I pop the question?) the ball's in our court. Even the final choice-free bastion for guys—fashion—has opened itself up. For most, work attire is entirely what you make of it, and even those in suits get Fridays to be creative. On weekends, remember that the ladies have judged you by the time they look at your shoes.

All these choices simply make it harder to get it right—but even sweeter when you do. That's where we come in. There are basic lessons, shortcuts and tricks in virtually every area of your life that can help you get more out of it. The aim of this book—and *P.O.V.* magazine every month—is to give you that coveted know-how, navigate a maze of options, and put you in the shoes she's looking for. It won't eliminate all the choices. And it may not make you the perfect person. But, hopefully, it will go a long way toward making the perfect guy.

—Randall Lane
June 1998

CHAPTER 1
STYLE

Q: BOXERS OR BRIEFS?

Some debates will never end. Bird or Magic? Hemingway or Fitzgerald? Tastes great or less filling? All of which is fine when it's just you and your buds chewing the fat at the corner bar. But are you prepared to defend yourself when what looks to be the best date of your life hinges on a simple query, "Boxers or briefs?"

Your answer could be the difference between a score and a shutout. While we all know women have very definite opinions on some things in your life—your shoes, your car, your mother—you might not realize just how important your skivvies are in her appraisal of you. Ask any woman and she'll tell you a man's choice of underwear speaks volumes about his self-confidence, style . . . even how she thinks he'll perform in the sack.

Ludicrous? Think about it. You go to a party and see two equally attractive women. You later find out one is wearing a matching silk bra and panties combo from Victoria's Secret, while the other is sporting I Can't Believe It's a Girdle. Which one are you going to pass the chip-and-dip bowl to?

Whether you like it or not, you're going to be judged by your underwear and how you look in it. And there's no more surefire mood killer in a seduction than dropping your pants and being

	BOXERS	BRIEFS	BOXER BRIEFS	NOTHING
BRAND	Joe Boxer flannel boxers, $12.99, 1 pair	Fruit of the Loom briefs, $4.49, 3 pack	Chereskin boxer briefs, $14.99, 2 pack	Nothing (free and easy)
FEELS LIKE	Having a comfy snuggle-soft blanket line your basket	Grammar-school gym class	Being vacuum sealed	A lot like Kramer— lettin' it all hang out
SEX APPEAL	Extra room makes her wonder what you're hiding	There's a reason why giant grapes and apples do the endorsing	Turns every man's soggy dough to buns of steel	Ain't nothing like the real thing, baby
DOWNSIDE	Bill Clinton	You argue, "Hey, I need the support"—can you back it up?	Good looks come with a price: they scrunch up like panty hose	Three beers + one girl = pup tent
FINAL ANALYSIS	Keeps your look loose and your sperm count high	Hey, if nobody's watching, wear what you want	Excellent for the indecisive— the surf 'n' turf of men's underwear	Tramps like you? Baby you were born to run

greeted with a snicker. With today's dizzying array of choices—from comfy flannel boxers to the ever-offensive thong—underwear has now surpassed ties as the gift for a woman to give her man for Valentine's Day. Take your drawers seriously. She does.

Q: HOW DO I BUY A GOOD PAIR OF SHOES?

When did buying shoes stop being fun? Since they stopped making anything your size with Velcro? When you realized it wasn't cool to wear the new pair out of the store? Or perhaps since your mom stopped paying for them?

It doesn't matter. The fact is that you're now faced with having to buy sensible, grown-up shoes and spending a decent chunk of change for the privilege. Don't fret. It's possible to find a pair that fit the criteria of being appropriate for the office, stylish enough for dates, and even comfortable. Now if you could just convince your mom to foot the bill . . .

The general rules for buying shoes haven't changed: when venturing to try them on (and always try them on), wear the kind of socks you're likely to wear with the shoes. Try to shop at the end of the day, when your feet are most swollen. And never rely on "breaking in" shoes; they should fit comfortably from the beginning.

Also, don't get preoccupied with size—shoe size, that is. Every brand runs differently. A good rule of thumb (or finger) is there should be about a half-inch of space between your heel and the back of the shoe. The tip of your index finger should suffice as a measuring tool. Also, if you have wider-than-average feet, buy wider-than-average shoes. Don't try to compensate by going one size larger.

What should your shoes be made of? Try to stay away from synthetic fibers—if the "upper" is the only thing that's leather (a common ploy), not only will your taste be questioned, your feet will sweat more than Ted Striker landing an airplane. Go for natural materials like leather and suede. These materials allow your feet to breath, reducing the chance of rash and athlete's foot.

Leather is also the best bet for soles because leather soles conform better to your walking pattern. If you walk a lot on asphalt and concrete and are afraid of wearing through leather soles, go to the shoemaker and invest ten bucks in rubber half-soles. Taps attached to the toe and heel are another good way to extend the life of your soles.

When it comes to style, you're on your own: it all depends on where you work and if you think Doc Marten's are still the latest. Square toes, split toes (with a seam in the front), monk strap closures (buckles), and rolled seams are all popular and often quite smart—it's all a matter of taste, where you work, and how much of a sense of style you possess. One of the fashion clueless? Oxfords, or lace-up shoes, are a good, dependable, and safe pick because they're timelessly classic and tend to be sturdier. Oxfords can also be laced several ways to loosen different parts of the shoe for individual comfort. One final word on style: Tassels? Keep moving.

Finally, there's the issue of cost. Shoes are an investment: you get what you pay for. Expect a decent pair to be priced in the hundred-dollar range. That said, you'd be wise to make them last. Alternate wear with at least one other pair of shoes, and use cedar shoe trees, which maintain appearance and form, prevent wrinkles, and can add years to your shoes' lives. (The scented wood is also perfect for absorbing moisture.) And polish the damn things, will you? While it may be true that nothing beats a great pair of legs, a buffed pair of killer shoes ain't bad.

BUILDING A CLASSIC WARDROBE

A BLACK TURTLENECK SWEATER: Women love 'em and no matter when the last time was that you made it to the gym, this'll make your shoulders look b-r-o-a-d.

Great masculine style is timeless, unchanging, and unfailingly traditional, right?

Well, actually, no. Men's clothing, like women's, is subject to the vagaries of the culture and the restless winds of fashion. Just take a look at a photograph of your father (or yourself) from the seventies, and you'll see. While changes in men's fashion tend to be evolutionary—with tiny incremental variations in, say, lapel and shoulder width each season—there is definitely an ebb and flow to the world of men's style. And one who fails to take note of this passing parade tends to be slightly out of it.

Contrary to the notion that manly men do not concern themselves with fashion, consider the fact that men of action throughout history have been in the forefront of sartorial innovation. Many of the hallmarks of men's fashion have a military heritage: the necktie or cravat (named for an eighteenth-century regiment of Croat soldiers who wore scarves around their necks); the lapel (early military uniforms); buttoned cuffs (Napoleon supposedly instituted them to keep his men from wiping their noses on their jackets); raglan sleeves (from Baron Raglan of Crimean War fame); and jacket vents (to enable cavalry officers to ride more comfortably). Today's sports stars are clearly among the most fashion-oriented men in the culture. It's safe to say that sports have had as profound an effect on contemporary dress as anything dreamed up lately in the design studios of Paris, Milan, or New York.

But what about the apparent irony that crowns men's fashion shows? After showing all manner of interesting cuts, wild patterns, and colorful furbelows on the catwalk, the fashion designer himself, the genius behind all this elegant energy, emerges from backstage to take a bow. Frequently—which is to say rather more than the mere laws of chance would dictate—that designer appears wearing a white oxford cotton shirt and khaki trousers. (T-shirt and jeans is another variation.) This is no coincidence, and it happens over and over again. The utilitarian virtues of this conspicuously nonfashion uniform for a designer are obvious: he can perform the frantic last-minute work of a fashion show unencumbered by any fussy style, while his own image will not detract from the message of his collection. But it also contains a hidden message for his consumers: that underlying all the moonshine of fashion, the purity of a white oxford cloth shirt and khaki trousers is absolute, and that such timeless essentials underpin even the most formidable and sophisticated wardrobes. Entire books have been written, and successful catalog businesses based, on this elementary concept.

Should your entire wardrobe be made of basics? Certainly not. But you can build from there.

The important thing for the well-dressed man is to be able to meet every occasion with the proper ensemble, and not to seem out of date within a year or two or even three of making a purchase. You neither want to be left behind nor totally be a slave to the moment. That doesn't mean you shouldn't buy one of the new body-fitted V-neck shirts or sweaters to go under your suit jacket, or spring for a pair of chic leather boots to wear with your flat-front pants. The question for any man is how to *adapt* the best fashions of his era to his own individual needs and, over time, to build a wardrobe composed of both solid basics and the more personal touches that mark him as a man of style. In this quest there is no substitute for taste, which can be acquired, and a respect for quality, which requires a bit of money. As critic Sir Max Beerbohm once wrote, "The stylish man must possess physical distinction, a sense of beauty, and either cash or credit."

However, plenty of men achieve a high level of personal style without spending a great deal of money. The artist and wildlife photographer Peter Beard always manages to float effortlessly through the most haute fashion circles, from the front row of Paris couture shows to black-tie galas at Lincoln Center, rigged out in what seems to be a wardrobe composed entirely of a few slightly shabby tweed and cashmere sport jackets, some oxford shirts, faded olive khakis, and leather sandals worn without socks, even in the dead of winter.

A WHITE SHIRT: Button-down or tee, under a sweater or alone, it's the one piece of clothing that really does look great with everything.

You might not be a louche socialite lensman with cadres of models hanging onto your every word, but the example is instructive. Less *is* more, especially in this circumspect age. Aggressive, trendy clothes nearly always subtract from the existential weight of the wearer. As the fashion designer John Weitz is fond of saying, *underwhelm* them.

Whatever the mandarins of Milan or the sultans of Seventh Avenue might be dictating for the season, the stylish man will always have certain things in his livery: a well-made, conservatively cut navy blazer; an English-type raincoat, either fly-front or trench, with a button-out lining; a sturdy topcoat in tweed, wool, or cashmere; a pair of cap-toed black or cordovan oxford shoes, and so on. He will very likely possess a revolving collection of a half-dozen carefully selected worsted-wool suits and a few more in cotton or linen; at least a dozen cotton dress shirts, several of which will be white, the rest in quiet pastel shades and perhaps a couple of French blues; and a generous supply of high-quality woven-silk ties. He will also have a dinner jacket or tuxedo of classic proportions; a set of gold or onyx studs; a few pairs of cufflinks (small); a tie bar or two; and shoe trees (either wooden or plastic will do).

AN OVERCOAT:
You don't look tough braving the elements in just your suit jacket. You look stupid.

These things, whatever the times and the fashions, come with the territory for the sartorially adept male. He may have a velvet evening jacket instead of, or in addition to, the classic black with grosgrain lapels; and he may have an ivory dinner jacket for summer wear. He may have a slim-fitting Gucci or Armani suit for chi-chi openings and nights on the town. He may have a deep collection of Hermès, Alan Flusser, or Gene Meyer ties. But the bones of the wardrobe will be in place. There is no real style without substance. It usually ends up being far more costly to buy what you consider a "cool" suit or sport jacket before you have established such a foundation.

The key to building a solid, enduring wardrobe is to purchase clothing that suits you particularly well—that complements your figure and face. If you are very heavyset, you should probably not wear patterned fabrics (except for pinstripes), and avoid double-breasted suits unless they are perfectly cut, since they can emphasize girth. Plaid is your enemy, suspenders your friend. Also, beware the button-down shirt, which makes a full face loom larger, and the Windsor knot, which, again, plays up the breadth of one's kisser. Short men should in most cases stick to dark-colored single-breasteds, with long lapels and natural shoulders. The athletic guy should shun wide shoulders and favor jackets with a low button stance. The tall, thin man can get away with a lot, but the new high-buttoning suits, with three, four, or more buttons, unfortunately tend to make him look like Ichabod Crane.

Clothing should also fit your station in life. The uptown businessman has a different set of sartorial needs than the downtown artist or the Silicon Alley pioneer. But even in these latter days of the twentieth century, when casual dress has invaded the sanctum sanctorum of IBM headquarters, the heart of a man's wardrobe (and, increasingly, a woman's) remains the suit.

Your first suit should be as timeless, as classic, and as perfect for your body as your wallet and shopping schedule allow. It should probably be blue, but dark gray is OK, too. (The black suit has recently come into vogue, but men of very fair coloring should pass on it.) The navy suit is the cornerstone of a man's wardrobe. Stylish, successful men typically own several. But if you own only one and you don't live in Alaska, it must be of tropical-weight wool, so that it can be worn virtually year-round.

The next building block in your wardrobe would be a gray wool suit, perhaps in a traditional bird's-eye or nailhead pattern. Now you are ready to loosen up a bit and introduce more pattern to your closet. Perhaps a glen plaid double-breasted, a houndstooth minicheck, or a nice pinstripe or chalkstripe is next. Once you have a foundation, you can begin to experiment.

How many suits should you own? Enough so that they can be effectively rotated. That is, you should have enough tailored ensembles, warm weather and cold, so that you never have to wear any one garment more than twice in one week (and *never* two days in a row). Good woolen suits, like good leather shoes, need to be aired for twenty-four hours after each wearing. Hang the suit separately, preferably on a wooden dumbvalet, before returning it to the closet. When you do this faithfully, your suits will need to be dry cleaned only rarely—about once a season will do (pressing can be more frequent).

What else do you need? Shoes—and plenty of them. They need to be rotated, too. Several pairs of relaxed dress trousers, including a pair of gray flannels to wear with a sport jacket, seem obligatory, as are sport shirts and sweaters. You will want your own personal array of casual clothes, including knockabout stuff.

Most of the male fashion icons of this century, from Fred Astaire to Ralph Lauren, have been experimenters with a classic point of view. Some of what you collect and wear will eventually prove to be

ONE GREAT SUIT: Special occasions, interviews, important client meetings. Splurge a little on just one and the confidence boost may seal the deal.

ephemeral, but such is the nature of all things. Once you have all the essentials covered, there will be noticeably less space in your closet for egregious fashion mistakes. Consider Thoreau's philosophical stance: "Beware of all enterprises that require new clothes." A man can expect to own and discard many suits of clothes while keeping up to date with his own changing tastes, his physical dimensions, and the swings of fashion. The ideal wardrobe is more a journey than a destination.

BASIC ACCESSORIES

A BRIGHT-COLORED SCARF:

A scarf is like a tie; it's your only chance to add some personality to that overcoat.

There's a scene in the movie *Steel Magnolias* in which Olympia Dukakis, portraying an old Southern belle, wraps up her own brand of Darwinism by eloquently declaring, "The only thing that separates us from the beasts is our ability to accessorize."

Chances are you don't remember the line, or the movie. (It was a chick flick.) But believe it or not, the sentiment ain't a bad one to keep in mind the next time you get dressed. Investing a paycheck in a smashing navy Brooks Brothers suit can be nothing but money down the vanity drain if you ruin it by pairing it with a cruddy pair of scuffed shoes or a cloth belt from your Boy Scout days.

Let's face facts: When it comes to most things that are truly important—love, sex, money, how to best spend an autumn Sunday afternoon—men are not like women. This is true in the fashion arena, as well. Any woman can regale you with enthralling tales of the perfect dress found jammed at the end of the 50-percent-off rack, or the day she unwittingly passed by a store window only to hear the shrieking wail of "Buy me!" emanating from a pair of Prada sandals behind the glass.

Men? We're a little different. For one thing, the voice a guy is most likely to hear is coming from a mug filled with some sort of lager. And by and large, men tend not to sweat the small stuff—their accessories—when it comes to pulling together clothes to wear. There are two reasons it takes women twice as long as we do to get dressed: they wear makeup, and we don't (Dennis Rodman excluded); and they spend countless hours fumbling through drawers and jewelry boxes trying to find the right stuff to go with their outfit.

It can be frustrating (especially if the movie you want to see starts in fifteen minutes), but there is a method to the ladies' madness—that's why she always looks better than you do. Take a page from her book and learn how to complement what you wear with touches that will enhance your clothes, whether you're sporting a power suit for the office or simply a T-shirt and jeans.

Picking good accessories involves a simple game of mixing and matching. You want to select items that you need, that you will have for a long, long time, that won't go out of style anytime soon, and that—given the previous three conditions—won't cause you to swallow hard when you have to shell out good money for them.

BELTS

Most guys make their biggest mistakes with belts. Belts come in two basic varieties: dress and casual.

Classic dress belts come in black, brown, and sometimes oxblood. If you see any in any other color, keep moving: you'll find them on the five-dollar table at Marshalls in six months, and for a reason. Every man should own one dress belt in black and one in brown. Typically, black ones have silver buckles, and brown ones have gold buckles. The rule of thumb of which one to wear is a simple one: the brown belts go with brown clothes; the black belts go with everything else. There are some exceptions to this, of course (say, a gray suit with thin brown pinstripes, where one should wear the brown belt to bring out the pinstripes), but it's basically a sound tenet.

Casual belts are usually thicker and are a staple of jeans and khakis. Very wide belts with clunky buckles can be quite smart, but should be worn only with jeans. For khakis and chinos, select thinner belts. Casual belts also offer the opportunity to play with textures, like distressed leather and even faux alligator. With most jeans and casual pants (with the exception of black ones, which must always be worn with a black belt), you can wear either a black or a brown belt. A final caveat: If your mom comes back from a trip to the Southwest with some Indian-made multicolored belt, make sure to thank her—then toss it in the trash. That type of look is strictly the domain of the guys wearing socks with sandals.

BLACK BELT WITH SILVER BUCKLE: Nothing says casual better than ditching the nine-to-five gold buckle.

WATCHES

In the last twenty years, watches have gone from being simple time-pieces to integral fashion accessories. Not too long ago, it was simply Rolex or Timex. Not anymore.

Mercifully, jewelers have come to understand that not all of us can collect timepieces the way Imelda Marcos used to collect footwear. One of the best trends in recent years has been the emergence of the dual-toned metallic watchband, typically a silver band with a gold metal stripe down the middle.

Who cares? You should. Your watch should always, always complement not just your clothes, but in particular, your belt. A dual-toned metal band does the same trick that the classic square, white-faced, black-leather band watch has done for decades: it allows you to wear your watch with basically any outfit or any belt. Now *that's* a good investment.

Generally speaking, the bulkier the watch, the less appropriate it is for business attire. Love your Swiss Army watch? Great! Wear it with your Gap T-shirt for the next twenty years. But if you're donning a suit and tie, either a metal band in silver, gold, or dual-tone or a black-banded watch are your best (and safest) bets.

Of course, a whole new breed of casual watches has flooded the market in recent years, hawked by everyone from the ubiquitous Swatch (strictly the province of fashionable thirteen-year-olds) to Timex, which still makes perfectly sensible and—pardon the pun—timeless designs. For a fun watch that won't break your bank account, consider Fossil, which now produces a wide range of watch faces in not only interesting colors but also provocative textures as well.

Finally, if you inherited an Elgin pocketwatch from your grandfather, consider yourself lucky—just remember to wear it only with a suit.

EYEGLASSES

Now most guys don't consider eyeglasses part of their fashion sense (given that they have any to start with). They'll agonize over the perfect set of four-hundred-dollar Revos at the local Sunglass Hut and then turn around and cheap out on the specs they need to actually *see* anything.

Gone are the days when Dr. Smith, the local optometrist, gave

HUSH PUPPIES: Hipsters don the chartreuse, bankers opt for basic black. A hue for you and comfy, too.

you four styles of frames to choose from. Today, it's chic to wear cool eyeglasses, as evidenced by the fact that Hollywood celebrities—Rob Lowe, Sylvester Stallone—with good eyesight regularly wear fake ones strictly as a fashion accessory.

Picking cool eyeglasses isn't really that difficult: If you've got a big face you need bigger ones, and if you have a small face you need smaller ones. End of story. Just beware of going too far in either direction. Ben Franklin may have been a hell of a statesman, but nobody ever stopped his horse-and-buggy to exclaim, "Ben! Cool specs!"

These days, most eyewear chains offer "specials" where you can come in and get something like an eye exam and two pairs of glasses for ninety-nine bucks. Beware: What they're not telling you is that the selection of frames that fit into the two-for–ninety-nine category tend to all look like they should be worn by some sixty-five-year-old retiree in plaid pants. Do yourself a favor and invest some money in your eyewear. Top designers like Ralph Lauren and Donna Karan now proffer some terrific frames that will look terrific on you. A good tip: When you try frames on, wear a plain T-shirt with a blazer over it. If the glasses look good with both the combination and just the T-shirt alone, buy 'em. You've got eyewear that'll look good with both your office and casual duds.

SHOES

Finally, there's the matter of your feet. Unfortunately, while in recent times men as a gender have loosened up considerably in enjoying the pleasures of shopping, indulging in a big binge for shoes remains taboo. It's a girl thing.

Don't be an idiot. Ask any headhunter the most common fashion mistake made by interviewees—he'll tell you instantly it's all in the shoes. Career-minded guys think nothing of dropping $500 on a beautiful tailored olive suit, and another $140 on a Polo shirt and a Nicole Miller tie to go with it. Then what do they do? Step into the same pair of beat-up old brown loafers they've been wearing forever. Buying good shoes shows attention to detail—and how many potential employers aren't looking for that?

Still, if you're financially strapped and you're only able to shell out for one decent pair of something, go with the classic black loafer. They'll do you for everything from your casual oxford shirt with black pleated pants to your jeans with heather-gray T-shirt. Just don't

THE RIGHT SOCKS:

Nothing ruins the spiffy lines of a new Italian suit better than a pair of white gym socks.

THE RIGHT SHOES:

See previous entry. The same goes for sneakers—don't try to train for a marathon in bottom-of-the-line New Balance sneaks.

wear them with a suit. Never. People always break this rule, and they always look like clods. Suits need lace-ups, like classic oxfords.

And remember that shoes are the finishing touch on any outfit, so keep that word in mind: finish. Not clash, not contrast. *Finish.* Black pants need black shoes. Brown pants need brown (or oxblood) shoes. Classic summer seersucker pants need light, cloth bucks. Penny loafers, like charcoal-gray pants and the burgundy necktie, will never go out of style—they're a can't-miss staple. And if you look at a shoe and it has a tassel on it, put it back. Tassels are for English lords and gangsters.

The right belt, watch, eyeglasses, and shoes can not only enhance your wardrobe, they can also take your clothes to the next level of style. And that may be enough to separate you from the beasts.

A BLACK LINEN SHIRT:

The fella's version of the Little Black Dress. Win-Win, any way you button it.

THE TEN COMMANDMENTS OF TAILORING

Girlfriends can come in handy in this department, but when it comes to buying a suit or sport coat, it's usually left to you and your taste. We'd like to offer a little help. Here are ten basic rules about fit and cut every man should know. Think of them as the Ten Commandments of altering men's tailored clothing.

1. SHOULDER. If it doesn't fit your shoulders, try a different size. Remember that sizes vary based on manufacturer and designer—a 40 regular Hugo Boss will be more generously cut than a 40 regular from Brooks Brothers.

2. COLLAR. Always check if the collar should be lowered—it is the most common alteration, besides hemming trousers. If the coat collar rides up, it leaves a gap between the coat and shirt. This problem is most visible on the newscaster who didn't check his coat's fit while he was sitting down—a mistake even if you're not on television five nights a week.

3. TORSO. To nip or not to nip? Err on the side of lean and narrow, but watch it: too much and you'll look like an Edwardian dandy. You should be able to hug yourself wearing a coat and not feel like you're wearing a straitjacket. Fitted doesn't mean tight.

4. SLEEVES. Sleeve-length is up to the individual. Dressier guys, wearing French-cuff shirts and cufflinks, might like the coat's sleeves to be a little shorter. Just don't get carried away. You don't want to look as if you're wearing the same coat your mom bought you in junior high to attend your friend's bar mitzvah.

5. LENGTH. Too long, and your jacket will look like an outerwear coat. Too short, and you'll look like a bullfighter. As a general rule of thumb, you should be able to run your fingers along the bottom of the coat with your arms dangling naturally—no reaching down or bending your elbows to shorten your arms' length.

6. VENTS. These are the slits that are sometimes in the back of a sport coat. Double vents look best on a tall, thin physique, a single vent has little consequence, and stocky people should stick to coats without vents because they are slimming.

7. DOUBLE-BREASTED. More formal, they require quality fabrics and a good cut. Since double-breased suits and sport coats emphasize the horizontal, any man under six feet was traditionally kept far from them. But clothiers now agree the cut can work on a man who is five feet eight inches tall as long as he is slender.

8. TROUSERS. Current fashion dictates trousers that are narrower in the leg, have a plain front and no pleats. Trousers should drape slightly, have a break before the hem and fit comfortably—that means you shouldn't show off the pockets' lining if you've gained weight.

9. CUFFS. A matter of taste. Every man should probably have at least one pair of dress pants with safe, standard one-and-a-quarter-inch cuffs. If you choose cuffless, watch trousers that are too short.

10. AND FINALLY... Always wear what is appropriate for your physical type, lifestyle, and career.

NICE JEANS: Clean and without holes— you'll be pleasantly surprised by how many places you can wear them.

MAKING THE DENIM DECISION

It's been 144 years since a Bavarian immigrant by the name of Levi Strauss arrived in San Francisco during the Gold Rush and saw gold in the pants of the scruffy miners scraping for metal. While there are few fashion rules regarding denim, there are also ways to get the most out of these most durable of pants.

◆ Jeans prices go from dirt cheap to ridiculous, so what's the difference? The answer: not much. Don't sniff at lower-priced models. Chances are 50/50 they'll fit you just as well as some designer label. Denim is denim is denim; any price differential is most likely caused by extra seaming and pockets, studs or a sandblasting or mill-washing process to fade the material—all stuff you don't care much about anyway.

◆ Black jeans are dressier but also take the biggest beating from fading. To combat it, fluff dry them to preserve color and then leave them out to air dry. To avoid stiffness, add an extra capful of fabric softener during the rinse cycle when you wash them.

◆ Jeans vary wildly in fit. Be patient, find a brand that is comfortable and looks great, and wear only that brand.

◆ White jeans are considered "winter white" and are acceptable for wear after Labor Day. They're best accessorized by smart lace-ups, such as saddle shoes from Johnston & Murphy or black suede oxfords.

◆ Regular fit jeans hug the contour of your body, so they're the best if you're in good shape and want to show off your derrière. Relaxed jeans give an extra half inch all around (translation: "Yes, I will have another helping"); baggy jeans offer as much as four extra inches in various spots. Fat guys think wearing baggy clothes will make them look thinner, and they're wrong. Going to the gym will make them look thinner.

◆ Denim shirts are OK, but *never* wear them with jeans. Only with khakis, and only taupe or black khakis at that. Paired with a print tie

HANES BEEFEE TEES:

Durable.
Versatile.

and a herringbone or checked blazer, the denim shirt offers a can't-miss uniform for casual Fridays at the office.

◆ Ripped jeans—in the rear, in the knees, wherever—are strictly the domain of musicians in rock videos and disaffected teenage girls. You wouldn't wear a shirt that's been ripped in half. So why would you wear jeans that look like they've just been through a paper shredder?

◆ Acid-washed jeans were big in the eighties. Leave them there.

LIFELONG LEATHER

The leather jacket is a loaded proposition. While guys wear these versatile coats everywhere they can, most of them don't have a clue of how to properly take care of them. Rest assured: ignoring the care of a leather jacket will cut the life of your purchase in half—and tag you as a loser.

◆ You can't protect something that already has a big gash down the arm. Give whatever you're going to buy a good once-over to see if it's scratched, ripped or discolored in any way; make sure to take your time, as textured leather can hide defects. And if you do happen to bring that leather peacoat home and discover a rip, return it immediately: repairs are tricky, expensive and hardly guaranteed.

◆ If you want to know, ask. Most leather or suede salespeople are trained to know how to handle the merchandise you are purchasing. Ask detailed questions. Salesperson doesn't know the answers? Leave the store.

◆ Leather jackets are cool; long leather coats are considered gauche (translation: major guido). Buy only the former. And stay away from those black leather jackets with all the zippers and metallic buttons; they went out with the Village People.

A LEATHER JACKET: Makes a statement.

♦ Black leather can dress up any outfit; brown leather goes only with casual clothes.

♦ Suede is just leather turned inside out and tanned differently. If you have your eye on suede, make sure you specifically buy a suede brush, which softens the suede and gets fine particles of dirt and grime out of this sensitive material. Always brush in *one* direction to keep the material from discoloring and fading.

♦ While leather and suede are both durable materials, they weren't made for braving monsoons—that's what raincoats are for. Still, if you get caught in a gale wearing your prized black leather jacket, don't panic. The easiest way to protect it is to treat it beforehand with a simple petroleum or silicone-based aerosol spray. A good choice: Pecard Leather Care Products (www.pecard.com.). The Pecard folks have been in the leather biz since 1902 and make a superior product.

YOUR COLLEGE SWEATSHIRT:
Comfortable conversation piece. She'll look great wearing it the morning after.

♦ Most dry cleaners can't guarantee the cleaning of leather. So it's a good idea to ask specifically, since a botched job could leave you with a leathery mess. And have you ever tried to sue a dry cleaner?

♦ Be careful with Guinness or grape juice. Unfortunately, some stains just don't come out.

BREAKING IN THE CAP

Baseball caps aren't really much about baseball anymore. Whether the look you're going for is boyish or rakish, a well-maintained baseball cap can be a handy fashion ally for those times when you want a little attitude or if you're simply having a bad hair day. Of course, you've got to buy the right kind. No mesh—that's for your tractor-drivin' grandpa. And be wary of fitted ones—they shrink when wet and then won't fit anymore.

Like baseball gloves, baseball hats need to be broken in to be worn with the best effect. Here's our exclusive foolproof method, suitable for caps both new and old:

◆ Adjust the cap to the proper size for your head and start bending the bill to make the cardboard inside more pliable. Then, with the cap off your head, spend between fifteen minutes and a half hour arcing the bill in the same fashion. The degree of the arc is entirely up to you. The slimmer your face and the sharper your jawline, the more rounded an arc you can get away with. A round face paired with a sharply arced bill will only make you look fat.

◆ Get a towel, wet it and start stuffing it into the presized cap. Work the towel into the hat and mold it to the round shape of a head. Smooth wrinkles by stuffing in more cloth. If the cap is wrinkled or creased during this process, the cap will be disfigured when you're done and your hat will end up sitting on a shelf—with the rest of your old lids.

◆ When you're done stuffing, wrap rubber bands around both the entire cap, to keep the towel from falling out, and the bill, to keep it curved and looking sharp.

◆ Place the cap in a dishwasher and set it to RINSE. *Do not add soap.* Soap will cause colors to bleed and/or fade. And make sure the dishwasher is otherwise empty: dirty dishes along for the ride could cause your precious hat to smell like last night's mac-and-cheese.

◆ After the dishwasher process is done, take the wet towel out of cap and replace it with a dry towel, securing it again with rubber bands. Reshape the cap and let it dry for approximately two days. Your hat should now fit like a glove.

A TUXEDO:
Invest in one and you'll never run in fear of the words "black tie" again.

TWENTY SARTORIAL TIPS TO TAKE SERIOUSLY

1. The most important fashion rule: what you wear should be an expression of yourself. It should make you feel more comfortable than wearing nothing. If it doesn't, something's wrong. Either you're trying too hard or you're not trying hard enough.

2. Buy good suits. Not enough can be said about the importance of a good suit—or two or three. You don't have to spend $1,000 on an Armani, though it wouldn't hurt. Most department stores carry Hickey-Freeman, Hart-Schaffner & Marx, or comparable brands, which run $400 to $600.

3. If you can buy only one suit, make it navy single-breasted in transitional weight wool. It's the most versatile.

4. If you can buy only three suits, buy navy and gray single-breasted wool suits and one summer-weight khaki.

5. For business occasions, conservative is generally better. At a meeting or an interview, you should be the one making the bold statements, not your suit. The IBM uniform—dark (navy or black) suit, white shirt and subtle tie—is the American standard in terms of respectability and professionalism.

6. With sports jackets, even though plain is boring, plain is better. Solid navy goes with khakis, jeans, shorts, everything.

7. Make sure your pants fit in the back as well as the waist. Take a lesson from Italian men, who are the best at wearing pants. Whether they're jeans or khakis or suit pants, they should drape back there, without sagging.

8. Avoid baggy pants. Full pants can work as a casual look for taller, thinner body types, but baggy suit pants will always look messy.

9. Formal suits get white shirts. Period. If you want to get more creative (and have the type of job where you can get more creative), try

A PAIR OF BLACK LEATHER LACE-UP SHOES:

Cross-trainers of the business set.

matching bright-colored shirts with darker ties in casual suit or blazer-and-slacks combinations.

10. The classic white oxford shirt will never, ever go out of style. If you don't own one, you should. Ditto for a pair of black, wool slacks.

11. The iron is your friend. Cotton needs to be ironed; wrinkled shirts are a sign of a total loser.

12. There is no one acceptable tie knot. Just make sure that it's proportional to collar and neck—big guys should have big knots, etc.

13. Color always says something. Black is the color of power, as well as mystery. Navy blue is the color of authority. Orange and red? These are warm colors that tend to attract women. They say, "Come talk to me."

14. In general, your safest bet is lighter shirts with darker pants, which narrow your waist and give you a more streamlined look. An exception is a black pullover with white pants, which can be a terrific look—if you're slender and can pull it off.

15. Vests should be long enough to cover the belt, without going longer.

16. You should own at least three white classic Ts. They may just be the most versatile garments you'll ever own, fit for stuffing your face before the television and also for contrasting colorful layers (vests, cardigans, blazers) on top of them.

17. Shine your shoes. Nothing ruins a cool suit worse than something beat-up on your feet.

18. Always make sure your shoes and your belt are the same color.

19. Running shoes are for running. Sweats are for sweating. If you're not doing either of these activities, you shouldn't be wearing either of these garments.

20. Jewelry. Wear as little as possible. A watch, a wedding ring, that's it. There's nothing worse than a man with too much jewelry.

A BAGGY SUIT:
You can stop
sucking it in.

CHAPTER 2

GROOMING/ HYGIENE

Q: CAN I STEM HAIR LOSS?

KIEHL'S SILK GROOM:

It'll make your longer locks scream for fingers to be run through them.

Unfortunately, male-pattern baldness is irreversible; once those hair follicles die, they're gone. Male-pattern baldness afflicts roughly 40 million men in the United States and 95 percent of the time, it's hereditary. Thank your grandpa. On the brighter side, the FDA has approved two second-generation hair restoration medications, targeted at preventing the shedding trend. Behold, captain comb-over: Propecia and Rogaine Extra Strength, the latest budding contenders in the $1 billion-a-year hair replacement industry.

Hair replacement medications work by beefing-up existing hair follicles. Available by doctor prescription, Propecia actually inhibits production of the hormone, DHT (dihydro-testosterone), that causes hair follicles to die. A study done by Propecia manufacturer, Merck & Co., found 83 percent of men who took the medication for one year, finished the year with the same or higher hair count. And—drumroll please—Propecia has proven effective in slowing the deepening M on the frontal part of your scalp. Rogaine has not.

Doctors prescribe Propecia in the form of once-a-day, 1 ml tablets. Prescriptions run roughly $50 per month. Sound too good to be true? Well, in some cases it is. Propecia packs with it a small chance of decreasing your libido and causing difficulty in achieving an erection.

Not willing to risk cooling your love engines? Rogaine's new, souped-up hair brew packs more than twice the active ingredient minoxidil as does regular strength Rogaine, theoretically accelerating the products' results. Where regular strength Rogaine users have had to endure four months of scalp nurturing to see new signs of life, Rogaine Extra Strength users have realized new hair after two. The dosage remains the same—1 ml applied directly to the scalp, two times daily. A month's supply of Rogaine Extra Strength sells over the counter for roughly $30. Like the regular strength formula, it may cause a dry, itchy, flaky scalp.

So for you balding badboys, there's some promise of new growth. Just remember these are treatments, not cures. And like the NCAA's use-'em or lose-'em eligibility clause, you'll continue losing your hair if you stop using your replacement medication.

Q: SHOULD I WEAR COLOGNE?

Even at $15 an ounce, there are perks inherent to dabbing. Sure it can make you feel ultramasculine, athletic, even rakish. But it's also downright seductive, allowing you to make an olfactory statement, which can be as strong as a fashion statement or a hairstyle. Once a woman links you with a specific scent, there's a good chance she'll conjure your image up each time she gets a whiff. Give her a T-shirt or sweater sprayed with your fragrance, and it's as good as the real thing being draped by her bedside.

The downsides? It can be tough to calculate how much is too much. (Hint: Apply it so only those leaning in to tell you a secret can detect it.) Douse yourself accidentally, and there's no turning back. Coworkers, friends, and relatives are rarely sympathetic to a malodorous offense of this kind. Allergic dates may end up gasping through

Remington
www.remington.co.uk/
men/shaving.html
A catalog of Remington products as well as tips and information on health and beauty.

Body Maintenence
www.bodymainte
nance.com
South Beach–based Body Maintenence takes its "keep it simple, keep it natural" philosophy online with tips for face, hair and body care. Browse the products. Get care advice. Purchase products.

www.cologneguy.com
Answers frequently asked questions about men's grooming (e.g., What's the difference between cologne and aftershave?). Reviews fragrances and stocks industry information.

**www.toserve.com/
fetish/shaving.htm**
Tips on shaving some of life's more private parts.

Clinique
www.clinique.com
On-line personal consultant tells you your skin type and which products are best for your skin type. Learn about Clinique's full line of men's skin supplies.

dinner, and you risk disgusting potential mates should their dads wear the same signature scent.

The good news: wearing cologne isn't plastic surgery. Give it a try. Head to your local department store and talk to the salesman at the cologne counter. This is the guy who will help you grasp the difference between "amber," "oriental" and "coniferous" fragrances, explain how your body's chemistry affects scent, and offer free samples. If you're still clueless, stick with the classics—Eternity for Men, Aramis, or Drakkar Noir. Or, you can always opt for the soap and deodorant, that cheap and foolproof duo.

A LITTLE COLOGNE:

The object is for a hint of scent— not to overpower those around you.

CARMEX:

No-nonsense approach to great lips (always appreciated). The stuff even inspired a rap song by Count Bass D.

DRY CLEAN:

No amount of ironing can compare.

Q: SHOULD I ENLARGE MY PENIS?

With the tacit acceptance of cosmetic surgery, the idea of getting a penis enlargement is being met with the same creepy Brave New World attitude largely reserved for sneaker ads: Just do it. By 1997, an estimated 15,000 American men had already done it, putting their thing under the knife for reasons ranging from personal virility issues to impressing the chicks. And for what?

The average penis size, when erect, comes in at 5.1 inches long, while fewer than 5 percent have less than 4 inches to work with. With those numbers, perhaps the greater question is: Why? Let's get one thing straight. If you're trying to impress the ladies, they're likely to balk if it's bigger than a bread box. An überpenis is not only somewhat of an oddity, it can be downright painful. Most women would prefer to spend an evening washing their hair than trying to fit a square peg in a round hole.

Nevertheless, when considering penis enlargement, you should have all the facts. For the $6,000 price tag, you're likely expecting to turn the little guy into the Goodyear Blimp. The surgical procedures available usually involve cutting the suspensory ligament at the base of the penis, which holds part of the penis inside the body (yikes!). The booty: about 1.5 inches. The other procedure, often done in addition to the lengthening procedure, involves having fat injected into the penis, or inserting strips of fat into the penis through two small incisions. The reward this time: a 30–50 percent increase in circumference. Sound harmless?

Not exactly. Some of the things patients have had to deal with include excruciating pain, lumpy misshapen masses of fat, inability to get an erection (remedied by the equally disturbing injection of the penis with hormones), penile bending (a.k.a. "banana syndrome"), infection, scarring, depression, suicidal tendencies, shrinkage to less than original size, tearing at suture sights, inability to perform sexually, and no feeling in the penis.

Some doctors insist that the likelihood of these things happening are slim. Fair enough. But for a vanity procedure, side effects should be looked at as real possibilities. When you're playing with your wanky, you don't want to end up on the losing end of the stats.

Chances are your penis is just fine. And when push comes to shove (heh heh), it's the motion of the ocean not the size of your ship that's gonna keep her coming back for more.

THE MEDICINE CABINET ARSENAL

We all look at a woman's morning routine with a mixture of curiosity, horror and puzzlement. Having a girlfriend stay over is like having an art studio open in your bathroom: the place where you shave and occasionally get cozy with *Sports Illustrated* is suddenly stocked with creams, palettes and brushes. You stare quizzically and wonder: *What is all this stuff?*

It's for her face and body, pal, and it's why she always looks twice as good as you do. While she exfoliates you figure that with a bar of soap, shampoo, deodorant and some hair gel, you're set.

Wrong. While no one is suggesting you become a regular at the Estée Lauder counter, adding just a few extra steps to your morning routine can pump up your looks almost overnight. Here are five simple ways to take your grooming to the next level.

MOUTHWASH:
Keep it in your desk. After you eat that pizza loaded with garlic and onions for lunch, your coworkers will thank you.

EYE DROPS:
You don't want dried out eyes to lead her to thinking you're coming on too strong (wink wink).

Q-TIPS:
Fact—swabbing feels good. And wax tastes terrible, so if you want a woman's tongue in your ear more than once, clean it out.

SHARPER IMAGE NO-FOG SHOWER MIRROR:
Shaving in the shower has never been easier.

RAZORGUARD:
An oil-based solution for storing your blades between shaves, it helps your blades last up to ten times longer.

ALUM BLOCK:
It's time you stopped plastering those little toilet-paper squares all over your face to stop shave-induced bleeding.

FIND A SIGNATURE SCENT. Most men drag out whatever they got last Christmas, spray it on for weddings and let the dust collect the other months of the year. But using fragrance to complement your looks stamps you as a man of style and confidence.

What to choose? Avoid anything that's cheap or smells like your dad (translation: no more Aqua Velva). And you are absolutely forbidden to buy anything with the word "musk" in the title. Select one and wear it all the time: you want a nice scent that people will pleasantly associate as smelling like *you*.

TAKE CARE OF YOUR HAIR. Some guys spend a small fortune on expensive gel and then ruin it by cheaping out on a Wal-Mart hairbrush. Hair care is important: brushing dry hair stimulates oil glands at the base of the scalp, lubricating hair; brushing oily hair helps lift away excess oils.

If you've got dry or normal hair, try an old-fashioned wooden-handle brush from Kent ($46), the British authority that made its first brushes when the redcoats were battling the colonists. For fine or thinning hair, consider the sensitive brush from Mason Pearson ($75), another English import. This brush features boar bristle tufts set on a pneumatic pad for deep penetration.

GET RID OF YOUR OTHER HAIR. There's just one word for nose hair and ear hair: gross. For the easiest way to get rid of it, check out the Personal Groomer by Panasonic ($32). It's safe to use with water, contours to both the nose and ears and rinses clean.

BE SKIN SMART. Your face takes a pretty nasty beating most weeks, especially if you're an outdoorsman, golfer, or sun worshipper. Fight back—supplement your soap-and-water drill with a basic moisturizer. Ask a skin consultant at your nearby department store for advice about what moisturizer suits your skin type.

NAIL IT. Since you're probably not going to saddle up for a salon manicure anytime soon, turn to Dovo, one of the world's finest suppliers of cutlery, for a classy leather-encased grooming kit designed to keep your cuticles gleaming. It's pricey ($115), but you'll have it until you retire. But leave the nail polish to the ladies: as with imported beer and Cowboys football, in male grooming there is sometimes too much of a good thing.

PREVENTING PIZZA FACE

Okay big guy, you spend eight hours a week in the gym, 20 percent of your paycheck at the clothing store, and no less than 30 minutes a day on your hair. So what's standing between you and babe magnetization?

Maybe it's your skin. Ask any girl: shaving, sunning, and swilling have left many a guy with a killer case of crater face. But even if you're guilty as charged, smooth, trouble-free skin is still attainable.

SHAVING

Razor bumps and red, irritated skin are often the price you pay for a smooth, close shave. Minimize them with the proper technique: wet your face with warm water, put the shaving cream on, then keep it on for a minute or two to fully hydrate the hair. Choose a shaving cream with moisturizers that allow the razor to glide easily.

Shave in the direction of hair growth to help prevent ingrown hairs, razor burn and cuts, and use a razor that swivels to minimize nicks. If you really need a closer shave, try shaving twice rather than shaving against the grain.

Aftershaves will not improve the state of shaving cuts or prevent infection. Most contain alcohol as the main ingredient, which, while refreshing to oily skin, can also irritate dry skin.

ACNE

You thought you'd left it behind in the seventh grade, but alas, many of us don't outgrow acne. Roughly two-thirds of adults are plagued by breakouts, which are caused by stress, fluctuating hormone levels, surface bacteria, and excess oil production. If that wasn't bad enough, men also have thicker facial skin and more oil glands than women.

Stress and hormones, as we know all too well, are not easily controlled. But you can minimize bacteria and oil by washing your face twice a day with an antibacterial soap.

If you wear a helmet for sports or if you have a phone pressed

VITAMIN B:
Seems to minimize the hangover.

ECHINACEA:
Keeps that pesky cold at bay.

SHORT NAILS:
Long nails look bad and can do damage to sensitive areas—yours and hers.

NAIL CLIPPERS:
No biting, no tearing.

against your face all day, beware of an irritation called acne mechanica. Try to alleviate pressure against the skin as much as possible and wash your face after long periods of contact.

To control acne, try over-the-counter treatments made with benzoil peroxide or salicyclic acid. For inflammatory acne, choose a product with a low concentration of benzoyl peroxide, such as Neutrogena's On-The-Spot Acne Treatment (2.5 percent). Products that contain high concentrations of benzoyl peroxide are often too drying for adult skin, and a harsh product can make the problem worse. Salicyclic acid, found in compounds such as Clinique's Anti-Acne Spot Treatment and Neutrogena's Oil-Free Acne Wash Cleanser, is more gentle. Both benzoyl peroxide and salicyclic acid also peel the skin—far better choices than grainy facial scrubs, which may aggravate acne.

If your acne doesn't clear up after using over-the-counter products, consider seeing a dermatologist. Prescription medications for adults include oral and topical antibiotics and topical Retin-A.

MOISTURIZER:
You may think it's girly, but cracking hands and elbows can hurt like hell.

TWO-PLY TOILET PAPER:
One-ply doesn't cut it.

SWEAT

Sweat itself does not affect the skin. But if you sweat under a thick barrier of sunscreen, you can worsen acne. The same is true when sticky hair gels drift down onto your sweaty forehead.

Similarly, when sweat combines with oil produced by the skin, the combination closes off the pores, creating a breeding ground for acne. Wash your face right before and after you sweat, and if it becomes a problem, use topical anti-acne drying preparations.

SUN

Gels and other sunscreens formulated just for faces are best, since they won't clog pores. While the sun can make acne less of a problem temporarily, don't bask without sunscreen, as that zit pales to the long-term risks: Even one severe sunburn doubles your risk of developing skin cancer later in life, including deadly melanoma.

Choose a sunscreen with titanium dioxide, which absorbs both UVA and UVB rays, such as Neutrogena's Chemical Free Sunblocker. Hats and sunglasses that block the damaging rays are also a good idea.

If you do manage to get burned, the best strategy to minimize swelling and redness is cool compresses, aspirin, and cortisone cream. It's also a good time to remind yourself that while tan is nice, neither a bright red face nor skin cancer is going to score you many points with the female skin testers out there.

SHAVING 101

◆ Start off hot. Shaving in the shower is great if you've got lots of hot water and a good, steam-resistant mirror. Otherwise, before shaving, douse your face in hot water or apply a hot towel.

◆ Apply a preshave moisturizer to open up pores and loosen hairs.

◆ Use a good glycerin-based shaving cream. Most foams and gels contain agents like menthol that actually close pores and stiffen your beard.

◆ Apply cream with a good shaving brush (badger hair is best). This is a necessity, not a luxury. Then lather, baby, lather!

◆ Always, always shave *with* the growth pattern of your hair. Shaving against the grain causes unpleasant razor burn and nasty ingrown hairs.

◆ End with a splash of cold water to close pores.

◆ Use an alcohol-free moisturizing aftershave, preferably with aloe. Alcohol-soaked cologne aftershaves can irritate skin.

◆ Finally, at least once, get a high-end barber-shop shave, and let a pro help show you the way. Spoil yourself, tiger. You've earned it.

CLINIQUE POST-SHAVE HEALER:

After your shave you need, well, an aftershave.

WAHL'S ELECTRIC CLIPPER:

Sideburns. Goatees. Mustaches. Beards. Twenty-five bucks means you never have to be fuzzy around the edges again.

GETTING A GREAT HAIRCUT

The white man's Afro. The bowl cut. The duck's ass. Those are but three of our nominees for the Bad Haircut Hall of Shame. If the mirror whispers that you, too, might harbor a contender, then it's time to shape up your head.

More than your clothes or your shoes, your haircut—how you wear that mop that shades your ears in the summer and keeps your brain warm in the winter—is the most important style decision you're ever likely to make. Like a belt, shoes or sunglasses, your hair should be treated like a fashion accessory. A good choice can take your look into high style; a bad one can destroy the coolest threads. You wouldn't wear Air Jordans with that new Armani suit, would you? (Would you?)

Your hair will only be as good to you as you are to it. It's time to ditch the five-dollar, one-cut-fits-all 'do from Frank the Barber and

HOW TO MATCH YOUR FACE TO THE RIGHT HAIRCUT

Which styles go with which facial structure? Here are a few suggestions that might save you from wearing that after-the-bad-cut hat.

SQUARE FACE
The George Clooney: Go short, *really* short—almost shaved—to balance sharp lines of your features. If you do go any longer, keep it to a medium length, and fuller on the sides.

THIN FACE
The Pat Riley: Go medium/long and slicked back. The key is to get that long face to *not* look long. "You definitely don't want any height on the top, because it will make your face look that much longer," Vitale warns.

FAT FACE
The Chris Farley: Truthfully, it depends on just how fat you are compared to your face. The best option? Go longer and thinner in the back and sides. And don't keep any height on the top.

RECEDING HAIRLINE
The Bruce Willis. Like your hair, your options are limited. Shave your head and grow whatever you can, such as a goatee.

step into a world where men go to salons, have stylists and, most importantly, know when to lose what good stylists routinely refer to as the "dork cut."

The biggest factor to consider when deciding on a haircut is your face. If you have, shall we say, a *rotund* face, then it's best that you stay away from that bowl cut or mop top, lest you look like Louie Anderson. Your hair should complement your face, not match it. Look at it like yin and yang—your locks should create a perfect balance for your upper torso. Square face? Think round haircut. Long face? Think short. Your personality counts for something here, as well. Jerry Garcia wouldn't have looked quite right sporting a crew.

There are, however, some stop signs on the coiffed-hair expressway. Stay away from the supertrends that usually last about half of an Andy Warhol fifteen, like shaving Vanilla Ice–style lightning bolts (or any words or pictures) in the sides, top or back of your head. And never go against the grain of your own hair.

Don't expect magic, either. If your hair is thinning, not even the most adept stylist can turn it into a dark, curly thicket. You best go short. Going gray prematurely? Suck it up and think about a dye job.

One final factor to consider: Is your hairstyle appropriate for the office? Obviously, you should stay away from longer or dyed hair if you're an account manager at Salomon Smith Barney. But if you're oh, let's say, a lowly editorial assistant at a men's magazine, then crazy hair can fly.

You don't have to be drastic to get results, but as Larry King has taught us, variety is the spice of life. Don't be afraid to look through magazines and rip out a couple of styles that you like. Bring 'em to your stylist and ask which one he'd recommend. Take the time now to get the 'do that's right for you—because in a few years those trips to Frank or the salon might not be necessary. After all, you can't style baldness.

REGULAR HAIRCUTS:
Something you can't hide— scruffy looks bad.

A GOOD LINT BRUSH:
What's the use of buying nice clothes if they all look like your dog slept on them?

A NOSE-HAIR TRIMMER:
Grooming's secret weapon.

TEETH: TO WHITEN OR NOT TO WHITEN?

George Washington knew something about discolored ones—his were made of wood. More than one Miss America contestant has been known to smear a healthy dose of Vaseline on hers, hoping for added glimmer. And Farrah Fawcett used hers to launch a million posters.

They are, of course, teeth, and these days everybody seems to want big, white, horsey ones. From that desire, a cottage industry has emerged: In 1996, Americans spent over $100 million on teeth whitening products, everything from tooth polishes to over-the-counter kits to dentist-applied bleaches. Whereas a decade ago teeth whitening was the sole province of showbiz folk, middle-aged corporate wives with too much time on their hands and the rich and vain, it has now come down to the masses.

Like hair replacement, the teeth whitening game is loaded with pitfalls. But the general rule seems to be a simple one: You get what you pay for. Shell out your life savings for pricey veneers—white covers that are fitted and then basically glued onto the front of your teeth, like Lee Press-On Nails for the smile—and you'll likely take a camera-ready grin to the grave. Cheap out and grab something off the drugstore shelf, and you're probably throwing your money down the spitting sink.

Discolored teeth are caused by many things: coffee, tea, cola, red wine and beer, along with blueberry pie, ketchup, mustard and basically anything more colorful than tap water. Cigarettes and stogies are also deadly—smoking just two cigars a day will yellow your teeth in four months.

Most yellowing, however, is the product of something much less preventable: aging. Like the rest of your body, which progressively goes to hell as the years pass, so do your teeth. And given that most folks can't afford veneers, which cost between $600 and $2,100 per tooth, professional bleaching, done by a dentist, has become the oral equivalent of plastic surgery: It's likely to do the trick, but not permanently. As with a face-lift, the effects of a teeth-lift will fade over time, and you'll need to go back to the dentist's chair to maintain the results.

Most teeth bleaching is done by custom fitting a mold to the patient's upper and lower teeth, filling the mold with a bleaching solution (often hydrogen peroxide) and letting the chemicals do their

GLIDE DENTAL TAPE:

Residual popcorn kernel? Broccoli stalk? One word: gingivitis. Glide brand floss breaks loose all those leftovers without tearing.

INDIAN TONGUE RAKE:

Kills bad breath by scraping the plaque from your tongue. Available from stores selling Eastern Indian wares.

thing. Depending on the dentist's technique, the procedure, which runs about $600, can take anywhere from 30 minutes to weeks of return office visits; some doctors give their patients doggie bags so they can continue whitening their teeth at home over the next few weeks.

Another popular choice for putting the pearly back in your not-so-whites is laser technology. Priced at roughly $1,100, the one-time procedure consists of placing a reactive chemical (made of chlorophyll, bleaches and other heat catalysts) on the patient's teeth, then flashing laser light on the surface.

TEETH WHITENING: ARE YOU A GOOD CANDIDATE?

As you age, so do your teeth. But just because they've turned yellow doesn't mean they have to stay that way. If the color of your teeth is really bothering you and you're committed to getting your teeth whitened, then at least know the facts.

OVER-THE-COUNTER WHITENING KITS

Price: $10 to $40

Process: Takes weeks. Consumer has to wear a Styrofoam mouth tray filled with bleach for hours at a stretch.

Safety: Generally not recommended by dentists (including the American Dental Association), who say that consumers who misuse the products could irritate their gums or destroy the enamel on their teeth. Some dentists say smokers should avoid the procedure altogether.

IN-OFFICE BLEACHING

Price: $350 to $700

Process: Patient stays in office while bleach placed in custom-fitted mouth tray sinks in. Some dentists perform the procedure over a period of weeks; others give their patients trays and chemicals to wear at night.

Safety: In 1993, Britain banned the procedure. Some patients experience gum sensitivity for a few days after the bleaching.

Bleach most often effective on: stains from coffee, smoke, antibiotics, gradual aging of teeth, or illness.

Bleach less effective on: porcelain or plastic—if you've got crowns, bridgework or fillings, they'll probably have to be replaced if you want to whiten up your smile.

As with most cosmetic surgery, self-esteem seems the product the dentists are really selling. Therein lies the rub: As with Rogaine for hair replacement, teeth whitening cannot guarantee the same results. Two people may have the exact same procedure done by the exact same dentist, but one may see more dramatic lightening of the teeth than the other. Most experts agree, however, that almost all patients who undergo bleaching will see some sort of result. It just might not be blinding in front of a camera.

If three- and four-digit dentist bills make you queasy, there is the drugstore alternative. Practically every pharmacy stocks kits that contain diluted versions of the whitening material used by dentists.

Of course, if you're wary of using peroxide-spiked paste to brush your teeth, try smearing on one of the dozens of chemically tamer "whitening" toothpastes on the market. They sell for between $5 and $10 and claim to whiten and brighten up to two shades lighter.

Do they? Not really. If you truly want to whiten your teeth, you're going to have to shell out the cash.

The American Dental Association remains curiously mum on teeth whitening, but most dentists claim that the procedure is reasonably safe, with few risks except, perhaps, the disappointment when you get out of the chair and don't have a smile like Jimmy Carter's. Not everyone's a good candidate: Think twice about having bleaching done if you've got any sort of preexisting dental condition, such as receding gums.

And keep in mind that the effects fade. No matter how much money you spend, the ravages of time and coffee will bring on the yellow again.

SLEEP:
At least six hours a day. A rested mind is a powerful mind.

BATTLING BACKHAIR

The mystery that is life is rooted in many things. And yes, hair is one of them. Men spend most of their adult life hoping to keep it; women are told that if it grows in the wrong way on the wrong spot, it makes them about as desirable as a roasted old lady (except in some parts of Europe).

Luckily, well-paid marketing executives know this. So it's no sur-

DON'T LOOK BACK

	HOW IT FEELS:	HOW IT GROWS:	MITIGATING FACTOR:
HOT WAX KIT: The time-tested way your mother removed the scruff on her face. Both Sally Hansen and Nair (my choice) offer a simple three-step process. Clean the skin, melt some wax, slap it on; wait a few minutes and rip it off.	Ripping hot wax off your body. Be glad no one's asking you to wear a bikini this summer.	Hair is being pulled out by the root, so you've bought yourself some time. When it started to grow back, it felt a little stubbly and grew in a bit thicker than the other methods.	Bond with your mom, or maybe grandma, over double-boiler waxing.
SWEET SIMPLICITY: As seen in the infomercial, this process involves slopping a gooey, honey-like mixture called the "brulee" (basically sugar and lemon) on the hairy parts and ripping it and your hair off with small, white, reusable strips.	Ripping hot "brulee" off my back was less fun than eating a caramel custard, but this honey-like mixture didn't feel too bad; a lot like having a sticky band-aid stripped from the skin.	Hair came in a bit coarser, though slightly thinner than its cousin, the wax method.	The infomercial that made this product famous ($30 million in sales to date) was recently spoofed on *Friends* (and the well-groomed ones even ate the brulee, which, admittedly, isn't bad).
NAIR CREAM: Rub it on, let it sit for about five minutes and let the chemicals go to work.	Cold and creamy with a little bit of a sting.	Smooth as a chafed baby's butt; mild stubble and a slightly quicker regrowth than the razor.	Serious empathy for those hordes of scared teenage girls slumped over the toilet trying to do their first bikini wax with this bottle full of chemicals.
RAZOR: Water, shaving cream and the blade—you know the drill.	Never expected Gillette to find its way back there.	Be it beard or back, stubble is an undiscriminating mistress.	Ten Bics for $1.59.

FINAL ANALYSIS: Think no pain, no gain and you'll have a pretty good idea of the principals at work when you consider how best to shed your back.

prise that keeping hair on and getting it off is a billion-dollar business—one that, unlike that thinning patch on your skull, is not going away anytime soon. With their faces, legs, bikinis and underarms, women have an awful lot of unwanted hair. Yet us guys come to discover that we, too, have unannounced guests on the temple that is the body.

What to do about the unwelcome rug on your back? Consider the four different removal methods on page 33.

CHAPTER 3

HEALTH/ FITNESS

Q: HOW DO I CURE A HANGOVER?

In ancient Greece, it was believed that if a heavy drinker donned a ring of parsley on his head, he could avoid a hangover the next morning. It's probably no coincidence that the lowly herb soon went from hangover "cure" to an innocuous and easily rotting sideline garnish, where it has remained for the last five thousand years.

Truth is, it's difficult to ward off the evils of The Morning After. And while you'll most likely feel less and less postpartying pain as the ugly college years recede from your memory, there are still those late kamikaze nights when you just know you're going to wake up feeling as if something angry assaulted your brain—and then died in your mouth. Here's how to help avoid that not-so-fresh feeling.

A PERSONALIZED TAPE:
Make one for working out, one for driving out, one for making out.

WHY, GOD, WHY?

As in, why do I exist? Why did I make a commitment to watching musical theater in six hours? And more importantly why, exactly, am I hung over? Modern science has your answer. According to the

American Medical Association's *Encyclopedia of Medicine,* the chief cause of hangovers are "congeners," byproducts of alcohol fermentation found in high concentrations in such typically evil culprits as red wine, bourbon, and brandy. Excess alcohol consumption also produces an overabundance of acetaldehyde, which poisons the system.

TAKE TWO AND CALL ME IN THE MORNING

Hangover cures are like hurling stories—everyone's got one. Remedies of lore range from sex and creative food concoctions (burnt toast with honey, extra-greasy cheeseburgers, egg rolls and milk) to more beer, masturbation, bong hits, and Bloody Marys. And although the "wake and drink" (a.k.a. "hair o' the dog") remedies work to a degree—primarily because they raise your blood-alcohol level and, since alcohol is a form of sugar, increase your blood sugar— if you're consistently curing your hangovers by drinking more, you're dangerously close to setting foot in Ed McMahon territory.

Instead, your best bet is to down a couple glasses of water *before* hitting the sack and take some anti-inflammatories, such as aspirin. The water rehydrates, the aspirin relieves that nagging inflammation of your brain, and, with luck, you wake up feeling like the Zest shower guy. From there, keep drinking—water. This highly underrated liquid remains your best source for reclaiming your life.

ACTIVATE THAT CARBON

We're sure you don't go out every night prior to a hangover and declare, "Tonight, I'm going to get plastered." (Well, not *every* night.) But if, say, you're going out for a business dinner that you know will entail networking/bonding/drinking like a fish, you may want to consider popping an activated-carbon pill. If taken before, during, and after drinking, activated carbon absorbs the toxins that cause hangovers. Best of all, it's available over the counter, under such brand names as Liverite and Nature's Way. Our favorite, Sob'r-K, can also be ordered by calling 888–774–2760.

Or, then again, you could always—gasp!—drink slower; a normal, healthy liver can break down about a drink an hour. Which is better than waking up and vowing, as we all do, "to never drink again."

It's a nice thought, at least.

Q: HOW DO I FIND A CHIROPRACTOR— AND WHAT WILL HE DO TO ME?

The ten-cent definition of chiropractic medicine is drugless, nonsurgical health care focused on the neuromuscular skeletal system. In English, that means chiropractors can't mess with anything on the inside of your body—no cutting, no pricking, no drugs. Their external techniques, however, can run the gamut from massage or ultrasound to physiotherapy methods like electronic muscle stimulation.

A chiropractor's primary tool is adjustment—a technique in which he or she determines the correct position of a joint and physically manipulates it into place. Sound uncomfortable? Um, well, yes. On the other hand, patients often say the long-term pleasure outweighs the short-term discomfort. (If your chiropractor is inflicting serious pain, it's probably time to find a new one.)

The best way to find a good chiropractor is through word of mouth—people tend to feel very strongly about chiropractors they feel have helped them. If you have no vertabraically challenged friends, however, call your state's Chiropractic Association or the American Chiropractic Association (800–986–4636). You also might want to contact your state's Board of Chiropractic Examiners to see if a chiropractor's license is current and if any disciplinary action has been filed against him or her. (All licensed American chiropractors must have at least a degree from a four-year chiropractic college program; some states have even more stringent requirements.) Finally, schedule an initial consultation, and make sure there is a rapport; after all, this is the guy you're trusting with your back.

database of docs and scientific journals, lots of advice, and a set of links evaluated by experts. Not so snazzy, but invaluable nonetheless.

Adventure Sports Online
www.adventuresports. com
Info on kayaking, backpacking, and other adventurous activities, plus the lowdown on expeditions of all sorts, whether you're interested in whitewater rafting on the Colorado River or mountain-biking in Barbados.

Thrive Online
www.thriveonline.com
Information clearinghouse on health and fitness subjects ranging from asthma and alternative medicine to stretching and climbing.

www.healthexplorer. com
Reviews of more than three thousand health-related Web sites, with thumbs-up signs highlighting the best sites.

Q: IS COFFEE GOING TO KILL ME?

You roll out of bed every morning to face your miserable life, and you're finding that you can't even begin to fathom the litany of responsibilities, girlfriends, and work-related crap without jumping the nearest Starbucks employee. You need coffee—and lots of it.

Chinese food, movie popcorn, all the other stuff the food police keep warning you against—you can live without them. But coffee? The conflicting reports regarding coffee consumption and health over the years have ruled out only the extremes: while coffee probably won't spell your demise, you're also not going to see Popeye shotgunning a potful any time soon.

The health concerns are a two-part affair: one stems from your old friend caffeine, the other from conflicting reports about the so-called carcinogens and chemicals floating in your cup.

Let's start with caffeine. An extensive review of caffeine and health by the International Food Information Council showed no significant link between moderate caffeine consumption and cardiovascular disease or cancer, the two big guns of health paranoia. That's moderate consumption. No one advocates consuming large amounts of caffeine and ignoring other nutritional needs. Nor does anyone deny the side effects—those uncontrollable shaky feelings, minor insomnia, and nervousness. Sound familiar?

How much is too much? Two to four cups of coffee daily is probably kosher, although individual reactions to caffeine vary wildly. Consider that coffee, with 155 milligrams of caffeine in a 5-ounce cup, has considerably more caffeine than tea (60 milligrams per 5 ounces) and cola soft drinks (18 milligrams per 6 ounces). Granted, tea is totally undramatic; British people drink it. But if you're trying to cut down on your caffeine consumption, it could do the trick. Herbal teas contain no caffeine at all—although sucking down something akin to a floral bouquet isn't always the most appealing 8:00 A.M. pick-me-up.

As far as chemicals go, the ballot has been cast. Yes, coffee contains lots of chemicals—though no specific ones have been found to be harmful. Reports have espoused trace carcinogens created by the high heat of roasting, but the lack of a significant link between coffee consumption and cancer seems to nix this theory as well.

SNEAKERS THAT FIT:
Avoid foot and knee problems. And *do* slip in odor eaters.

Still, if the phrase "trace carcinogens" makes you uncomfortable, it might behoove you to check out organic coffee. Growers of organic coffee must comply with government standards that forbid the use of any chemicals to produce the coffee for three years.

The key to coffee, like most of life's pleasures, is moderation. While decaf has its benefits, with three milligrams of caffeine in a five-ounce cup, it's kind of like nonalcoholic beer or the Bowl Alliance. What's the point? You'll get a bigger buzz off chocolate milk. We know the reasons you drink coffee in the first place—for the nausea, the jitters and to feel the blood coursing through your veins—and we understand. Just take it easy.

Q: HOW DO I GET MY EIGHT GLASSES OF WATER EACH DAY?

H_2O AND EXERCISE: Before, after, during.

You've had the same morning routine since college. Sixteen ounces of dark-roasted love in the morning, Diet Coke around eleven, then another at lunch, and you've already covered more than half your daily fluid needs, right?

Not exactly. Though it's true that adults need to consume at least eight glasses (sixty-four ounces) of water each day, caffeinated beverages work against the count—even if you're all clear at the bathroom stall. Yes, coffee and soda consist of mostly water, but, like alcohol, they contain diuretics that induce water loss.

Roughly 60 percent of the adult body is water and, like the old cookie jar, it needs constant replenishment. Your body needs water to maintain body temperature, breathe, digest food, transport nutrients through the body and to rid the system of waste products. The mythical eight glasses makes up for the water you lose each day through urine, sweat, and even breathing. When you don't have enough water in your system, your cells begin drawing water from the bloodstream, which eventually will lead to dehydration. When you have too much water in your system, the only consequence is dependency on nearby bathrooms. (But hey, you're a guy. Trees abound.)

It's especially key to hydrate when exercising. A good rule is to drink two cups of water two hours before exercise; one cup thirty minutes before exercise; one-half to one cup about every twenty minutes during exercise; and then one to two cups afterward. Every pound you lose during exercise represents about two cups of water.

Fruits and vegetables are legitimate sources of water, as are beverages like fruit juices, herbal teas and watered-down sports drinks. The only rub is the fact that these drinks also pack sugar and extra calories.

In the end, there's no hitch-free substitute for pure water. And when really think about it, sixty-four ounces is not that big a deal. After all, you rarely balk at the idea of knocking back six beers in one night. And water won't inspire you to wear the lampshade.

CLEAN MACHINES:
Basic gym etiquette. Learn it. Love it.

THE SKINNY ON FAT

Going to the grocery store these days is an intimidating experience. What with all the "low-fat," "reduced-fat," "zero-fat" and "so-skinny-that-when-you-turn-it-to-the-side-you-can't-even-see-it" products on the shelves, you feel kind of guilty every time you haul pork rinds to the counter in preparation for the big game. The fixation with fat—formerly reserved for females—has now become a national coed obsession. Yet even with the $25 billion our country spends on low-fat food every year, the average guy still looks a lot more like the Goodyear Blimp than, well, a much more svelte aircraft. What gives? With all the fat-free stuff out there, shouldn't we be thinner than ever?

FAT CHANCE

Um, no. At least one-third of Americans are overweight, according to the latest statistics, and some estimate it's higher than that. The reason: too much consumption and too little exercise. Your body stores extra calories as fat whether or not the food you're stuffing down is labeled low-fat.

Add to this the fact that your body recognizes and scoffs at low-fat substances. Sure, those Baked Lays may taste like the full-fat version.

But when your body breaks them down, it senses that something's missing and sends a memo to your brain asking for replacements. In a recent study, researchers found that subjects who ate meals with fat substitutes like Olestra for a day responded by eating almost twice as much fat as usual the next day. Thus, you get hit with a double whammy: you eat more than you normally would because you think there won't be any consequences, and your body turns those extra calories into fat. The next day, your body craves *real* fat, so you wind up fixing yourself thirty pounds' worth of Spam sandwiches.

(FAINT) PRAISE FOR FAT

Know what? You need fat. Particularly to cushion your organs, keep your skin healthy and help in the absorption of certain vitamins. It might do more than that, in fact: Researchers have found that a diet that is extremely low in fat may increase the likelihood of stroke, as well as reduce your testosterone to levels previously attained only through repeated viewings of *The Joy Luck Club*.

So you need it, but how much? The figure that's bandied about most often is no more than 30 percent of your calories from fat. Some physicians give even a little more leeway depending on what kind of fat you're eating. There are a number of fats that are actually *good* for you. Although saturated fats (think red meat, dairy, and most fast food) and trans-fatty acids (most prepackaged snack items and, yes, fast food) have been linked with everything from heart disease to increased cancer risk, they aren't the only kinds of fat out there. Monounsaturated fat, which you'll find in olive oil and canola oil, actually helps protect your cardiovascular system. Meanwhile, omega-3 fatty acids (found in seafood, green leafy vegetables, and certain kinds of nuts) are body-friendly as well, lowering the likelihood of heart attacks, stroke, cancer, and other diseases.

OK, SO WHAT THE HELL AM I SUPPOSED TO PUT IN MY STOMACH?

1. DIVERSIFY. Maybe you can't afford to do it with your stock portfolio, but it's a lot easier to do at the dinner table. Eat some of those fruits and vegetables you've been avoiding since the second grade. When you go out to a restaurant, try ordering fish for a change. Instead of smearing your bread with butter or margarine,

A TRAINER: Splurge for at least a few sessions to set up a routine and check your form.

dip it in olive oil. It tastes better, and you replace negative trans-fatty acids with healthier monounsaturated fat.

2. QUICK FIXES. No way you're going to overhaul the way you eat? There are some small steps you can take to minimize the damage. For example, if you're just not going to eat fish or vegetables, you should consider taking one fish oil capsule and one multivitamin daily. That'll give your body some of the omega–3, vitamin, and mineral benefits. (Check with your doctor before starting with the fish capsules, however. They act as a blood thinner, and can be harmful in high doses or to people with certain conditions.) Likewise, if you cook with vegetable oil or shortening, switch to olive oil. You won't notice a difference in how it tastes. Order a baked potato instead of french fries. Spend two seconds blotting the top of your pizza with a napkin. Eat a big lunch instead of a big dinner.

MORNING WORKOUT:
Chances are it's your only free time all day.

3. KEEP FAT IN PERSPECTIVE. While "30 percent of your calories from fat" is a nice goal to have, it's not going to make a difference if you gobble boxes of SnackWells and haven't exercised since the Reagan administration. Total calories are an important part of the equation, so you have to keep an eye on how much you're eating.

Some guidelines: your fist is about a cup serving of pasta, a three-ounce portion of cooked meat is the size of a deck of cards, and an ounce of cheese is the equivalent of four dice. That's usually the serving size listed on the package. And exercise, for God's sake. Yes, we're talking to you, cubicle boy.

4. CHILL OUT. Eating and taking medicine are not synonymous. So make the changes you can, and then relax. Eating is supposed to be enjoyable.

PREVENTING SPORTS INJURIES

When "work hard, play hard" means a sedentary week followed by weekend feats of athleticism, you're cruising for a bruising—literally. It may be tempting to jump into a basketball game after a winter on the couch, but infrequent exercisers sustain three times as many sports injuries—usually strains and sprains—as regular exercisers.

Similarly, poor stamina, the affliction of many a weekend warrior, leads quickly to fatigue, and thus poses a major injury threat: If you're tired, you tend to lose your form. It's no coincidence that a majority of skiing accidents happen at the end of the day.

Sports injuries also occur due to cold muscles. As much as it sounds like a waste of time, warming up really does help. Cold ligaments and tendons can snap like icicles without a little body heat, and a ten-minute brisk walk or jog is all it takes. Once muscles are warm, you've hit the optimal time to stretch, which is also de rigeur. An added benefit of stretching: You'll be more comfortable taking risks on the field, since you won't need to worry as much about pulling a muscle when you lunge or leap.

There are others tips to prevent injury that are specific to each sport. So we sought out Dr. Peter Bruno, a top sports medicine specialist at Beth Israel Hospital and the Insall Scott Kelly Institute for Sports Medicine and Athletic Trauma in New York City for some advice. Of course, that's a lot of resumé mumbo jumbo. Bruno also advises the New York Knicks on injury prevention. And anyone who can keep Patrick Ewing's knees and Larry Johnson's back in shape through an 82-game season is good enough for us.

STRETCHES

Fifteen to 20 minutes of stretching before each game helps keep the Knicks in shape. Before you hit your game, try the following stretches:

QUADRICEPS STRETCH:
Holding a chair or wall for balance, reach for your right ankle with your right hand and lift it to your buttocks. Push forward with the

WORKOUT PARTNER: Keeps you going and pushes you further. Ever hear of friendly competition?

AEROBICS: Weights are great, but you want that heart to keep on tickin'.

front of your thigh. Do not move your lower back. Hold for five seconds and repeat five to ten times with each leg.

ILIOTIBIAL BAND STRETCH:

Stand with your right side to the wall. Hold the wall with your right hand for support. Cross your right leg behind the left leg and place your left hand on your left hip. With your weight on the left leg, lean your right hip forward toward the wall, keeping your right leg straight. You will feel the stretch along the outer thigh. Hold for five seconds and repeat five to ten times on each side.

SPORTS INJURIES

	Common Injury	Remedy	Tip
Basketball	Jumper's knee (patellar tendinitis, a tiny tear of the tendon that connects the kneecap to the shinbone). Repeated running and jumping cause the injury.	Stretch your quadriceps before and after exercise.	Jammed fingers, perhaps the most frequent and hard-to-prevent hoops injury, should be iced immediately or they may stay permanently enlarged.
Biking	Iliotibial band syndrome, or stabbing pain on the outside of the knee, caused by repetitive stress on the band, which runs from your pelvis to shinbone. It often occurs when your seat or pedals are not the proper height for you or the tendon is too tight.	Go to a bike shop and get your bike adjusted to fit your body. Stretch the iliotibial band before and after biking.	Quadriceps take a pounding on uphills. When a gentle burn turns to searing pain, get off, stretch, and take it easy, or you'll strain one of the quads.
Racquetball	A hamstring, calf muscle or Achilles tendon pull. These painful back-of-the-leg strains usually occur after a fast leap or lunge.	Keep your muscles warm by moving constantly on the court. If you start to feel a pull, get off. Stretch hamstring, calf and Achilles tendon well before and after you play.	You might have faith in your own abilities, but what about your partner's? Wear protective eyewear, especially in a fast game.

HAMSTRING STRETCH:

Lie on your back with your knees bent and feet flat on the floor. Place a towel under the ball of your right foot and hold one end with each hand as you bring your right knee to your chest. Slowly raise and straighten the leg while keeping your shoulders flat on the floor. Hold for five seconds and repeat five to ten times on each side.

	Common Injury	Remedy	Tip
Running	Shin splints, which are irritated tendons crossing the shinbone. The continual jolts to the shin when your feet hit the ground cause the muscle to pull on the bone, creating tendinitis. Continued irritation can lead to stress fractures.	You may need new running shoes, which should be replaced after every 500 miles, when they lose 30 percent of their cushioning and elasticity. Build mileage slowly, maintain a controlled motion when running downhill and stretch your quadriceps, hamstrings and calves before running.	Check wearing pattern on the bottom of your shoes to see which side you favor. If they're worn out on the inside, you need a running shoe with a good arch; if they're worn on the outside, you need less arch support.
Skiing	Ligament and cartilage tears in the knee are usually the result of a fall. The most dreaded: the ACL (anterior cruciate ligament) and meniscus (cartilage) tears, which may require surgery or months of physical therapy.	A good biking program (stationary or outdoor bike) to build up your quadriceps. Strong quads can take the impact of bumps and jolts so your ligaments are spared. Warm up the quadriceps and hamstrings with stretches to prevent muscle strain.	If you're going down, don't break a fall with your poles. This will protect your thumb, which many skiers needlessly injure during a spill.
Weightlifting	Muscle tears (usually biceps or deltoids) that may keep you out of the gym for weeks. Even worse: Lift too much weight with cold muscles, and it's not uncommon for the bicep to snap completely and require surgical repair.	Before you lift, do 15 minutes of easy jogging or stair climbing and upper body stretching to warm up. Alternate upper-and-lower body weight training to allow muscles to repair themselves.	Start with an amount of weight that you can easily handle and slowly increase. As the weight increases, don't arch or you'll wind up with back strain.

CALF STRETCH:

Sit with your legs straight out in front of you, one foot apart. Place a towel around the ball of your right foot and hold one end with each hand. Pull the towel until you feel a gentle stretch. Hold for five seconds and repeat five to ten times with each leg.

ACHILLES STRETCH:

Kneel on your left knee. Place your right foot next to your left knee with your heel flat on the floor. Push forward with your right shoulder until right heel raises slightly off the floor. Try to push the right heel down as you lean forward. Hold for five seconds and repeat five to ten times with each heel.

RICE

Sometimes, even well-conditioned athletes get injured. Fortunately, most recreational injuries can be treated at home with RICE. (And we don't mean Uncle Ben's.)

REST. Rest allows your body to heal itself. When injured, stop exercise immediately. Don't put weight on wounded limbs; use a sling or crutches as needed.

ICE. Apply ice to injured parts as soon as possible. Cold causes torn blood vessels to shrink and helps stop internal bleeding. This allows a minimum amount of swelling at the injured site.

COMPRESS. Wrap the injury with an ace bandage or cloth to keep swelling down and reduce motion, which adds stress to the injury. It should be firm but not tight.

ELEVATE. Raise the injured area above the level of the heart, if possible, so that gravity drains excess fluid away. Elevation also minimizes swelling and pain.

WEIGHT BELT:
Spare your back, muscle boy.

TWENTY-POUND DUMBBELLS:
Simple, cheap, versatile at-home workout enhancer.

THIRTY-MINUTE POWER WORKOUT

Building big, powerful muscles fast is tricky business. It usually takes the better part of a year to turn an unconditioned body into a muscle-bound machine. If that sounds like forever, don't sweat it. There's a faster way.

The secret is building both strength and stamina. This magic combination can lead to visible muscle mass in about six weeks. If you're already doing regular cardiovascular exercise, you'll get speedy results with three weekly thirty-minute weight training sessions, provided they are properly designed. (For that, read on.)

The effects are much smaller if you aren't keeping in aerobic shape, though, so hanging around the weight room isn't enough. The heart, not the bicep, is the key muscle to greater strength. By running, biking, or playing hoops for just a few days each week, your heart is able to deliver more oxygen to the other muscles, making them more efficient and thus allowing you to build up faster.

You don't need an expensive gym membership for this workout, either, since it's done with free weights. If you're strapped for cash as well as muscle, invest about seventy dollars in five-, ten-, fifteen-, and twenty-pound pairs of dumbbells.

Though the twenty-pounder may seem easy to lift, don't necessarily start with it. Too many weight training neophytes make the mistake of doing too much too soon. Choose a weight that you can lift ten times but becomes difficult around the eleventh. When you begin, do three sets of twelve repetitions with the weight you choose. Allow just one minute of rest between lifts. When you can do all three sets without strain, it's time to move to the next weight. For bulkier muscles, alternate fewer repetitions with more weight.

How you lift is just as important as how much you lift. Quality beats quantity, so take your time: handle the weights with slow and controlled movements, and use your full range of motion. This allows you to train a greater percentage of muscle mass (which means bigger muscles) and prevents strain. You know you're overdoing it when you feel yourself start to cheat, or pull in other muscles to help lift the weight. Even worse is when you engage your lower back or shoulder joint for support—that's when you're likely to wind up getting injured. If you feel the urge to cheat, stop yourself before you get hurt.

EXERCISE MAT: Roughly ten bucks, and you no longer have to do sit-ups on that dirty hardwood floor.

THE PROGRAM

Do three sets of twelve to fifteen repetitions for each exercise. Start with five-pound dumbbells, and increase weight as needed.

CHEST AND BACK

1. PUSHUPS. Place hands slightly wider than shoulder width apart on the floor. Extend the body in a straight line. Press shoulder blades together, and keep abdominals tight. Lower the body until elbows form a right angle. Raise the body up as far as possible without separating the shoulder blades.

2. BENT-OVER ROWS. Place feet hip-width apart with knees bent. Bend over from the waist until the upper body is parallel with the floor. Pull dumbbells toward hips and press shoulder blades together, then lower weights slowly.

JUMP ROPE: Classic, effective aerobic exercise; also useful when your niece drags you to the playground.

BICEPS/TRICEPS

1. CURLS. Stand with feet hip-width apart and knees bent. With one weight in each hand, palms up, curl weight up as far as possible without allowing your elbows to leave your side.

2. LYING TRICEPS EXTENSIONS. Lie on your back with knees bent and elbows facing the ceiling. Hold one dumbbell in each hand, and lower and raise the weights without moving the upper arm.

SHOULDERS

1. FRONT RAISE. Place feet hip-width apart, and bend knees slightly. Hold weights with palms facing body. Raise arms in front of you until they are parallel to the floor, and then lower.

2. SIDE RAISE. Place feet hip-width apart. Bend knees slightly. Hold weights with palms facing body. Raise arms to the side until they are parallel with the floor, then lower.

3. BENT-OVER RAISE. Place feet hip width apart. Bend over until body is parallel to the floor. Hold weights with palms facing body. Raise arms to the side until they are parallel to the floor, then lower.

LEGS AND BUTT

1. LUNGES. Place feet hip width apart. Hold weights by your side. Step back with one leg, bending both knees at the same time. Stand up using front leg only.

ABDOMINALS

1. REVERSE CRUNCH. Lie on your back, with your hands at your side and knees bent. Roll your hips toward your chest and then lower them slowly back down again.

2. CRUNCH. Lie on your back with your hands at your side and knees bent. Place hands behind the head (do not clasp fingers). Slowly press the lower back into the floor as you raise your chest to your hips.

TRAINING TIPS

- Maintain good form. Keep your back straight, abdominals tight, knees soft, and shoulder blades together as you lift.

- Practice proper breathing. Do not hold your breath. The more regularly you breath, the less quickly you become fatigued. Exhale during the muscle exertion, and inhale during the release.

- Have a loose grip. Do not grip the weights tightly when lifting. This works the forearms, which cheats the larger muscles you've been trying to build.

- Stay in control. Allow the exercise to be performed over a full range of motion in a controlled manner. Be careful not to hyperextend a joint.

- Don't overdo it. Try not to cross the line between challenging yourself and straining your muscles and joints. Stop exercise immediately if you start to feel a strong exertion turn to searing pain.

BUILDING BIG ARMS AND A POWERFUL CHEST

Since we know you weren't tuning in, here's a *Baywatch* update: David Hasselhoff has been told to keep his shirt on. His chest just wasn't cutting it.

This proves good news on two fronts. Besides making the show eminently more watchable for most guys, it serves as an important lesson: even a guy who knows a billion people are checking him out every week loses his upper body physique if he's not smart and disciplined about his training regimen. And be warned: the upper body is a key asset on the sports field and with the ladies. Not only will a sculpted chest, back and arms make you stronger, they will give you the powerful look of a Greek god.

Too often, guys who haven't lifted since high school head to the weight room and make the classic mistake of starting with heavy sets and low reps, a routine that is more likely to lead to pain, injury, and frustration than big muscles. The theory now is to build your body like a house: start with light resistance to build the foundation, add medium resistance to create the infrastructure, and finally, use high resistance to make it strong enough to weather any storm.

With the accompanying workout, you'll reach every major muscle in the chest, back and arms. To figure out how much weight you should start with, take 70 percent of the maximum you can lift. If it's a hundred pounds, for example, use seventy pounds. If you're using dumbbells, drop another 10 percent to sixty pounds (thirty-pound weights for each hand). Now you're building the foundation. To add intensity, keep it slow: four seconds to lower and four seconds to lift.

For the best results, change the sequence of the exercises so that your muscles don't adapt to a pattern, which makes it too easy for them. Stick with the program and you can expect noticeably bigger muscles in four to six weeks.

PUSH-UPS AND SIT-UPS: Herschel Walker never lifted weights. You don't have to either.

THE PROGRAM

You'll need a gym equipped with a bench, weights, and chin-up bar. Increase your weight by 5 percent to 10 percent as soon as you can go above the set number of reps with good form. Start with one set of each exercise, and add more sets gradually.

FIRST 3 WEEKS: 15 TO 18 REPS

WEEKS 4 AND 5: 12 TO 15 REPS

WEEKS 6 AND 7: 8 TO 12 REPS

WEEKS 8 AND 9: 6 TO 8 REPS

CHEST

INCLINED CHEST PRESS (WORKS UPPER CHEST).

Lie on a bench set at a forty-five-degree incline. Hold a dumbbell in each hand next to your armpits. Straighten your arms out in front of you with dumbbells rising up over the upper part of your chest until they touch; squeeze your pectoral muscles, and slowly lower to the starting position.

DUMBBELL FLIES (WORKS MIDCHEST).

Lie on a flat bench. Hold a dumbbell in each hand with elbows bent at a ninety-degree degree angle and pointing toward the floor. Contract your chest muscles, and slowly bring your hands together in a semicircle, keeping your elbows slightly bent. Return to starting position.

DECLINE PUSH-UPS (WORKS ENTIRE CHEST).

Put your hands on the floor, shoulder-width apart, and place your feet up on the bench behind you. Bend your elbows out to the side, and lower your upper torso so the top of the chest touches the floor. Straighten your arms, and return to the starting position.

BACK

CHIN-UPS (WORKS UPPER BACK, BICEPS, FOREARMS).

Hold the bar above you with an underhand grip, hands at shoulder width. Bend your knees so that you are fully extended, then pull yourself up until your collarbone is at bar level and your chin is over the bar. Pause for a second and lower.

DUMBBELL PULLOVER (WORKS UPPER LATS, LOWER CHEST, AND TRICEPS).

Lie on a flat bench with your knees up. Hold a dumbbell in each hand at hip level. Raise your arms straight over your head so that the

A LOW-KEY WORKOUT BAG: A fluorescent yellow Fila bag might fit right in at the gym, but people will look at you funny if you bring it to the office.

elbows come back by your ears. Slowly pull the weights back over to the starting position.

INCLINE DUMBBELL ROW (WORKS THE RHOMBOIDEI, TRAPEZIUS, LATS, AND BICEPS).

Lie chest down on the bench, and hold a dumbbell in each hand, with your arms hanging down below you. Pull your arms straight back, so the elbows are by your sides. Pause for a count and return to the starting position.

SHOULDERS AND ARMS

LATERAL RAISES (WORKS THE MIDDLE PART OF SHOULDERS).

Stand with your feet hip-width apart and hold a dumbbell in each hand with your arms by your side. Bend the knees and elbows slightly, and raise the arms straight out to the side until they are parallel to the floor. Pause for a count, and lower back to starting position.

SHOULDER PRESS (WORKS THE FRONT PART OF THE SHOULDERS AND TRICEPS).

Sit on the bench, feet flat on the floor, back straight, with a dumbbell in each hand. Bend your elbows at a ninety-degree angle, lift the weights to your ears, and then straighten the arms so the dumbbells touch over your head. Pause for a count, and lower slowly to the starting position.

SEATED DUMBBELL CURLS (WORKS BICEPS).

Sit on bench with feet flat on the floor, elbows by your side and dumbbells in each hand, palms up. Bend your elbows so that they go no higher than ninety degrees, pause for two counts and slowly lower to starting position.

DUMBBELL TRICEPS EXTENSION (WORKS THE TRICEPS).

Sit on the bench, with your elbows by your side and a dumbbell in each hand. Slowly lift your arms over your head, keeping elbows by your ears. Pause for a count and lower the dumbbells behind your head toward your neck, keeping elbows in by your ears. Extend arms straight up to return to starting position.

TRIAL-SIZE EVERYTHING:
Two-inch shampoo bottles may not last long, but they eliminate a lot of bulk.

NOTHING BEATS A GREAT PAIR OF LEGS

All too often, men neglect their lower half in an effort to build their chests and arms. The result: bird legs. Fine, if you intend to spend all your time at the beach underwater. If not, it's time to turn those sapling legs into mighty trunks. Well-muscled legs add strength and stamina to practically any workout. And, as any lady will tell you, good-looking legs get noticed. This workout focuses on your leg muscles, while still leaving time for your upper body. Call it an opportunity to create a balanced physique.

A major benefit of balanced workouts is injury prevention. Overtrain the quads at the expense of the hamstrings, and you're asking for a tendon pull or knee problems. An even set of quadriceps, hamstrings, and calves, on the other hand, helps absorb impact in running, skiing, and basketball, to name just a few sports, which in turn protects your joints, tendons, and ligaments from injury.

The program here combines aerobic workouts with anaerobic training, a strategy that puts your body in a prime state for building muscle mass. Your best bet: do aerobic exercise plus weight training on the same day, twice a week. For example: a twenty-minute bike ride followed by ten minutes of weights and five minutes of stretching. Biking and stair-climbing are two of the best exercises you can do to build leg muscle, and they'll take you a long way toward aerobic fitness.

No gym membership? No worries. All you need is a bicycle (if you lack one, the stairs are your friend), a backpack, and a set of dumbbells. Several of the exercises below, such as the Gear Shredder (bike exercise) and Two-Step (stair exercise) use your body instead of weights for resistance. Others, such as the Stiff-Legged Dead Lift and One-Legged Squat, can be done with or without weights.

A word to the wise: After each workout, stretch your Achilles tendon—that snappable piece of fiber above your heel—as well as your hamstrings and quads. Strength training with weights puts tremendous pressure on all three areas, and pulled muscles take a long time to heal.

Try the following exercises for six to eight weeks, and get ready to ignore the whistles from women as your muscle-bound legs stride down to the park in those sleek new running shorts.

A GOOD PAIR OF SWEATBANDS: Terrycloth is a gym rat's best friend.

AEROBIC LEG WORKOUT

GEAR SHREDDER (WORKS THE QUADRICEPS MUSCLES IN THE FRONT OF THE THIGHS AND THE CALVES).

Set your bike at a low gear and pedal for five minutes as a warm-up. Then switch to a high gear, and stand on the pedals (gear down for uphill climbs to avoid falling). Pedal as fast as you can for fifteen minutes, then gear down, sit back on the seat, and keep pedaling fast. Slow down to dismount, and move straight ahead to your strength-training workout.

TWO-STEP (DEVELOPS THE QUADRICEPS MUSCLES AND THE HAMSTRINGS IN THE BACK OF THE THIGHS).

This exercise requires some serious stairs (not a stair-climbing machine, just stairs). A football stadium is ideal, because it gives you one long set. The goal is to climb at least sixty individual steps. If you work in a multistoried building, try the back stairs.

Go up two stairs at a time; two-step climbing develops the whole leg (quadriceps, hamstring, and gluteus—nice butt!). Go down by running in a smooth, flowing motion, and be careful not to spin out on the landings. Grab the railing if you need to, but avoid hanging on—you can put too much stress on the knee closest to the rail. Repeat for twenty minutes.

WEIGHTED CLIMB (BUILDS THE QUADRICEPS, HAMSTRINGS, AND CALVES).

This is the same as the Two-Step, only with a pack on your back. Put ten pounds of weights in the pack, increasing the amount five pounds every week until you reach a maximum of forty pounds. Descend carefully, one step at a time, to save your knees. Stop if you feel a sharp pain in any part of the knee. Repeat for twenty minutes.

RESISTANCE LEG WORKOUTS

STIFF-LEGGED DEAD LIFT (WORKS THE HAMSTRINGS IN THE BACK OF THE THIGHS).

Stand on a pair of phone books (one under each foot) or on a block of wood. Hold a set of twenty-pound dumbbells in each hand. Bend slowly at the waist, with your knees straight, but not locked. Keeping your back straight, lower your upper body until the weights are

FLIP-FLOPS:
Nothing's worse than taking a shower and inviting the attack of that nasty athlete's foot.

below the level of your feet or until you feel the hamstring stretch. Now rise up slowly, keeping your back straight. Repeat ten times. When you can do ten reps, add five pounds to each dumbbell.

ONE-LEGGED SQUAT (BUILDS QUADRICEPS, HAMSTRINGS AND THE GLUTEAL GROUP IN YOUR BUTTOCKS).

Stand on one foot, tucking the other behind your ankle. Keeping your back straight, squat as far as you comfortably can. Raise yourself slowly, and repeat twelve times. Your quads should feel like they're on fire. When you can do the set easily, try doing it with a five-pound dumbbell in each hand. Repeat on the other leg.

CALF RAISE (WORKS THE CALF MUSCLES).

Raise yourself up on tiptoe, hold for a second, and lower slowly. Repeat ten times. When you can do a set easily, hold dumbbells in both hands, adding five pounds to each dumbbell every week, building to twenty pounds of weight. For fuller calf development, try an advanced calf raise: holding weights in both hands, stand on a step, lower your heels past the stair level, and then rise up on tiptoe. This gives you a good stretch, too.

THE BELOW-THE-BELT WEEKLY SCHEDULE

DAY ONE:
20 minutes stair climbing (the Two-Step)
10 minutes resistance training (Dead Lift, One-
   Legged Squat and Calf Raise)
3 minutes stretching

DAY TWO:
Upper-body exercise

DAY THREE:
20 minutes biking (the Gear Shredder)
10 minutes resistance training (Dead Lift, One-
   Legged Squat and Calf Raise)
3 minutes stretching

DAY FOUR:
20 minutes light exercise, such as a brisk walk or
   easy bike ride

DAY FIVE:
20 minutes serious stair climbing (the Weighted
   Climb)
3 minutes stretching

DAY SIX:
Upper-body exercise

DAY SEVEN:
Rest

FIVE MINUTES TO WASHBOARD ABS

When scrawny Michael Keaton needed washboard abs to play Batman, the producers took the easy way out—they bought him an armorlike suit. Since that's likely out of your price range, you'll just have to make do with the real thing. But don't worry. They'll be much more appreciated and can be developed almost as simply.

Today's crunches isolate the abdominal muscles so well that you can create a sculpted torso with just five minutes of ab work each day. With that small a time commitment, you've just run out of excuses.

Strong abs are more than a hot asset. They're your core strength. This group of four muscles—the rectus abdominis, external obliques, internal obliques, and transversus abdominis form a wall of support on the front and sides of your torso that helps you do everything better, from throwing a ball to lifting weights. And a good set of abs acts as a pillar of strength for your back, which means you're less likely to suffer lower back problems later in life. This muscle group also gives you better posture, which makes it easier to stand up to your full height and regain the inches lost to slouching. (Admit it, you're guilty.) Three specific exercises form a complete ab workout. You don't even need a gym. To build a muscled midriff all you need is workout space and a few minutes to do some targeted ab work.

These are not the sit-ups you did in high school. In fact, they're a lot easier. All you have to do is lie flat on your back, lift your legs up, and contract your abdominal muscles. And you don't need endless reps.

To keep the tempo slow as you do the exercises, focus on your stomach. Think about pressing the small of your back into the ground, and visualize the muscles you're working on. Don't allow yourself to use momentum to lift off, which is tempting but ultimately a waste of time. Keep it slow, do them daily, and you'll see results in just a few weeks.

There's just one catch: nobody will be able to see those newly defined abdominal muscles if you're carrying a few extra pounds around your middle. Regular aerobic workouts are essential, as well as a diet low in high-fat foods. After that, it's Micheal Keaton, eat your stomach out.

SPRING-LOADED HAND GRIPS:
Forearms like Popeye, without all that spinach.

THE AB RIPPER

For the maximum benefit, go from one exercise to the next with no more than ten seconds of rest time.

1. CLASSIC CRUNCH. If you have time for only one, do the classic crunch, which works all of the ab muscles. Lie on your back with your knees bent and your feet flat on the floor. Cradle your head with your hands so that your elbows are out to the sides. Contract your abs to lift the upper body until your shoulder blades clear the floor, then lower and repeat. Try not to lower all the way down to the floor after each repetition.

2. OBLIQUE CRUNCH. The oblique muscles run along your sides, near the love handles. Add this one and you'll get extra torso definition. Lie on your back with your knees bent and your feet flat on the floor. Bring your left shoulder toward your right knee, keeping your arms back and open, until your shoulder blades clear the floor, and then lower. Alternate these with the reverse: lift the right shoulder to the left knee and lower.

3. REVERSE CURL. This exercise focuses on the lower abdominal area, the transversus abdominis. If you can master this one, the most challenging of the three, you'll see a dramatic change in the shape of your stomach. Lie on your back with your legs straight up in the air. Use your abs to lift your tail bone and hips off the floor, keeping your legs straight. Don't allow your legs to fall toward your head. At the same time, curl your upper body off the floor toward the legs (shoulder blades clearing the floor). Keep a slow and controlled motion throughout the exercise.

YMCA: Financially, there's no excuse not to work out.

THE HOTEL ROOM WORKOUT

The glamour of being a business traveler fades quickly. Who among us has ever flown the Concorde? More like cramming into coach on the red-eye to Dubuque, desperately hoping that once there you'll be able to find a Stuckey's that's open twenty-four hours. With a steady diet of air travel, stress, and "home-style" road restaurants, it's no wonder that so many business travelers bloat up faster than Elvis.

There's a simple way to avoid this fate: exercise. With the right routine, you can not only combat the negative health effects of business travel, but you can put yourself in better shape than ever before. Not staying at the Four Seasons with its spiffy gym? No problem. You can do this killer workout in any hotel room (even at the Motel 6). The only other resource needed: twenty minutes.

This exercise routine is based on a style of training called Peripheral Heart Action. What you're doing is moving blood through all the muscle groups of your body in sequence. By forcing you to move quickly from one exercise to the next, this method ensures that you'll receive cardiovascular as well as muscle-toning benefits.

These exercises aren't supposed to hurt (except in that vaguely pleasurable exercise way) unless you're doing something wrong. If at any point during the routine, you find yourself yodeling in pain, stop immediately. Second, to obtain those cardiovascular benefits, you'll need to limit yourself to only thirty seconds' rest between exercises. Any more than that and you risk turning into Willie Loman.

One last thing. Make sure to incorporate some cool-down stretches. (You can use the stretches from the warm-up.) Also jot down how many reps of each exercise you did so you've got a target to beat for next time.

And take a shower before going to that sales meeting, OK?

TWO BIG GYM TOWELS:
One for you, one to wipe off the machines.

WARMING UP

Start off with trunk-side bends. Standing with your hands behind your head, bend to the left. Hold for four seconds, return to a neutral position, and then bend to your right for four seconds. Alternate sides for one minute. Now do calf raises: raise yourself onto your tiptoes, moving your heels as high as possible, and then lower. Repeat for one minute.

Next, stretch your quads by raising your right foot behind your body and grasping it with your left hand. (Stand a few inches away from a wall so you can support yourself with your other hand.) Keeping your thigh perpendicular to the floor, slowly pull your heel in toward your backside until you feel the thigh muscle stretch. Hold for thirty seconds, and then repeat with the left leg. Finish with a one-minute set of jumping jacks.

SQUAT THRUSTS WITH PUSH-UPS (WORKS LEGS, CHEST, SHOULDERS, ARMS).

Stand with your arms at your sides, feet shoulder-width apart. Bend your knees until you're squatting with your hands on the ground. Kick your legs back into a push-up position and do the push-up. (Remember to stare at the floor while doing this. Looking up can strain your neck.) Pull your legs back into the squatting position, then stand. Repeat. Continue this for one minute. (To make it tougher, add a jump to the end of the movement.)

CRUNCHES (WORKS UPPER AND LOWER ABS).

Stare at the ceiling with your knees bent and feet flat on the floor. Your hands should be laced together behind your head, elbows out. Focus on keeping your lower back glued to the floor as you curl your head and shoulders up. (Don't use your hands to pull up your head.) At the same time, slowly lift your legs and pelvis, tucking your knees into your chest. Return to starting position, then repeat. Continue for one minute.

WIDE- AND NARROW-STANCE PUSH-UPS (WORKS CHEST, SHOULDERS, AND ARMS).

Begin with your hands wider than your shoulders, your body at roughly a forty-five-degree angle to the floor, and your weight supported by only your palms and your toes. Do push-ups for thirty seconds. Switch to a grip with your hands narrower than your shoulders; do push-ups for another thirty seconds.

ALTERNATE CRUNCHES (WORKS OBLIQUES).

Return to the crunch position. This time, as you curl your head up, bring your right shoulder toward your left knee. Return to starting position and then repeat, bringing your left shoulder toward your right knee. Alternate for ninety seconds.

SQUATS (WORKS LEGS, BUTT, HIPS, AND BACK).

Keeping your back straight, squat until your thighs are parallel to the floor. If you're having trouble balancing, it may help to hold your arms straight in front of you, palms facing down. As soon as you reach the bottom position, return to your original stance, and repeat in a nonstop motion. Continue at a quick pace for the next two minutes.

A WRIST HEART-RATE MONITOR: Check up on your aerobic progress.

DIVE-BOMBER PUSH-UPS (WORKS CHEST, ABS, SHOULDERS, AND ARMS).

Unlike regular push-ups, your feet should be stationed slightly wider than your shoulders. Place your hands the same width as, and slightly in front of, your shoulders, your body at that trusty forty-five-degree angle, with your weight supported by your palms and toes. Pretend you are arcing under a fence twelve inches in front of you and twelve inches high. Arc down and back up to your starting position, as if you're rewinding the previous move. Continue for one minute, and then lie facedown on the floor for the final exercise.

BACK EXTENSIONS (WORKS BACK).

Staring at the carpet, place your hands behind your head, and raise your chest off the ground. Hold for two seconds, and then return to the starting position. Repeat for one minute. Collapse in a sweaty heap.

SNOWBOARD:
The ultimate winter workout.

TRAIN FOR A MARATHON

If you were surprised to find out the paunchy guy in the next office—the one whose proudest earthly possession is one of those beer-can-holder helmets—has run a marathon, don't be. With proper training, anyone in decent physical condition can finish the world's classic endurance test. No longer the sole province of gaunt ascetics, the 26.2-mile run has become a cross-section of our society, populated not only by Olympic hopefuls but also by octogenarians, amputees, paraplegics, organ-transplant patients, and, yes, even Oprah.

Longing to wear the metallic I-just-finished-a-marathon cape? Just follow this simple training guide, and in five months, you will be lining up next to beer-cap boy.

The keystone of marathon training is the long run. It strengthens heart and leg muscles and teaches the body to deal with fatigue. Carefully begin at a comfortable distance, and then increase the length of your weekly long run in small increments. Never add more than two miles to your longest previous run.

Your pace during these runs should be relaxed, approximately one minute per mile slower than your customary training pace—running any faster can lead to injury and excessive fatigue. Do not be afraid to stop and walk for periods of up to five minutes during these runs. And fluids are essential before, during, and after these runs—figure one or two cups for every thirty minutes. Either water or a sports drink such as Gatorade will do the trick, and you should err on the side of overhydration. You're better off making a few pit stops in the bushes than ending up in the emergency room.

As wretched as you may feel the day following your long run, you should go for a short one. Don't worry if you feel like you are running with a refrigerator strapped to your back; the purpose of this session is not to go fast but to loosen your muscles and chase away soreness.

As you train, picking an appropriate pace becomes important. As a first-time marathoner, your paramount goal is simple: finish the race. Don't worry about a fast time; this will come if you decide to run additional marathons. Thus, during your training runs, your aim is to cover a certain distance, regardless of how long it may take you. You should run at a pace where conversation is possible. Running with a friend will help you follow this rule.

If you train in an area frequented by other runners, be careful not to let them influence your pace. Plan your workouts in advance and stick to them.

Speed work is not necessary, but some runners like to throw in an occasional up-tempo workout for variety's sake. This is fine, but don't overdo it. Run speed workouts no more than once a week, and make sure that you have at least one day to recover between your tempo runs and your long runs.

Just as you must be anal about training after your weekly long run, you should not train every day. Two nonconsecutive rest days each week provide your body with a chance to rebuild the muscle fiber that you have torn down. If you are feeling particularly tired, take a third or fourth day off. The key here is to listen to your body—if you are experiencing pain, illness, or fatigue, back off.

Feel free to substitute other types of aerobic exercise for running once or twice a week. Bicycling, swimming, in-line skating, aerobics, stair climbing, cross-country skiing, and rowing all provide good cardiovascular workouts without the pounding of running. When you cross-train, remember that your goal is to run a marathon, not to become an Olympic cyclist or rower. Thus, be sure to keep your

A GOOD PADLOCK:
Protect yourself in the locker room.

effort moderate (i.e., about the same exertion level as your normal run and no longer than one hour) to avoid compromising your marathon training.

As you get more comfortable running, consider an occasional road race. These events can serve as tune-ups and give you a yardstick by which to measure your fitness level. They will also serve as speed work, breaking up the monotony of training. Perhaps most importantly, races simulate the marathon experience, teaching you how to deal with obstacles such as nerves, crowded starts, water stops, and those most dreaded marathon hardships, port-a-potties. They also help beef up the old T-shirt collection.

Choose tune-up races from five miles to thirty kilometers, and race no more than twice a month. Always go for a short, slow recovery run on the day following a race. On weeks that you race, eliminate your long run.

Two weeks before your marathon, cut back on your training, allowing your body to heal itself and store energy for the big day. In the week before the marathon, run no more than 30 percent of your normal mileage. And during the final three days, keep your runs to three miles or less, and make sure that they are very easy and comfortable. Do not hesitate to take one or two of these days off.

Your diet during this period should not change drastically, since this may upset your system. On the day before the marathon, don't stuff yourself. Make lunch your largest meal, and eat an early dinner. Both meals should consist primarily of carbohydrates like pasta. Drink plenty of fluids, and avoid alcohol and fatty foods (unless you want to emit noxious fumes for twenty-six miles).

Throughout this final period, get plenty of rest. Don't worry if marathon anxiety keeps you from sleeping well the night before the race; if you are well-rested, one poor night of sleep will not hurt you. And here's some good news: recent studies indicate that the age-old ritual of prerace abstinence is mere superstition. So if sex relaxes you, there's no reason to become a priest the night before the marathon.

Now you're finally there: race day. Try to eat a light meal (approximately four hundred calories) two to four hours before the marathon. Stick with carbohydrates like bagels, bananas, or sports bars. If you are feeling queasy, use a sports drink as a liquid breakfast. Be sure to consume fluids until your urine is clear.

Never try to break in a new pair of shoes during the marathon; wear a pair of broken-in (but not broken-down) training shoes. Dress on the light side; it's better to be cold at the beginning of the race

A WALKMAN:
It really does
make the time on
the treadmill fly
by.

63

HEALTH/FITNESS

than hot for the last twenty-three miles. And here's a little trick if you like the spotlight: write your name on the front of your shirt. Unless you're Michael Jordan, how many other chances will you have to hear thousands of fans scream your name?

When the gun goes off, you will feel a tremendous rush of adrenaline. The crowd will surge, and you will feel the urge to take off like Carl Lewis. You must resist. The worst mistake you can make is to run too aggressively at the beginning of the race. There is no worse nightmare than running out of gas with ten miles left. (Trust me.) No matter how good you feel, run the first twenty miles of the race conservatively. If you still feel like gangbusters at this point—highly doubtful—then pick up the pace a bit.

Drink at every aid station. Your body will need 150–300 calories of carbohydrates every hour after the first hour of running. If you plan to get these calories through sports drinks, make sure that you have tried them during long runs prior to the marathon. The last thing you want to do is to start hurling Gatorade after twenty-five miles.

You will feel sore for several days after the marathon. Don't be surprised if you walk downstairs backwards and find that the "Walk" sign on traffic lights becomes painfully short. Do no workouts of any type for one week following the marathon. If you wish to resume your running after this, start with weekly mileage no greater than 25 percent of normal. Rushing things will only increase your risk of injury, so build up your mileage in small doses. After that, it's on to the next one.

TWENTY-ONE WEEKS UNTIL THE STARTING GUN

This sample mileage schedule should serve as a guide, not a bible—don't be afraid to alter it. If you take a few days off, resume training according to schedule; don't attempt to make up for lost mileage. If your long run currently exceeds two miles, begin with the week on the schedule that contains your present long run. If you cannot run two miles, begin with workouts that alternate running and walking (e.g., run two minutes, walk two minutes, repeat five times). Once you can run two miles without stopping, begin the schedule.

Week No.	Mon.	Tue.	Wed.	Thu.	Fri.	Sat.	Sun.
1	0	2	2	2	0	3	2
2	0	2	2	2	0	4	2
3	0	2	3	2	0	5	2
4	0	3	4	2	0	6	3
5	0	3	4	3	0	7	3
6	0	3	5	3	0	8	3
7	0	4	6	3	0	9	3
8	0	4	6	4	0	10	3
9	0	4	7	4	0	5	3
10	0	5	7	4	0	12	3
11	0	5	7	5	0	6	4
12	0	5	7	3	0	14	3
13	0	5	8	5	0	7	4
14	0	5	7	3	0	16	3
15	0	5	8	5	0	8	4
16	0	5	7	3	0	18	3
17	0	5	8	5	0	9	4
18	0	5	7	3	0	20	3
19	0	5	8	4	0	10	4
20	0	4	6	3	0	8	4
21	0	4	0	3	0	2	Marathon

CHAPTER 4

CONSUMABLES

Q: SHE'S COMING OVER FOR A ROMANTIC DINNER. WHAT DO I COOK?

DINNER PARTY:
Have everyone
bring something
and still look like
a sport.

It's the big night. You've done The Lunch, The Movie, The Drinks, and The Museum. The small talk's out of the way. It's clear you like each other and are ready for something, well, a little more intimate. Your place, perhaps? Taking this relationship to the next level now rests solely on one hidden talent: your cooking.

Of course, we know you: You haven't turned on your stove since you reheated that pizza last year, and you feel a certain pride when you simply get most of the microwave popcorn to burst. That's where we come in: if you can follow simple, three-step directions, you can cook up a healthy, highly impressive meal. These two original dishes won't make you a gourmet, but they're more than good enough for bluffing.

Some things to keep in mind: prepare as much of the food as you can in advance, so you'll be ready to serve before she dozes off. Both dinners are complete meals and need no more than fresh bread and perhaps a green salad to accompany them. For dessert, go easy on yourself, and buy a pint of ice cream, fresh fruit, or biscotti.

On the big night, don't forget to set the scene. Have a chilled bottle of white wine or a room-temperature bottle of red ready to go. Set the table with all three utensils and most importantly, candles.

As you cook, have a little appetizer, such as cheese, bread, and olives sitting on a plate so she won't starve waiting for you to finish your masterpiece. And give her periodic taste tests of your work in progress, just to make sure.

GRILLED SWORDFISH STEAKS

2 swordfish steaks, 1 inch thick, about a half-pound each
4 tablespoons fresh lemon juice
4 tablespoons soy sauce
3 tablespoons minced scallions (white part only; save green stems)
3 tablespoons fresh grated ginger root
3 teaspoons sesame oil
salt and pepper

STEP 1: Mix the lemon juice, soy sauce, ginger and scallions in a small bowl. This is the marinade.

STEP 2: Place the fish in a bowl, pour the marinade over the fish, then refrigerate for 30 minutes, flipping the fish once. Meanwhile, turn the oven to broil, and let it pre-heat for about 15 minutes.

STEP 3: Transfer fish to a shallow baking dish and broil for eight minutes on each side. Serve immediately. Garnish plate with green scallion stems.

PROSCIUTTO-MUSHROOM CHICKEN

2 boneless chicken breasts
1 small onion, minced
½ pound mushrooms, chopped
½ pound prosciutto, chopped
¾ cup white wine
4 tablespoons olive oil
salt and pepper

STEP 1: Heat one tablespoon of olive oil in a skillet. Add minced onion and stir until you can see through it. Then add two more

COOKING CLASSES: Nothing impresses a girl more than homemade *anything*.

tablespoons of olive oil and sliced mushrooms, and stir 10 more minutes. Finally, add prosciutto, and stir two minutes. Now remove your new sauce from the skillet.

STEP 2: Heat another tablespoon of olive oil in the same skillet. Sprinkle chicken with salt and pepper, then place the chicken and the white wine in the skillet. Cover and cook for about 15 minutes, turning once.

STEP 3: Top chicken with mushrooms and prosciutto, and serve.

MACARONI MADNESS

There are some things Italians are not very good at: war, politics, stoicism. Pasta, however, is one thing they have down.

Italians practically came out of the womb boiling rigatoni. Conversely, most of you were probably introduced to cooking pasta through the two-step method. Step one: boil spaghetti. Step two: open jar of Ragu. While we applaud you for keeping up the illusion that you are indeed cooking for yourself, you're not. And while you probably ate pasta in college because it was like your girlfriend—fast, cheap, and pretty tasty, trust me: knowing how to make a good pasta dinner will impress. Anything out of a jar, however, won't. It's time to move on to big-people's pasta. So if you don't know al dente from Al Gore, here are some tips to bring out the Italian Stallion within.

First of all, let's get one thing straight. It's called *macaroni*—not pasta. Spaghetti? Get over it. Macaroni comes in hundreds of shapes for a reason: different shapes hold different sauces better. There is indeed a method to the madness.

Tubular shapes, among them penne, mostaccioli, ziti, and rigatoni, are best served with meat sauces or chunky vegetable sauces—because they're cylindrical, they hold them like glue. Since they can survive serious heat without losing shape or firmness, they are also good for baked dishes (hence the ubiquitous baked ziti).

Ribbonlike pastas such as fettuccine—about a quarter-inch wide—and the thinner linguine are best with creamy Alfredo or seafood sauces, because they're sturdier than spaghetti and its strandlike ilk.

If you must have spaghetti, consider some of its thinner relatives, such as capellini (a.k.a. "angel hair") or slightly thicker vermicelli. These are best dressed with delicate sauces; they're too thin to carry anything chunky.

And speaking of sauce, let's pry that jar of Prego out of your hands. When you're talking macaroni, the sauce is the thing. We're not asking you to put on a housecoat and stay inside all day, boiling down a sauce from fresh tomatoes while watching Rolonda. Even we can see that's too much to ask. And while it's easier to open a jar—especially since it doesn't taste all that bad—you can still make a "quick sauce" rather easily without having to endure the predictability of a store-bought brand.

Since fresh vine-ripened tomatoes are about as common as small-pox, try using canned whole tomatoes that you puree yourself for a few seconds in a blender. If you buy already pureed tomatoes in cans, you're risking a tinny, flavorless, sour product—go for the whole ones. For a quick tomato sauce, start with some olive oil in the bottom of a pan. Then sauté either chopped onion, garlic or both, depending on what you want: onion will give you a sweeter sauce; garlic, a more robust flavor. Add the pureed tomatoes, salt and pepper and herbs of your choice. Obviously, fresh herbs tend to be superior, but if that's too much to ask, dried will do just fine (except for dried parsley, which has the flavor and consistency of fish food).

If you want to branch out from tomato sauces, pesto sauces and cream sauces are surprisingly easy. (We've included two good ones below.) Or add vegetables, meat, or seafood. (See Fusilli Della Russo, below.)

Last—but not least—the brand of pasta you buy is more important than you think. Fresh pasta (the soft kind, in the refrigerated section of your grocery) is the best, but its price-to-flavor ratio isn't really worth it. Among dried brands, there have been veritable wars waged between American companies such as Creamette, Prince, and Ronzoni and Italian competitors like De Cecco and Barilla. Opt for the latter, which are made from the good stuff, 100 percent durum semolina flour, and cook up great al dente (which literally means "to the tooth," or rather, firm to the bite). American brands tend to be grainier, and absolutely should not be overcooked—unless you're looking to spackle your walls.

Some final cooking advice: Give your macaroni plenty of water to boil in, and add a little salt or oil after the water boils. When test-

Vegetarian Pages
www.veg.org/veg
Internet guide for vegetarians and vegans packed with vegetarian news, events, and recipes.

Lobster Net
www.thelobsternet.com
Order live Maine lobsters and lobster bakes in a can.

Virtual Vineyards
www.virtualvin.com
Direct marketer of fine food and wine on the Internet.

All About Beer
www.allaboutbeer.com
Brewing recipes, tips, theory, and a database of more than nine hundred brew pubs.

ing for doneness, don't throw it against the wall. (Who started that anyway? And what does it mean?) Take a bite. If you like it, it's done.

STEAK TIPS

Consider this: The Center for Science in the Public Interest—a consumer advocacy group that once described fettuccine Alfredo as a "heart attack on a plate"—recently reassured carnivores that the occasional steak dinner doesn't mean that your cardiologist will soon be flying to Tahiti, funded by the tattered remains of your arteries.

Incredulous? The CSPI analyses concluded that a 12-ounce sirloin steak has 15 grams of fat and 390 calories after it is trimmed of fat, and a trimmed filet mignon has 18 grams of fat and 350 calories. Compare this with a 10-ounce serving of barbecued chicken breast, which has 280 calories and only 5 grams of fat. The "problems" begin with prime rib and strip steaks. A trimmed 12-ounce New York strip steak has 34 grams of fat and 570 calories, and a 16-ounce prime rib has 62 grams of fat and 980 calories. Yikes!

So what's the beef? Have a favorite cut of steak? Do you care? Not to sound like your mother—or your cardiologist—but you should. The price of meat, like anything else you buy in life, is dictated by the rules of quality and quantity. The more tender the steak, the more expensive. If you know your animal anatomy, you're better prepared to select a good steak for grilling or broiling and you'll likely save some cash.

The cuts we see labeled "steak" in most meat cases can be divided into three categories.

TENDER

These are steaks naturally tender enough to just toss on the grill; the cuts come from a section right in the middle of the back called the "short loin." When the bone is left in, it yields three different steaks: porterhouse, T-bone, and club. When the bone is removed, the steaks are often called "New York" steaks or "shell" steaks, and the most tender muscle of the short loin is, not surprisingly, the tenderloin,

IN-AND-OUT BURGER:
If only because you can order your meal, "animal style."

PLASTIC CHOPSTICKS:
Great cooking tool and good practice for your next sushi date.

a.k.a. filet mignon. You can save money on tenderloin by deboning the porterhouse yourself. The two areas flanking the short loin in either direction grow gradually less tender, but they're still very good and flavorful and less expensive. Behind the short loin lies the sirloin, which is a fine meat to grill or broil. And just in front of the short loin is the rib section, from which prime rib is cut.

NEXT-TO-TENDER

A few steaks just outside the "tender" zone can be grilled with great results with a little tenderizing, which involves one of those scary square hammers with the pointy bumps on both sides. This group includes "chuck" steaks, the first cut after the tender rib section, and, from the other end of the carcass, the sirloin tip and top of the round. With the help of a little tenderizing, both cook well either broiled or grilled.

NOT-SO-TENDER

These are steaks that are awfully close to tough and are better stewed or braised—simmered long and slow in a rich sauce—than broiled or grilled. These cuts include "flank" steak and "corned beef" from the brisket section just below the shoulder; and the "oven roast" and "oyster" steak from the bottom round, which is located, well, you know.

BISTECCA ALLA FIORENTINA

(A ridiculously simple classic Tuscan treat.)

1 24-ounce T-bone steak (or two smaller ones)
½ cup red wine
2 tablespoons extra virgin olive oil
2 teaspoons balsamic vinegar
fresh ground pepper
1 pound fresh arugula
coarse Kosher salt

Rub steak(s) on both sides with a generous amount of coarse salt, then sprinkle with fresh ground pepper. In a heavy-bottomed skillet (preferably cast iron), heat olive oil over a medium-high flame for

TURKEY BURGERS:

A painless way to cut down on the red meat.

PEPPER:

vs. salt.

about one minute. Sear steak on one side for about four minutes (two minutes if using two smaller steaks), shaking pan occasionally to make sure the meat is not sticking. Flip steak, and repeat. Flip again, and lower heat to medium; cook through according to preference. (In Italy, steak is never served cooked beyond medium-rare; for more American tastes, cook the steak for another two minutes on each side for the classic style, four minutes on each side for medium-well.) Wash arugla thoroughly and then arrange on plate, undressed. Remove steak from pan, and place on top of arugula. Add the balsamic vinegar and wine to the frying pan, and bring to a boil. Lower heat, and reduce the mixture until syrupy. Top the steak quickly with the reduction and serve. (Yields two servings.)

GOOD BEER IN THE FRIDGE:

You never know when someone may stop by—or when you might like to treat yourself.

DRAUGHT GUINNESS:

Oi! The most strength you'll ever get out of a can.

BREWMASTER'S BASICS

To 1.5 million special-interest voters, Jimmy Carter is the greatest president of the twentieth century. No, they aren't gas-station owners or peanut farmers. We're talking home brewers, many of whom genuflect daily to the man who legalized the beer version of moonshine back in 1978, helping to unleash the American beer renaissance.

Bogged down by your bar tab? Many homebrewers start out using a simple process called extract brewing, based on a prepackaged kit. All a kit consists of is a malt extract formulated to produce a particular kind of beer, such as British pale ale or Irish stout. Available through a catalog such as the Home Brewery, or at your local beer stores, most kits run about twenty-five dollars.

So with the chemistry taken care of, home brewing becomes a question of preferences. There are two major beer styles: ales, which generally hail from England and include stouts and porters; and lagers, which originated in Germany and take longer to brew. Whatever style of kit you choose, make sure the yeast has been refrigerated and isn't out of date.

Once you've chosen a yeast kit, you need the necessary equipment. A proper beginner's set, which should run between forty-five and sixty-five dollars, should include fun-looking tools like fermenters and hydrometers. Everything else you'll likely find in your kitchen, except for bottles, which can be purchased at a beer store. A normal five-gallon batch will require about forty-eight bottles, and brown bottles are best since they filter out potentially damaging ultraviolet rays. Green bottles are more vulnerable, but they're still better than clear bottles.

Whichever route you take, just make sure they are clean—working with sanitary equipment is a paramount concern when brewing. You can soak the bottles in buckets with a mild bleach solution or boil them.

Clean the bottles. Fill the bottles. Drink your beer. Repeat.

SELECTING A FINE WINE

Big night. Date of your dreams. Snagged a table at one of the hottest restaurants in town. Cocktail conversation was irresistible. Navigated the menu like Magellan through the Straits. The night is *yours.*

And then, calamity. A supercilious twit brings over the wine list. You thumb the pages, recalling the way you felt during high school calculus tests. You look at the listings. They might as well be the schematics for your PC. Sweat beads on your brow. She asks if you're OK. Cut. End. Finish.

Well, not necessarily. Luckily, restaurants are changing the way they present and serve wine to their customers. There used to be three types of wine lists: those in French restaurants, which showcased exclusively French wines; those in Italian restaurants, which listed only wines from Italy; and those in American restaurants, which set forth homegrown bottlings—with a few overseas selections thrown in. The European lists invariably read like atlases, divided into geographic regions you probably had never heard of, under which flowed the names of producers you definitely had never heard of. The American list at least had wines classified by grape type, but still offered no help in figuring out quality; you were left clueless as to whether that twenty-dollar bottle was the good stuff or Thunderbird in a pretty package. It almost seemed as if restaurateurs were daring you to order a bottle.

Now that's changed. More and more restaurants are printing

KIT AND CABOODLE
Mail-order kits and equipment

The Barley House:
800–760–4062

The Barnegat Bay Brewing Co.:
800–HOP–ON–T

The Brewmeister:
800–322–3020

The Filter Store Plus:
800–828–1494

The Home Brewery:
800–321–BREW

Just Brew It!:
800–936–7191

New York Homebrew:
800–YOO–BREW

Wine Hobby USA:
800–847–HOPS

William's Brewing:
800–759–6025

For more information, The American Homebrewers Association is an organization with 25,000 members dedicated to the craft. Inquiries: 303–447–0816; email: orders@aob.org or http://www.aob.org/aob.

WINE 101

There's nothing more impressive to friends and mates alike than possessing a minimal command of wine knowledge. It should be right up there with knowing last night's scores, how to change your oil and how to make her scream your name.

Tackle the subject in true male fashion: make it an adventure. Know this from the get-go: When it comes to choosing wine one can never be certain that every bottle will deliver what's expected. Is it going to be too sweet? Too dry? Too young? Too fruity? The worst thing that can happen is that you don't like the wine (and hopefully didn't spend too much); the ultimate scenario is that you make a fabulous discovery along the way.

GETTING STARTED

While lounge culture has transformed many of us into swaggering cocktail swiggers, perhaps the worst drink to have immediately before a meal is a martini. That powerful jolt of practically pure alcohol can deaden the palate and dull your senses (if not make you fall asleep). Consider instead a light, refreshing aperitif, which is—no surprise—a French word for a drink served before meals. This can include a dry sherry, an aromatized spirit such as Campari or a fortified wine such as Dubonnet or Lillet. Of course, the ultimate aperitif is a glass of sparkling wine, or Champagne.

SIMPLE FACT

Champagne comes from the region in France for which it is named; sparkling wine from anywhere else in the world is technically not Champagne, rather sparkling wine. The difference? Price, primarily. While Americans make great sparkling wine, the Spanish wonderful Cava, and the Italians primo Prosecco, the French make the best bubbly and charge accordingly. Let your wallet be your guide.

WEIGHT WATCHING

Have you heard the old rule regarding wine that says, "White wine with fish, red wine with meat?" Well, file that one with "Don't swim for at least one hour after eating." Sure, both "rules" are foolproof, but they certainly don't enhance your sense of adventure. When it comes to matching wine with food, your only concern should be simply balancing the weight of the two, regardless of color. Think of it this way: Delicate foods, for instance, fare better with lighter wines, while heartier dishes merit richer, heavier wines for balance.

The following cheat sheet should serve as a guide, nothing more. Trying to pair every nuance of a dish with a perfect wine becomes an exercise in anxiety. Relax. When a wine comes to the table without great expectations, you'll at the very least be pleasantly surprised. If it stimulates intelligent conversation with that lucky lady, you're already a winner. If the bottle is unexpectedly greater than you could have every imagined, you're the king. Now dry your hands and enjoy yourself—and her.

	LIGHT WHITES	LUSCIOUS WHITES	LIGHT REDS	HEAVY HITTERS
SOUNDS LIKE:	Muscadet, Pinot Blanc from Alsace or the U.S., Pinot Grigio/Gris from Italy or Oregon, Riesling from Germany, California or Washington, Chardonnay (from Chile or South Africa), and Macon or Bourgogne Blanc (both of which are Chardonnays from France).	Albarino from Spain, Gavi from Italy, Sancerre or Pouilly-Fume from France, Sauvignon Blanc from California or New Zealand, Gewurztraminer from Alsace, Condrieu from France, Viognier from California, Chardonnay from California or Australia.	Beaujolais from France, Gamay from California, Dolcetto from Italy, young Rioja from Spain (not labeled "Gran Reserva"), young Chianti from Italy (not labeled "Riserva" or "Gran Riserva"), Cotes du Rhone, Pinot Noir from California or Oregon, Merlot from Chile or Italy.	Barbera from Italy, Merlot from California or Washington, red Bordeaux from France, Zinfandel from California, New World Cabernet Sauvignon, Northern Rhone from France, Australian Shiraz.
TASTES LIKE:	Possess crisp, refreshing acidity, ranging in flavor from citric to herbal and from floral to fruity.	Lush, ripe, juicy fruit, and smoky or vanilla accents.	Fresh and fruity, bright acidity with moderate tannins (the astringent quality that makes red wine taste dry when young), wonderfully diverse and accommodating to most foods.	Ripe fruit flavors of berries and plums, often accented with smoke, toast, vanilla or spice from having been aged in oak barrels. Although they can be tannic when young, the fats in foods help soften them.
GOES WITH:	Raw bar treats; delicate fish (soul, snapper); pates; grilled veggies; pastas with pesto or oil-based sauces; goat cheeses.	Ice-cold crabs or lobsters; salmon or tuna; roasted chicken or turkey or pork; baked ham; pastas with cream sauces; Brie or other semi-soft cheeses.	Fish dishes prepared with red wine sauces; game birds (squab, quail, pheasant); chicken or turkey roasted with red wine; veal with mushrooms, pasta with meat sauces (alla Bolognese); risotto with wild mushrooms; pizza with the works; Swiss and other mild-but-firm cheeses.	Poultry or game birds; beef; hearty stews; roasted veal or pork; bean-based dishes (cassoulet); pastas with hearty sauces; Parmigiano-Reggiano and other hard, hearty cheeses.

their wine lists with some description of what the wines are like. Thus, diners are finding guidepost headings such as "Aromatic Whites" and "Soft, Versatile Reds." Others restaurants are even going so far as to recommend specific bottles to go with specific dishes. But it's still more fun—and impressive—if you take charge. Even if you encounter the most Jurassic of wine lists—say in a good but old-fashioned French place, where the list looks like it was inspired by a fifth-grade geography text—you can still rule.

Know zero about wine? Your best bet is to find out if the restaurant has a sommelier. If there is, ask to see him and check him out. If you begin to feel as if he's just a big show-off out to intimidate you into ordering some thirty-dollar bottle, thank him politely for his advice—and then discard it. If he seems congenial, listen to his suggestions, and ask a couple of pointedly innocent questions—"Do you really think this will be best with the steak *au poivre*?"—so you look good. If he's doing his job right, he'll let you get away with it. Just watch the price, and you'll be OK.

If you know something about wine already, you can be more independent. You know Chardonnay and Cabernet, right? Then even on a traditional French list, you're almost home free. The two classic wine regions of France are Bordeaux and Burgundy, both of which produce great red and white wines. The simple rule of thumb is that red Bordeaux are primarily Cabernets; white Bordeaux are primarily Sauvignon Blancs; red Burgundies are Pinot Noirs; and white Burgundies are Chardonnays. The characteristics will be slightly different from American bottlings, but they're still consistent enough that you can order based on what types of qualities—fruitiness, bite, dryness, and so on—you want with your dinner.

Another great gambit is to look for wines by the glass. Really smart restaurants will offer by-the-glass tastings of some bottles on their list. This gives you the opportunity to experiment before investing in a whole bottle. And you can start before you eat. Order a glass that you think you might like instead of a cocktail, and see if you like it. She can do the same; then you'll be able to sample two wines without having committed to a single bottle. You can even go one step further by ordering a glass to go with your appetizers. This way, you have yet another chance to audition a wine for the main event. Or you can try something different with the entrée, which is especially appealing if, say, you want a fish starter and then to move on to meat.

Still wine-list wary? Here's the ultimate fallback option. If all you

A GOOD WINE:

Avoid the fear factor when you're invited over someone's house—find a good bottle and write down its name.

know is that you want a red, order a Zinfandel. With its up-front fruit and spicy backbone, Zinfandel is easily adaptable to a wide range of foods; it's also a wine that is more consistently reliable from year to year than vintage-sensitive reds like Cabernet. If it's a night for white, go for Sauvignon Blanc. Pleasantly aromatic, it can be counted on for slightly tangy fruit and just enough acidity to make a congenial match for most seasonings. And like Zinfandel, it is reliably good from year to year.

Finally, don't become preoccupied by vintages. True Cabernet-based wines will improve with age as their tannins soften. But the prevailing style of winemaking these days is such that most wines are ready to drink when they come to market.

And if none of this helps? It's back to the brew-pub, pal.

Here are some of the main ingredients you're likely to encounter on most menus—and wine pairings that should work admirably.

PASTA

With pasta, it's really the sauce that determines the wine. For something rich, like a classic meat sauce with those zesty Mediterranean seasonings, Zinfandel is right on the mark; for a vegetable-based sauce, say pesto, choose a Sauvignon Blanc. And if it's seafood, Chardonnay is the way—unless it's really spicy. In that case, go for a Zinfandel.

CHICKEN

If it's a plain roasted chicken or chicken that's mildly sauced, go for a mild red like Pinot Noir. If it is aggressively seasoned, opt for Zinfandel.

SHELLFISH

Lobster, which is a rich meat, almost invariably goes well with Chardonnay. Scallops also invite a pairing with Chardonnay, or, if served without heavy saucing, Sauvignon Blanc. Shrimp also go well with Sauvignon Blanc.

FISH

Oilier fish, such as salmon and tuna, go beautifully with Pinot Noir (this also gives you a chance to show that you're a rule-breaker—

PASTA STRAINER: One step and you're ready to serve.

DIGIORNO FROZEN PIZZA: King of the freezer section, plus you get to watch the dough rise.

white wine isn't always the best choice for fish). More delicate sea fare, like sole and flounder, are fine with Sauvignon Blanc.

BEEF

If it's a fairly straightforward preparation like a steak, go for a Cabernet Sauvignon. If there's a lot of seasoning, such as in steak *au poivre*, put it together with a spicier Zinfandel.

LAMB

Almost always goes well with a brawny Cabernet.

FRESH FRUIT:
Ingredient for healthy diet and tasty margaritas.

EXTRA-LIGHT OLIVE OIL:
Multipurpose cooking oil composed of the good kind of fat (monosaturated). Use it instead of vegetable oil and shortening.

THE HARD STUFF

Beer and wine are fine, but for proper style points at a bar, hard liquor is still the king. With dozens of vodkas, tequilas and single-batch bourbons flooding the market, choices abound. So it's time to advance your libation education beyond what you and your bros sucked down at the frat house. Let's belly up to the bar, son:

WHISKEY

First, let's get our terms straight. Bourbon, rye, Scotch—it's all whiskey (or whisky, sans the *e*, as folks in Canada and Scotland spell it). But each possesses qualities based on the grain it's fermented from. Bourbon comes from corn, Scotch from barley, and rye from (surprise!) rye. Whiskey is an elixir that is directly affected by its environment, from the local water to the shape of the stills to the type of barrel it ages in.

So how about starting with some rye? No, let's ditch the rye. Rye is a heavier whiskey, though Canada, rye's traditional homeland, makes a lighter product. Rye's time has largely passed. When was the last time you ordered a Seagrams's Seven and ginger-ale highball that wasn't for your grandma?

A bourbon then? Well, if we're looking for something on the

sweeter side—and feeling patriotic—let's do bourbon. Born in Kentucky over two hundred years ago, it's America's only native spirit. Its rich amber color and sweetness come from aging in new oak barrels, which are charred in order to carmelize the wood's natural sugars and bring them to the surface. Variations depend on what's added to the mash. W. L. Weller Kentucky Straight Bourbon is known for its subtle whisper of wheat, while Jack Daniels has its secret sour mash recipe.

OK: blended or single malt? Here's where it gets tricky. Blended whiskey is a mixture from as many as forty separate distilleries, while single malt is the product of a single distillery. This is an art form in Scotland, where single-malt is king.

Did someone say Scotch? Perhaps, in your youth, you reached for Dewar's White Label, a blended Scotch whiskey—it's only fitting. Hopefully, by now you've matured in your ability to keep Scotch down and accordingly become more demanding. Go for depth of character, the crash of the sea upon the peat bogs. Go for single-malt Scotch, neat, straight up, and hold the umbrella.

Why all the hype about single malts? That's like asking about the difference between a bottle of red Gallo table wine and a Robert Mondavi Cabernet Sauvignon from the Napa Valley. The purer the drink, the more distinct the taste. Each Scotch maker has its own formula, its own way of drying the malted barley over a peat fire, its own type of cask (used sherry or bourbon barrels are common), its own aging schedule. The rest of the brown drinks are like training wheels for the single malts. You need them to get here, but once you've arrived, you may never turn back. Perhaps no other spirit, Cognac included, even comes close to the way an exquisite single-malt can consummate the marriage between power and athleticism on the palate.

So what'll it be? Perhaps a seaweedy, salt and peppery Talisker ten-year-old. Or maybe a flowery eighteen-year-old made by Glenlivet. Or a smoky twelve-year-old Cardhu. Make it a double.

VODKA

Americans have been in love with vodka since James Bond declared that he preferred his martinis made with vodka rather than gin. Bond seduced the nation, and in 1967 vodka surpassed gin in popularity. Yet while we've cut back slightly since the high-flying eighties, we Americans still managed to drink a whopping 294.3 million one-

A SIGNATURE DRINK:

Bond has his martini. What's your poison?

liter bottles in 1996 (the last year for which statistics have been tabulated), according to *Adams Liquor Handbook 1997*.

The flavor characteristics of any liquor can be determined by the proof at which it leaves the still. With vodka, the crisp, clean character is achieved by distilling the spirit at very high levels of proof.

The production of vodka begins with the distillation of a fermented mash composed of grain or vegetables at a very high proof of about 190, which helps eliminate cogeners, the toxic impurities that form during fermentation. The neutral distilled spirit is then subjected to several processes that impart a subtle character, but not too much, lest the Bureau of Alcohol, Tobacco, and Firearms—the government arm that regulates booze, cigarettes, and guns (basically, all the stuff that's bad for you)—deems it unfit to be called vodka. According to the BATF definition, vodka is a spirit "without any distinctive character, aroma, taste, or color."

While several methods of distillation exist (many of which are considered "top secret" by each distiller), the end result is to achieve a subtle spirit with nuances that are discernible on the palate by way of mouthfeel rather than flavor. So the notion that you can taste the difference between vodkas when blended with fruit juice—in a screwdriver, for instance—is pretty ridiculous.

Why is vodka so popular? The easiest answer would be its accessibility. Also consider its lack of distinctive odor and flavor—making it the perfect libation among businesspeople partaking of the now-tisked-at three-Martini-lunch. Even former President Gerald R. Ford once declared: "The three-martini lunch is the epitome of American efficiency; where else can you get an earful, a bellyful, and a snootful at the same time?" How did this guy lose the 1976 election?

In the 1990s, cocktail culture has transformed vodka's appeal, taking the classic dry martini to new heights of flavor and complexity. Today, vodka comes in more flavors than Starbucks coffee, and popular distillers are introducing superpremium alternative styles to their already popular brands in a frenzy to outclass each other.

In addition to Glacier, a vodka made from spuds (in this case from Poland), there is Chopin, named for Poland's favorite son. Skyy vodka's creator, Maurice Kanbar, continues to claim that his spirit is created with a secret four-column distillation that substantially reduces the chance of side effects or hangovers. (Hear, hear.) Of course, that theory doesn't fly if it's mixed with sweet, hangover-inducing juices. One of the most distinctive of the newcomers is Rain vodka, purportedly the only vodka quadruple-distilled from

BOTTLE OPENER:

For the times when there's no nearby surface on which to pop off a bottle cap.

organically grown American grain—complete with the harvest date on the bottle.

Thankfully, all of this competition makes for a lively tasting environment in which, inevitably, we get to experience a wide range of interesting spirits—and perhaps come away feeling as focused as our fathers did after a good business lunch.

TEQUILA

Tequila is the oldest distilled spirit in the Americas. When the Spanish conquistadors arrived in Mexico nearly five hundred years ago, they found the natives drinking *pulque,* a coconut milk–flavored beverage made from fermented agave. The Spaniards threw the pungent brew into stills, and tequila was born. You probably know to drink it by the shot—with a slice of lime and a lick of salt to mask the harsh taste.

Today tequila is undergoing another transformation. Once the drink of choice for the rowdy, it is now a sophisticated sipping beverage rivaling fine scotches and brandies. This latest generation of refined, superpremium tequilas is far removed from the throat-searing beverage of just a few years ago. Made exclusively in a limited region of Mexico from blue agave, these superpremium tequilas have gutsy, earthy, and herbaceous flavors that set them apart from other spirits.

Where vodka and gin strive for smoothness, for a gentle and almost neutral flavor that hides the taste of alcohol and the origin of the ingredients, the best tequilas aim to bring forth as much flavor as possible from the plant itself and its soil—what the French call *goût de terroir.* Southwestern and Mexican restaurants have always stocked a wide variety of tequilas, but these days, a good selection is as essential to any bar as premium scotches, Cognacs, and bourbons.

So how to choose your tequila? Start by skipping the "gold," the salt, and the slice of lime. The finest (approximately 1 percent of total production) are produced only from the blue agave (and labeled "100 percent agave"), while others may contain up to 49 percent added sugar. While a 100 percent agave designation doesn't guarantee great taste, most of the best tequilas are made this way.

Like grapes, agave is sensitive to the land and environment in which it grows and, as with wines, many exotic flavors can be found in top-flight tequila. It's not unusual to detect hints of everything from mushrooms and smoke to vanilla, pepper, oak, and even mint in the best.

Patron is among the most successful of the premium tequilas, and

A MANHATTAN:
A serious drink that separates you from the pack.

its beautiful, hand-blown bottles have contributed at least as much to its recent popularity as its taste. At the other end of the price spectrum, Sauza's Hornitos, a highly regarded *reposado* (or gold tequila), offers good value for the money; a 750-milliliter bottle runs around $16.75. Herradura's tequilas generally earn high marks for their purity and intensity of flavor; El Tesoro de Don Felipe's silver and añejo are elegant, artisan tequilas with delicate, floral flavors.

The high end of the market is seeing some intense competition as companies strive to outdo one another. The race began with Porfidio's "single barrel" cactus bottle, which costs about $75; then came Jose Cuervo's similarly priced Reserva de la Familia, an intensely dark, bourbonlike tequila. More recently, Lapiz produced a striking blue pyramidal bottle holding a good-tasting añejo of 100-percent agave. At the very top of the market is Herradura's Selección Suprema, at a whopping $275 a bottle. The newest entry in the superpremium category is El Tesoro's Paradiso, "tequila with a French accent," according to owners Robert Denton and Marilyn Smith, who brought in master Cognac blender Alain Royer to craft this scintillating and palate-pleasing mix of silver and añejo tequilas aged in a variety of woods.

Mezcal is less well known than tequila. It uses a different variety of agave (espadin rather than blue) and is pit-roasted over hot rocks, not baked in ovens, often yielding a smokier flavor. Encantado ("enchanted"), the first superpremium mezcal available here, blends more than a dozen mezcals produced in remote villages around Oaxaca for a distinctly spicy, peppery liquor. Del Maguey offers a collection of four "single village" mezcals, each a pure, organic, and unblended spirit from small distillers in Oaxaca with exceptionally crisp, vivid flavors, each bottle in a traditional, hand-woven palm-fiber basket of Zapotec or Mixtec design.

Every sip of tequila or mezcal is like a trip across the border. But if you're really able to make that journey, the Ritz-Carlton Cancún may have the best selection of all—with more than three hundred tequilas and mezcals on its list. Just don't try too many at once. Like their cheaper brethren, the best tequilas still taste pretty bad coming back up.

RUM

Rum has pretty much always been a sleeper at the American bar. It doesn't have the cachet of imported vodkas, single-malt scotches, and

ROSE'S LIME JUICE:

You've got the vodka, the glasses and the ice. And don't say Gimlet—unless you have some.

single-batch bourbons. Most Americans mix rum because it usually tastes so rough. (This is a drink, after all, that was originally christened "kill-devil" in its birthplace, Barbados.)

In the last few years, though, more serious rum has been making it to market and even into mainstream bars. In addition to Caribbean varieties, rum is now crafted in countries ranging from Venezuela to Guatemala. What's interesting is how so many islands have rums that reflect their own character.

Jamaican rums like Appleton are stronger and more robust, the rastas of rum. As Puerto Rico is a commonwealth of the United States, its rums are not surprisingly the most polished; the Dominican Republic's product has more character. And rum from Trinidad, the most industrialized island in the Caribbean, is just like its origins: rough around the edges and almost raucous.

Probably the most fascinating rum is Barbancourt from Haiti, which is also like that island: it's the voodoo of rum—mysterious and perfumey, more like a brandy or a scotch than its Bajan counterpart. Pour a few tumblers of Réserve Spéciale at a party and you'll fire up the kind of buzz good dope once did. This is not an elixir to be squandered even in a rum punch. It has to play solo.

Any of these rums are a step up from what you learned to oversweeten with Coke in college, but some distilleries are also exporting new labels in an effort to tap into the connoisseur market, as scotch and bourbon begin to fade as trends of the month. Cockspur has VSOR, Appleton has an Estate Extra, Bermuda sends Gosling's Black Seal, and the Dominican Republic ships Brugal; even Bacardi Añejo (aged) and Reserve are trickling north. They're all being marketed as alternatives to cognac for cigar lovers, but unlike cognac, which can't mix, these rums can be diluted for an inexperienced palate.

All of these rums start out the same way—as a byproduct of sugar-cane processing. Molasses or cane juice is fermented in huge vats and then heated to make a concentrate that is mixed with water and aged in oak barrels. It goes in white and takes on a golden color from the wood, but real darkness comes from caramel added later on. As with any alcohol, whether wine or whiskey, the longer the rum stays in the wood, the better the flavor. One year is the minimum, but five is even better. (The age should be listed somewhere on the bottle.) Some distillers, who obviously don't know when to leave great enough alone, also produce flavored rums, with coconut or spices. Remember the cardinal rule: If it smells like grandma's kitchen, it's not good rum.

DIM SUM:
The Chinese way to brunch—for when you wake up and crave something exotic.

If you want to be sublimely seduced by dark rum on the first taste, shake up a rum punch.

Combine four jiggers of dark rum with two jiggers each of freshly squeezed lime juice, water, and simple syrup (sugar boiled with water). Add a couple of dashes of bitters and crushed ice. Shake vigorously. Pour over more ice into two tall glasses, and grate nutmeg thickly over the top. Two servings.

CLASSIC COCKTAILS

LOLLIPOPS:

Enduring reminder that at one time in your life going to the bank was not always about bounced checks and money orders.

Yes, the martini is back. Bigger than ever. Any self-respecting establishment now offers martini options by the dozen, and way beyond the world of olives and twists. Bars throw martini parties; faux-trendy magazine cover stories gush over "martini culture"; Tower Records now stocks an impressive array of "martini" CDs, apparently designed to get you to slip on a smoking jacket and croon like Sinatra.

Ho-hum. The truth is that the martini, staple of the Eisenhower era and James Bond movies, is only one of many once-popular cocktails that made "going out for a drink" something much more interesting than today's version, when the big question of the night is basically, "Wine, microbrew, or something from the Bud family?" It's time to go beyond the martini. When was the last time you heard someone order a stinger or a scorpion, except in a black-and-white movie? Any slug can pop open a Rolling Rock. But creating a Tom Collins, properly garnished with a slice of orange or lemon, poured into a tall, slender glass? Now *that's* class.

But through the years the cocktail, like society, has become dressed up and dumbed down, resulting in the advent of such lame concoctions as the Russian Quaalude, the Screaming Orgasm, and a Slow Screw Up Against a Wall. So we decided it was time to save the classic cocktail.

To begin, it is important to note that in the world of cocktails, there is a critical distinction to be made. There are the typical "girlie drinks" (think of anything with Amaretto, Kahlua, or creme de cacao drunk by groups of slender blondes from the steno pool at happy hour). And there are *real* drinks, whiskey- and bourbon-based fare such as the stinger, a sweet yet potent three-to-one blend of brandy and white crème de menthe, and the scorpion—citrusy, a little sour, and fruity — which is served in a large bowl with a fragrant gardenia floating on top. We'll get to the girlie drinks later.

How to choose a *real* drink? Think about it: Would Indiana Jones sip from a scorpion bowl full of alcohol? Real drinks—guy drinks—taste like their ingredients. They don't try to mask the alcohol under sweet and fruity flavors. And their garnishes are practical: an olive; a twist or wedge of lemon; no plastic monkeys, parasols, and other junky ephemera. Real drinks appeal to men who like to drink, while girlie drinks try to camouflage both their purpose (getting you drunk) and their ingredients.

Whatever your pleasure, you'd better start drinking soon: the federal Endangered Species Act doesn't include cocktails. Perhaps some of us should commit these recipes to memory and walk around reciting them, like the characters in Ray Bradbury's *Fahrenheit 451* who memorized complete novels. Perhaps only then will these potent cocktails survive to see another generation. But remember: memorize first, then drink. It definitely won't work the other way around.

Here are a half-dozen good ones to memorize for your next party. Make sure to use the right glass—as with romantic seductions and annual reports, presentation is everything.

SIDECAR

Pour one ounce of brandy or Cognac, one ounce of Cointreau, and half an ounce lemon juice into a shaker filled with cracked ice. Shake and strain into a martini glass, first dipping the rim of the glass in sugar. Add a twist of lemon peel.

STINGER

Mix an ounce and a half of Cognac (or brandy) to a half-ounce white crème de menthe in a shaker filled with cracked ice. Shake and strain into a cocktail glass. Garnish with a sprig of fresh mint.

OLD-FASHIONED

In a cocktail glass, mix together one cube of sugar and one teaspoon of water and stir. Add a dash of bitters, two shots of whiskey and one piece of lemon peel. Add ice and stir.

SIGNATURE DISH:
Perfect excuse to invite her to your place.

HOMEMADE MASHED POTATOES:
Heaven is in a big vat being stirred by a large woman at the OK Cafe in Atlanta, Georgia.

NAVY GROG

Fill half of a large cocktail glass with shaved ice. In a cocktail shaker, blend half an ounce lime juice, half an ounce orange juice, half an ounce pineapple juice, half an ounce Falernum, two ounces of dark rum, one ounce of light rum, and half a cup of finely cracked ice. Pour into glass.

TOM COLLINS

Combine three quarters of an ounce of lemon juice, one teaspoon of sugar, and one and a half ounces of gin. Shake well. Pour over ice cubes in a Collins glass (tall and skinny). Fill with soda water.

FOG CUTTER

**BLUE
POWERADE:**
Tremendous
hangover
remedy.

Combine one and a half ounces of light rum, a half ounce of brandy, a half ounce of gin, one ounce of orange juice, three teaspoons of lemon juice, one and a half teaspoons of orgeat syrup (almond). Shake and strain into a Collins glass over ice cubes. Top with a teaspoon of sweet sherry.

WATER:
64 ounces daily.

DRINKS FIT FOR AN UMBRELLA

A momentous episode in American mythology: at Betsy's Tavern in Yorktown, New York, an Irish lass named Betsy Flanagan served up a secret concoction of spirits she called a "bracer" to the American and French soldiers of Washington's army. She decorated her creation with a rooster's tail feather garnered from a local Tory farmer. According to legend, it was one of the Frenchmen who raised a glass to Betsy and exclaimed: "Vive le cock tail!"

The trouble is, *tail* isn't a French word. Here's the real historical significance of this incident: the first use of a tacky drink decoration. Yes, folks, it appears Betsy Flanagan invented the umbrella drink. But it took until the 1950s for this monument to tackiness chic to achieve widespread popularity. During the Korean conflict, a madam named Mai Lae dressed cocktails for American soldiers with sensual fruit designs, modestly covered with rice-paper umbrellas. Then Trader Vic's in San Francisco claims to have come up with the pineapple-bedecked Mai Tai as a tribute to Polynesian culture. And Elvis fans will tell you the King popularized tropical fruity drinks in *Blue Hawaii*.

Here are three drinks for your next barbecue:

TOP OF THE MARK

Made famous by Dennis Mullally, bartender extraordinaire at the Cub Room in New York City.

2 ounces Absolut Vodka
1 ounce Grand Marnier
½ ounce fresh lime juice

Combine all ingredients in a mixing glass over ice and shake. Strain into a chilled martini glass that's been rubbed around its rim with a lime wedge. Garnish with an orange or lime wheel balanced on a hokey swizzle stick across the rim.

What it says about you: you're just coming out of hiding and willing to demonstrate a little daring by ordering a bastardized gimlet (itself a corrupted martini) with a moderate garnish. You're getting there.

THE TYPHOON TF'N'T

Made famous by Chuck O'Connor, bar manager at Typhoon Brewery in New York City.

2½ ounces Tanqueray gin
½ ounce fresh Keffir (or regular) lime juice
½ ounce Frangelico
2 ounces Schweppes tonic water

Combine ingredients in a mixing glass over ice and swirl. Strain into a chilled martini glass. Garnish with a slice of ginger floating on top and a lime wheel speared with an umbrella on the rim.

What it says about you: you're well on your way. You don't mind

COFFEE:
Always keep it stocked. If you're not an addict, plenty of your friends are.

the umbrella on your TF'n'T because you're feeling confident. You assure yourself that you like the ginger slice because it reminds you of Gilligan's Island.

LEE'S HAWAIIAN ISLANDER MAI TAI

Made famous by Steven Lee, owner of Lee's Hawaiian Islander of Lyndhurst, New Jersey.

2 ounces Trader Vic's Mai Tai mix
2 ounces Meyers rum
2 ounces white rum
1 ounce orgeat syrup (almond flavor)
1 ounce orange Curacao

Combine all the ingredients in a mixing glass over crushed ice. Blend and pour into the tallest, cheesiest glass in the house. Garnish with fruit wedges on an extra long straw; umbrella optional.

What it says about you: you have arrived, and you're one confident mother. OK, even if you aren't, you'll be so blitzed after two of these that you won't care what anybody has to say—if you can even hear them.

VITAMIN C:

Keep your immune system in check.

JINGLE BELL CROCK

So this is the year you've decided to throw a big holiday bash. You're going to do it right: full bar, interesting wine, elegant hors d'oeuvres, maybe a baked ham. And, as a special touch, eggnog. All that will be missing is Tiny Tim, hobbling in and crying, "God bless us, each and everyone!" It'll all be there.

Well, maybe not. What will separate your party from the pack? It's about the 'nog. That ultrapasteurized, superhomogenized stuff in the waxed carton has about as much resemblance to the real thing as liverwurst does to *terrine de foie gras.* Spike it to the moon with hooch, sprinkle cinnamon all over it, it won't do any good—the grocery store version will surely taste like crap and languish in the corner next to the fruitcake. You have an option, however: made from scratch, good eggnog fuses creamy, mouthfilling tastes and textures with a bracing backbone of good liquor. If you really want to show your friends that you're a man who knows the swill from the swell, take the time to make the eggnog yourself.

This raises two interesting questions: Just what *is* eggnog? And how exactly *do* you make it? While it conjures images of a Yule log in the Old Country, eggnog is actually a very patriotic drink: it originated in the United States during Colonial times, when wassail, the classic holiday specialty of merry old England, failed to capture colonists' rebellious palates. The basic ingredients were eggs, sugar, milk and/or cream and alcohol (rum, a staple of the Colonial economy, seemed to be the liquor of choice).

As for the making—better you should ask how to build a perfect martini. The one thing everyone agrees on is the egg part. After that, it's a Hatfield-McCoy hotbed of controversy. Do you use the whole egg or separate the yolks from the whites and reunite them later on? Or do you just use the yolks? And what spirit is best? Rum? Bourbon? Whiskey? Cognac? Sherry? Port? Madeira? There are ardent adherents for all of them. Should the consistency be thick? Not thick? Solid enough to eat with a spoon? The noggin boggles. But don't fret: just follow these recipes, and there will be no doubt as to whose Yule is the coolest.

GEORGE WASHINGTON'S EGGNOG

Since the drink emerged when the United States was a tike, why not try the Father of Our Country's fave? (G.W. made a better general than bartender; the original directions are vague to the point of driving you to drink—drink anything but this eggnog, that is. We've adapted them in the way that makes the most sense to us.)

1 dozen eggs
1 dozen tablespoon sugar
1 quart milk
1 quart cream
1 pint brandy
½ pint rye whiskey
¼ pint Jamaica or New England rum
¼ pint sherry

CLIF BARS:
Substitute candy bars with a delicious, low-fat alternative. Your heart will thank you.

Separate the yolks from the whites and beat the yolks with the sugar until the mixture has a creamy consistency. Add milk, brandy, rye whiskey, rum, and sherry. Stir until thoroughly blended. Separately whip both the cream and the egg whites until almost stiff. Fold both into the mixture. Serve chilled.

ALL-AMERICAN EGGNOG

Because this is a homegrown libation, we like to make it with that great down-home spirit, bourbon (which is undergoing a well-deserved new wave of popularity).

BEN AND JERRY'S CHOCOLATE CHIP COOKIE DOUGH: Rapturous ice cream.

1 dozen eggs
1 cup sugar
1½ cups milk
2½ cups bourbon
½ teaspoon salt
2 pints whipping cream
grated nutmeg

ABOUT 30 SERVINGS

LACTAID ULTRA: A lactose intolerant's saving grace. Two small tablets insure your date will be a blast for the right reasons.

Separate the eggs. Using an electric mixer, beat the sugar and yolks until the mixture is creamy in texture and lemony in color. With the mixer on low, slowly add the milk and the bourbon. Chill this mixture for two or three hours, covered, in the refrigerator. Add the salt to the egg whites, and beat until just stiff. Whip the cream until it just forms peaks. Fold the cream into the yolk-bourbon mixture. Then fold in the stiff egg whites. Chill for one hour. When you serve, sprinkle the top of each with grated nutmeg.

GET EGGNOGGED-UP

Make the eggnog fresh:

2 pounds powdered sugar
20 eggs separated (whites in one bowl, yolks in another)
2 gallons of milk
1 pint heavy cream
2 teaspoons nutmeg

In one bowl whisk egg whites with heavy cream. In another bowl beat yolks with sugar and milk. Fold whites and cream into yolk mixture and add nutmeg. Chill.

2 gallons eggnog
2 quarts Berentzen Apple Jack liquor
1½ pints dark rum
½ pint Southern Comfort

Mix all ingredients in large punch bowl and chill for four hours. Prior to serving, stir gently. Garnish with sprinkle of cinnamon.

Fearing a visit from the fat police? Substitute 1-percent milk for whole milk, and add only one pint of cream instead of two. But believe us, it ain't as good.

SUPERIOR STOGIES

Cuba may be dirt-poor, but it's got one hell of a public-relations team behind it, endlessly flogging the supremacy of Cuban cigars. It's easy to get caught up in the hype.

Cuban cigars are illegal, which gives them a sexy, forbidden-fruit quality. Fidel Castro, the only man in the hemisphere who can make a Grizzly Adams beard into a political statement, quit smoking yet still parades around with his beloved homegrowns.

Unfortunately, it's largely a crock. Sure, they make some killer smokes, but buying the real Havana on the cigar black market is as big a gamble as going swimming at the Jersey Shore. For every euphoria-inducing Cuban smoke, there are three that are capable of driving even the most devout smoker away from tobacco for at least a month (an eternity in nicotine minutes). And with the price of Cubans running upwards of twenty dollars a cigar, they're a risk worth taking only on the most special occasions.

Long-time cigar smokers know that you can get premium-quality cigars, usually from the Dominican Republic, for as low as three to five dollars a smoke. (The real cheapies, for a buck and under, are an even bigger gamble than the Cubans.) We contacted a half-dozen

BREAKFAST:
Pancakes, French toast, and sausage links just don't taste the same at 5:00 P.M.

STRAWBERRY QUIK:
A throwback in liquid form.

cigar experts—guys who can insert the phrase "my walk-in humidor" into a sentence without breaking a sweat—and asked them about their favorite low-budget smokes. You can find most of these at any premium cigar store. Alternatively, you can try a mail-order company like New Jersey's JR Tobacco (800-JR-CIGAR).

ROLLED GOLD

THE EXPERT:	Bill Camire	Jeff Moffie	Jack Cummens	Michael Fauci
THE CREDENTIALS:	President, Cigar Connoisseurs of Cape Cod	President, Cleveland Cigar Club	Founder/President, Milwaukee Cigar Society	President, Triple Cities Cigar Club
THE CIGAR:	Macanudo's Hyde Park Cafe	Vilizon's Excalibur #1	Fonseca Triangulares	La Gloria Cubana Charlemagne
THE SCOOP:	"One of Macanudo's best. They come boxed loose, without cellophane. It's a very light, creamy cigar, smooth and easy on the palate with a delicate coffee flavor, nice spice, and a smooth finish; a cigar for during the day—anytime after noon you can light one up."	"I like a big cigar, and this one is a 54 ring by seven and a half inches. It's heavy, full-bodied, with a very nice aftertaste. It smells great, feels good, tastes good, and that's really what it comes down to."	"It's a very different-looking cigar, about five inches long with a 60 ring gauge, well over an inch in diameter, with a big end on it; it tapers down like a torpedo. It's very smooth, because there's so much tobacco to work with. It's light, with a spicy or nutty taste to it, but it's a very clean smoke because there's so much tobacco. It cools itself off because of the filtration."	"This is a premium handmade cigar from Miami, very full-bodied, reminiscent of Cubans. It's a very balanced cigar, so you don't get stuck with a cigar that has a lot of bottom and little top, or a lot of body and no bottom, or vice versa. A big ring size, 54, but it has all the great characteristics."

CHAPTER 5

AT WORK

Q: HOW DO I BEAT A DRUG TEST?

The "just say no" babble may seem like a distant memory, but left in its wake is a more concrete reality: If you plan on switching jobs occasionally, you're going to run into a drug test. Two-thirds of all new hires now get the plastic cup challenge, according to a survey by the American Management Association. Sure, your current boss may be a card-carrying libertarian who couldn't care less what you do on your own time, as long as it doesn't affect his. But your next *capo*—perhaps at IBM, AT&T, Intel, Xerox, Boeing, Chevron, Citibank, or another of the name-brand corporations on your short list—might not be so understanding.

And, of course, like any official program that peeks into your personal life, the priorities are all out of whack. Coke fiends and heroin junkies almost have to snort and shoot the morning of the test to get caught. The occasional pot smoker—this means about 20 percent of the young male population—might lose his chance at a dream job for that foggy night spent watching a Marx Brothers flick two weeks ago.

What to do? First, forget about the witch remedies. Some smok-

AN UP-TO-DATE RÉSUMÉ: You never know when your next day might be your last.

ers swear by Goldenseal, a foul-smelling root reputed to cleanse out your system. But most experts say it's worthless, as are most teas, herbs, and mail-order elixirs. They all come with instructions to drink lots of water—which is the real trick. Fill yourself to the bursting point with water or other fluids an hour or two before the test. Or consider swallowing fifty or a hundred milligrams of vitamin B_2 to color your urine yellow—some labs are suspicious of clear urine. Kent Holtorf, a doctor who spent many hours in the lab researching his book *Ur-Ine Trouble*, recommends eight to ten thousand milligrams of vitamin C four to six hours before testing and again two hours before the test.

Want to spike the proverbial punch? Bleach, Visine, or commercially sold adulterants like Klear will makes things murkier, but the labs are onto such games. SmithKline Beecham testing sites, which administered 6 million tests in 1997, up from 2.5 million in 1990, goes so far as to close off the hot water tap, dye the toilet water blue, and place a temperature strip in the plastic cup, all to prevent any monkey business.

The truth is, the only way to be sure you'll pass the test is to be clean. So either take Nancy Reagan's advice or make sure several days pass between toking and testing—more if you are a heavy user. If you can't wait that long, maybe you really didn't want that job anyway.

Q: SHOULD I SIGN A NON-COMPETE AGREEMENT?

Thought you were too low on the corporate totem pole to be asked to sign a noncompete agreement? Think again. They're not just for senior executives anymore.

The economy keeps getting more and more service-oriented, and at an outfit that doesn't actually make anything—a consulting or accounting firm, for example—the most important asset is the company's relationship with its clients. Frequently it's a midlevel schmo like you getting the face time with a client and developing that relationship. If you take that relationship to a competitor, especially if your bosses spent time and money training you to do your job, then your employer's lost an important asset.

That's why noncompetes, which usually prevent you from moving to a rival firm until you've been out of the business for a year or so, are now making their way down the corporate ladder, to the level of salesmen, account executives, and the like.

So should you sign it if one is thrust in your face? That depends on two things: first, how badly do you want the job? And second, what state do you work in? The enforceability of so-called "restrictive covenants" varies widely from state to state, so do your homework. As a general rule, the farther west you go, the better off you are. In California, for example, noncompetes are not enforceable for nonshareholder employees. Enforcement standards for Florida and Minnesota, on the other hand, are two of the toughest in the nation. Noncompetes in New York, Virginia, and Pennsylvania are enforceable, but not the most stringent.

If you do sign a noncompete agreement, pay heed: you may have to live up to it. So disregard your father or your father's real-estate lawyer friend telling you, "Oh, they can't enforce that. No one can prevent you from earning a living." They're wrong.

Also, don't be afraid to negotiate. Sometimes, the noncompete contract an employer is handing you is a boilerplate agreement they originally concocted for senior executives. Your agreement can probably be much narrower. For instance, if the contract says you won't be able to work for a rival anywhere in the Midwest, ask if it can be limited to your city or state. Frequently, what a prospective employer is handing you is simply a wish list, and they'll be more than happy to take a wish or two off the table.

RÉSUMÉ CHECK

Let's set the record straight: no résumé—not even one that brands you a world-traveled, Olympic-bound, Nobel Prize winner—can guarantee you a job. Résumés can only convince a potential employer you are worthy of an interview. While the prospect of filling an entire page with past achievements may seem daunting, it ain't

a modem for your home-office PC. With areas on working from home and changing careers, the site's in tune with the changing nature of work.

TOPjobs USA
www.topjobsusa.com
Targets mid- to upper-level professional jobs and offers one of the easiest user interfaces around.

CareerPath
www.careerpath.com
Compiles the help-wanted sections from the nation's top forty newspapers.

Overseas Jobs Web
www.overseasjobs.com
The patriarch of the international job-hunting family, offering a compendium of international job information.

Dream Jobs
www.dreamjobs.com
Killer jobs that you would never hear about unless you have a lot of plugged-in friends. One position listed daily.

rocket science. In fact, dozens of books spell out formulaic methods of listing and embellishing your experiences, from selecting active verbs to creating proper margins. But there are other make-or-break ways to juice up your résumé that go entirely unmentioned. Using them just might land you in the executive suite.

1. MAKE THE CONNECTION.

Don't try to stupefy potential employers with bigwig titles and fancy positions; your goal is to prove—on paper—that there's a logical connection between your experience and the job you're applying for. A multimedia company looking for tech-support cares far more about your high-school tutoring job than the poem you had published in last semester's literary journal. Unsure exactly what the company is looking for? Find out. Call the company's human resources department, and ask for a detailed description of the position. Then tailor (and, if necessary, rewrite) your résumé so your experience and activities demonstrate that you're the ideal match.

2. KEEP IT SIMPLE.

You may salivate over your computer's new calligraphy font, but trust us—it's not going to wow the recruiters. Their goal is to read through résumés free of hassle, so they can fill the position as quickly as possible. Don't make reading your résumé an obstacle course of gothic type. Choose fonts that are clean and easy to read. (When in doubt, stick to Times Roman.) Keep your page neat by using bullets instead of indenting, bolding instead of italicizing, and leaving a healthy dose of white space. And shoot for one page—only use two if your one-page résumé looks like a page from a phone book, and you have some serious, serious experience to back it up.

3. USE CAUTION WHEN GETTING PERSONAL.

Including personal info in your résumé is definitely a crapshoot. Still, weigh in the amusement factor. Someone who sifts through a truckload of identical résumés, all as dry as tax returns, could find your résumé's funny or personal comment intriguing; it could be the bait that gets you reeled you in. The more creative the job, the more leeway you have; wannabe investment bankers, consequently, should refrain from listing "coed naked fencing" and other frivolities.

If you're not sure whether to list something, don't. And never include your age, ethnicity, political affiliation, marital status, photo, or a physical description—all of which are off-limits for employers.

OFFICE ROMANCE:
Makes the day go faster. But be warned: If you're gonna play, you're gonna pay.

LEAVING ON TIME AT LEAST ONE NIGHT A WEEK:
You know what they say about all work and no play.

4. DOUBLE-CHECK AND TRIPLE-CHECK.

Like, duh. Who's not going to double-check a résumé before sending it out? The problem, however, isn't whether people proofread, as much as *when* they do it. The worst time: immediately after writing it and making changes. Your eyes will pick up what you expect to see, not what you actually see. Run a spell-check after saving your copy, print it, and let the résumé sit on your desk for at least a few hours. Then check for typos, weird spacing, and problem punctuation. Always ask someone else to proofread it as well—preferably someone proficient in grammar.

5. PAPER COUNTS.

You've got yourself a flawless résumé that does you proud. Don't blow it with el cheapo computer or copy paper. Flaunt it on twenty-pound white or cream stock, which has some solid weight to it but won't jam résumé-scanning machines. Use your own laser printer if it produces clean, crisp printouts. If not, get the local print or copy shop to do it for you. And when it comes to ink selection, it's black or bust.

MAXIMIZING THE ON-LINE JOB HUNT

There has been a lot of ink spilled about the Internet as a tremendous source of job growth, and rightly so. But here's some interesting news for the 90 percent of you who consider the Web a toy or tool, rather than a potential way to make living: Even if the Web can't get you a career, it can get you a job.

Take a visit to the Excite search engine (http://www.excite.com), and ask it for Web sites that deal with employment. You'll have 650,000 options—which are 649,999 more than the poor sap sitting next to you who limits his job search to the newspaper classifieds. Clothing designer. Software designer. Interior designer. It makes no difference: the Internet offers listings, tips, and sources for any and all career fields. The wheat's out there, it's just a question of separating it from the chaff.

Your best move is to start with the employment clearinghouses

ROGET'S THESAURUS: "My, that mendicant certainly does have well-trimmed dundrearies. . . ." Dropping the occasional five-dollar word reminds management they're dealing with a pro.

sprouting up daily on the Web. It would take a week to sift through them all, and most aren't worth your time or connection charges. But the very best are invaluable, starting with the Monster Board (http://www.monster.com), which lists more than fifty thousand jobs across the United States, searchable by job type or keyword. Top Jobs USA (http://www.topjobsusa.com) targets mid- to upper-level professional jobs and offers one of the easiest user interfaces around. And CareerPath (http://www.careerpath.com) compiles the help-wanted sections from the nation's top forty newspapers (including the *New York Times, Los Angeles Times, Boston Globe, Wall Street Journal,* and many others) in a completely keyword-searchable format. Using these three sites effectively will put you ahead of most of the job-seeking horde from the get-go.

Thinking globally? Then start at the top, with the patriarch of the international job hunting family: OverseasJobs.com (http://overseasjobs.com). The site offers a compendium of international job information. It posts its own listings, boasts articles about working abroad, provides links to more than 750 career sites in forty countries (indexed by the language used on the site, among other topics,) and allows potential employees to post their résumé to a site that's visited by twenty-five thousand individual users a month.

Already have a job, but open to the right opportunity? Head on over to Dream Jobs (http://www.dreamjobs.com), for the kinds of killer jobs that you would never hear about unless you have a lot of plugged-in friends—jobs that offer personal as well as professional satisfaction. Dream Jobs lists just one position a day.

A number of these sites employ one the Web's most fascinating (some would argue frightening) new technologies. "Agents" are search engines that function like artificial-intelligence machines. The more information you tell it about you (The Monster Board's agent is called "Jobba-the-Hunt"), the better suited it will be to find you a perfect job match. At some of these sites, you don't need to search them daily—the agent will E-mail you whenever a new job listing is posted that fits you like a glove.

The Career Site (http://www.careersite.com) uses agent technology like the Monster Board, but asks much more pointed questions and looks for creative ways to connect you with potential jobs. It also sends an anonymous profile of your background and experience to those employers in its database that have job openings most closely mirroring your résumé data.

You probably already have a résumé, and it is likely saved in some

A FRAMED PICTURE:
Show your workmates you have a life away from the office.

sort of electronic format. (If not, you need an education, not our help.) Getting your résumé out there is a smart start to begin your on-line hunt—and create one that contain keywords that gets to the heart of who you are and what you're looking for. Keywords are how recruiters sort through résumés, so know the buzzwords of your field. *Manage* and *hiring* make sense for a human resources position; *journalism* and *edit* for a publishing job. And don't worry about fancy fonts. If you're going to E-mail a résumé to a company or recruiter, a plain ASCII text file is *de rigeur.* Formatting will likely create problems for the recipient.

Traditional tools of job hunting—a résumé, a personal interview, having contacts within a company—are still an important part of the equation. And even as the world becomes increasingly wired, there's probably no better substitute for that thing you do when you keep your eyes open and put the word out to everyone from your neighbor to your dad's old college roommate. The word for that, ironically, is *networking*.

THE HEADHUNTER RULES

They call themselves "executive search consultants" or "recruiters," but the rest of the world knows them as headhunters. It's an appropriately mercenary term. While they may bill themselves as corporate matchmakers, these guys are hired guns who act much more like real-estate brokers. They can be pushy. They may try to sell you a job you don't want. And no matter how benevolent they seem, their ultimate goal is a commission check, which is generally a hefty 25 percent of your starting salary if they find you a job.

Now that you know the score, the real question becomes: How can these guys help you? Well, a good one can help ease a job search, offer access to contacts otherwise unavailable, and even dispense some valuable career advice. Once in a while, they may even help find you a dream job.

Headhunters operate in one of two ways: they find you, or you find them. In the case of the former—more common for upper-tier jobs—they might phone you to try to lure you away from your job to a position at another company. It's known as a cold-call and goes

OPINIONS:
That is to say, well-founded opinions.

GOALS:
Give meaning to the big picture.

something like this: "Hello, I am an executive recruiter for your industry here. Have you got a moment to talk?"

In the second instance, you go to them, much in the way you would to an employer—résumé in hand, interview suit on your back. This is the more likely route for those just out of college. Ads for executive recruiters abound in the help-wanted section of most Sunday newspapers.

While working with a headhunter saves time, it's anything but a quick route to a job. Only around 10 percent of all managerial positions are obtained through headhunters, and most tend to be on the upper rungs of the corporate ladder. People with no prior work experience will likely not get anything from a search firm. Companies are not going to hire pricey headhunters to find candidates for an entry-level position when they can run an ad in the newspaper for three hundred dollars.

What's more, many headhunters find out about openings the same way you do—in the (surprise!) Sunday classifieds. If a headhunter finds you a job you could have found by yourself, money that may have gone toward a higher salary might instead be used to pay off the headhunter.

Working with headhunters is also not an altogether painless process. You may spend hours on the phone with fast-talking and sleazy ones before finding one you are comfortable with. Some sleaze agents may even send you on interviews for jobs you're not interested in. Misrepresenting jobs is a common practice among headhunters. Like a real-estate broker shopping a crummy apartment, they have to figure a way to get you in the door. The biggest complaint among those who work with headhunters—especially among those early on in their corporate careers—is false promises and unreturned phone calls.

The bottom line in dealing with headhunters is remembering that their main objective is a commission check, not your happiness. In the best of all possible circumstances, their fee and your satisfaction are tied together. Here are some things you can do to make that happen:

♦ When looking for a headhunter, ask others in your field (maybe not your boss) for some recommendations. Find someone who will spend some time with you and who understands the field. The most effective headhunters with the most contacts are veterans of the industries they recruit for.

STOP SAYING "I'M SO BUSY":
Do you know anyone who isn't?

◆ Find out whether a headhunter is on contingency or retainer. A headhunter on contingency is paid only if he or she fills the job. A headhunter on retainer is paid on a contract basis to fill a certain number of openings per year. Working with a headhunter on retainer—typically less than a third of them—is usually more likely to lead to a job.

◆ If a recruiter calls and you're not interested in the opportunity, don't close the door to future ones. You may not be in the market right now, but if you befriend a recruiter, you may get a call when are.

◆ No legitimate recruiter ever requests a fee from you.

◆ Most important, don't rely on headhunters to find work for you while you go off to the golf course—unless your dream job is being a caddy. As much as you might like the idea of having an agent who's out there finding you a job, headhunters should be used only to complement your own search. That's the best way to keep control of your situation. Even if the headhunter finds a hot prospect, your own search will allow you to make a more qualified decision on whether or not you can do better. Remember—the only person looking out solely for you is you.

ELECTRONIC ORGANIZER: Organize your life and slip it in your pocket (just be sure to back it up on your computer just in case your life slips out of your pocket).

TOTAL NAME RECALL

So there you are: the company Christmas party, the annual sales meeting, or just a simple cocktail social. You're feeling good. You've got a martini in one hand, a Macanudo in the other. Then, out of the corner of your eye, you see what's-his-name. You met him at a business dinner months earlier—did you get his card? Maybe. It really doesn't matter, because you don't have time to ponder the question. In fact, the only thing you can be absolutely sure of is that you have no idea what his name is.

You rack your brain, but it's too late. As he approaches all you can do is say, "Hey," extend a hand, and utter something inane. As Homer Simpson might say—*doh!*

While the human brain is marvelous at remembering things like what color bra your prom date wore and how many homers Mike Schmidt smacked in 1980, it can be woefully inadequate when attempting to recall more important information. Scientists have been battling the mysteries of memory for years but have yet to completely connect the dots and figure out why we remember what we remember and forget what we forget.

But that doesn't mean that you can't train your brain to become your own traveling Rolodex, complete with shiny knob and mental index cards that don't fall out—no matter how fast you spin the damn thing.

1. NOTE PERSONAL TRAITS.

When you first meet someone, take a minute to acquaint yourself with some of his or her distinctive physical features. If you're introduced to a guy named Harry and he's got a handkerchief in his front pocket, register it: from now on, recall him as "Handkerchief Harry." Of course, you don't always have to be polite: recalling someone as "Buck-teeth Elaine" or "Fat Ed" is fine, as long as you never say it out loud.

2. REPEAT, REPEAT, REPEAT.

Repeat someone's name as often as possible when meeting him or her; as with your multiplication tables, repetition equals retention. For example, when meeting someone and replying with the standard, "Nice to meet you, I'm Harold Smith," try something like, "Nice to meet you, *Joe*. I'm Harold." And keep pounding away as you converse. Don't feel silly when you hear yourself saying "Joe this" and "Joe that"; most people are vain, and this repetition makes them feel important. Repeating someone's name also lends a more cordial, personal tone to your conversations—never a bad move in business.

3. ASK QUESTIONS.

The ability to greet someone you've met previously and recall his *last* name will impress for its exhibition of a razor-sharp memory. Let's say you meet someone with the name of, oh, Larry Wishkenewsberg. Don't see it as a horrific last name you're thankful your children will never have to bear. Instead, see it as an opportunity. Ask Larry about his family history. When did the first Wishkenewsberg dock at Ellis Island? Is he related to the Wishkenewsbergs of Kentucky fame? The only thing you need is one answer that will ring a bell the next time you meet.

BEASTIE BOYS SCREENSAVER: Available for free from (www.capitolrecords.com).

4. ATTACH A PICTURE TO THE NAME.

For those who may be more artistically inclined, Kevin Trudeau has a method. He's the author of *Mega Memory,* which he flogs on an infomerical you may have seen at 3:00 A.M. some Saturday night when you were doing your best to *forget* everything. When it comes to remembering names, Trudeau suggests breaking them down into pictures and then stringing them together. Meet an exec named Hazel Mercer? She'd be Hazy Elephant Mercenary. Sure it's stupid—but also surprisingly effective.

5. ALWAYS ASK FOR A BUSINESS CARD.

As an extra step, jot down some pertinent information about the person on the back, such as where you met him and who introduced you. (Obviously, *don't* do this in front of him.) Such info could come in handy during a subsequent conversation. Just keep in mind that if you're going to ask for somebody's card, it would behoove you to have a card to hand back. In business, having someone remember *your* name is just as important as remembering his.

SMILE:
Your boss will think you like your job.

POST-IT NOTES:
A way of life.

DELIVERING A MASTERFUL SPEECH

When Arkansas governor Bill Clinton, in his nominating speech for Michael Dukakis at the 1988 Democratic National Convention, spoke the words, "In closing . . ." a roar went up in the hall; he was *finally* finishing. Fortunately for him, he's a quick learner: his 1992 speech accepting his own nomination was much more to the point—and got much better marks. In fact, some pundits said it was the most important speech of his political career: not only did Clinton set the tone for his first presidential campaign, but he also erased once and for all the memory of that dud four years earlier.

That story has three important points. One, you're never too good or too experienced to ignore some of the fundamentals of good speaking. Two, you can give an occasional poor speech and still reclaim your agenda and stature. Three—and most important—the ability to communicate well to groups of people can make a critical difference in your career.

In fact, a study conducted by AT&T and Stanford University revealed that the top predictor of professional success and upward mobility is how good you are at, and how much you enjoy, public speaking. Yet surveys also continually show that the number-one fear of most adults—even above death—is talking in front of a crowd. Now there's a contradiction for you: the best thing for anyone's career is also what we fear most.

The ability to speak confidently is one of the most marketable skills you can acquire. Organizations continually seek individuals who can sell products, present proposals, report findings, and explain ideas effectively. It's no coincidence that more than half of Toastmasters clubs are in-house corporate or government groups. Audiences, now accustomed to slick media, are less tolerant than ever of marginal presentation skills. So the ante has been upped on what level of public speaking is needed to get your message across. Here are some tricks of the trade.

AN EXTRA UMBRELLA UNDER YOUR DESK:
And remember to bring it back in after a surprise rainstorm.

1. CARE ABOUT YOUR SUBJECT.
Passion is the starting point of all good public speaking. Peggy Noonan, President Reagan's celebrated speech writer, describes a speech as "poetry: cadence, rhythm, imagery, sweep! It reminds us that words, like children, have the power to make dance the dullest beanbag of a heart." So pick a subject that has an inordinate impact on you, a subject you'd like to share with others because you know, intensely, that they could benefit from your knowledge. Your enthusiasm will show through.

2. BE BRIEF.
The best way to impress an audience is to finish early. "My father gave me this advice on speechmaking," said James Roosevelt, son of FDR: "Be sincere . . . be brief . . . be seated." So hit it hard, hit it well, finish strong and, for maximum impression, keep it short. The less opportunity you give your audience's minds to wander, the more it will appreciate you and remember what you had to say.

3. MAKE USE OF MEMORY JOGGERS.
You can keep attention high and help people remember your message if you use enough examples to transmit your message powerfully. Similarly, statistics, if used sparingly and presented simply, can

add drama and credibility to your message. Comparisons can help your audience evaluate different options quickly and logically, and testimony—personal stories of credible people—can make your message more memorable and believable.

4. REMEMBER THE PAUSE THAT REFRESHES.

The sweet sound of silence, the power of the pause, can be artfully used in any speech. Pauses are not really empty spaces. Instead, they're opportunities for the audience to respond to your words with their own thoughts, images, and feelings. "The right word may be effective," Mark Twain said. "But no word was ever as effective as a rightly timed pause."

5. DON'T DAWDLE AT THE FINISH LINE.

Good speakers understand that the end is just as important—maybe more so—as the beginning. This is your chance to sum up your best thoughts, words, and images and imprint them indelibly on the audience's collective brain. Don't miss that opportunity by running beyond your time limit or fumbling your final message. Know what you want to say and say it. Then say good night.

FINAGLING A PAY RAISE

There's nothing better than a big, fat pay raise—and nothing worse than having to ask for it. Most people needlessly stumble when confronted with this touchy issue. Here are five steps to help nail that raise without wimping out or letting self-doubts get in the way:

1. THINK LIKE A CHIEF EXECUTIVE.

Before you pop the question, research your business to learn how profits are measured. Know the key financial reports that the president relies on to assess how your job helps the company make money. In the insurance industry, a loss ratio is a key benchmark. Airlines monitor their load factor. Hotels track their occupancy rates. By understanding how your boss thinks, you can speak the language of executives who must administer salary increases within limited

TAKING A CLASS: Meet new people, and have more to talk about than work.

A COPY OF AYN RAND'S *ATLAS SHRUGGED*: You'll never look at your career— or the world—the same way again.

budgets. Better yet, you can show how your resourcefulness has translated into stronger numbers for your division.

2. ASK YOUR BOSS TO MEASURE YOUR PERFORMANCE.

Work with your supervisor to set short-term, objective measurements that indicate how your work directly affects the bottom line. Set goals and establish timetables so that you can periodically review your progress. Explain that you want to chart your performance as a team player whose top priority is to maximize your contributions to your employer—then deliver results that prove your worth. This will give you hard data (low staff turnover, sales per square foot, quarterly revenue growth) to back up your rhetoric. And that makes it much harder for management to say no to you.

3. FOCUS ON MUTUAL GAIN.

Emphasize that your interests are aligned with the company's best interests. This will undercut any attempt by the boss to object to your raise on the grounds that "you're already paid more than your coworkers" or "we're cutting costs right now." You make the boss look good and greatly increase the likelihood of a raise by tackling tough or thankless projects. Reassure your manager that your desire for increased pay, a bigger office, or a better title reflects your eagerness to grow with the company and pave the way for future success. Also emphasize that your job satisfaction comes from improving how the firm performs or trounces the competition—and the rewards that spring from that.

4. THINK IN THREES.

Many employees tend to talk too much when conversing with their bosses, especially when they're asking for something. To avoid overselling, select only the three most powerful points you want to make. Come into your meeting with a clear, concise outline that summarizes your trio of ideas. When you express three compelling benefits, you offer enough meaty reasons for your raise without going overboard. But it's important to clam up afterward. Resist the urge to brag by recounting all of your achievements; your boss may tire of your incessant, self-congratulatory chatter. What's worse, if you let slip just one point that your boss finds objectionable, you may lose the whole argument. Thinking in threes reduces the chances of self-sabotage.

WATER BOTTLE: How else are you gonna get those eight glasses a day sitting at your desk?

5. ANTICIPATE OBJECTIONS.

Some bosses instinctively try to shut down discussion of pay raises or promotions by resorting to automatic rejection responses: "We're in a freeze"; "Let's wait till next quarter to discuss this"; "It wouldn't be fair to others in your department." Plan ahead and prepare for such predictable comments. Disarm your boss by acknowledging the objection and plowing on. Reframe negative obstacles as creative challenges that need to be overcome ("The fact we're in a budget freeze now is all the more reason to reward employees who propose sensible ways to cut costs"). Never argue when greeted with an objection; instead, welcome the chance to respond. Recognize the objection not as something bad to be attacked, but as a barrier that you need to gently maneuver around. Your aim is not to show how your boss is wrong as much as to analyze the situation in a broader or more creative light.

BUSTING-OUT ENTREPRENEURIAL STYLE

A MONT BLANC FOUNTAIN PEN: When you're on your way up, it helps to have accessories that make it look like it.

More young people are starting their own businesses today than ever before. Hell, we'll bet you personally either know someone who is thinking about it or has already made the leap. A recent study by a Babson College professor, Paul Reynolds, found that 10 percent of Americans between the ages of twenty-five and thirty-four are trying to start their own businesses, compared to only 3 percent of those thirty-four to forty-four. And a recent Roper Starch Worldwide study found 63 percent of eighteen-to–twenty-nine-year-olds polled said they actually wanted to start their own business; a similar number viewed such ownership as a status symbol.

There's a big leap, though, from dreaming about it to doing it. A recent survey by the U.S. Department of Labor Data suggests that while some 30 percent of the population think about starting a business, only about 4 percent make an actual attempt. But stats, schmats. If you're reading this, you're at least thinking about it. And we think you ought to just do it.

Face it. The real reason you're thinking about starting your own business is you. Do you like being a wage slave? Do you really relish waiting obediently for the next corporate downsizing? Or do you want to be master of your own universe? Timing is everything. And there's no better time than now, before a spouse and kids and a mortgage make taking a risk that much more daunting. What's to lose at this point?

First, though, a disclaimer: When you're running your own show, the buck, quite literally, stops with you. And if you don't think you're a grownup now, wait until you have clients knocking on your door, vendors waiting to be paid, and employees looking to you for the paycheck that feeds their kids. Yikes! There's no calling in sick. There's no dodging the unpleasant task, no throwing your hands up and quitting. And in the beginning, you can forget about your social life.

Further cause for caution: most start-up enterprises fail within the first three years. Why? There are as many variables explaining that as there are businesses, but by far the most common is a shortage of money, usually brought about by shoddy planning before the business doors ever open.

Still interested? Then read on. We've developed a handy-dandy six-stage guide to booting up your own enterprise. Keep in mind that this is only a rough outline; the details will vary dramatically depending on what kind of business you're starting. But the basics hold true: whether you're providing an information service out of your garage or manufacturing widgets in a factory, you still need a viable business plan, start-up capital, accurate forecasts, and the know-how to manage growth. It's not going to be easy. But if you succeed, you'll find yourself in control of your life and future.

A MENTOR:
You can't know *everything*.

GETTING STARTED

A wise man once said that to have a successful business, you must find a problem and solve it. So step one is finding your problem, i.e., your business idea. Sounds obvious, but too many first-time entrepreneurs don't have a clear idea of what their business is: whether you provide a service, manufacture a product, or convey information, it must be focused. Your business idea could spring from something you're already doing for somebody else. (You know you can do it better.) It can grow out of specialized research or academic work you're doing. You can fill holes left by changing laws or markets.

Or, if you're lucky, an idea could also walk in your front door.

KNOW THY MARKET

So you've got yourself a killer idea. Great. Who are you going to sell it to? A brilliant idea is not a good business idea until you have a customer. You have to adopt a marketing approach.

Before you even think about spending time and money for real market research—the kind you'll want to show potential investors—you need to make a few inquiries yourself. Start by picking up the phone and talking to potential future customers and people in the business. How big is your competition, and what are they not doing? What's the market share, and how much of it do you want? Is your service or product something people need? Something they want? And most important, will they pay for it? Make it your business to know your market intimately.

FORECASTING THE BUCKS

So now you've got the idea, and you've found a customer (hopefully lots of them). It's time to start looking at other details, like guesstimating how much money you'll need between the time you launch and the time your business is healthy enough to cover its own costs. For some businesses, this is three months, for others three years. A lot of it depends on your personal situation. Do you have enough socked away in the bank to forego taking a salary? Will you be able to keep your day job initially, while running the startup at night?

Whatever the circumstances, err on the side of pessimism. It's sort of a business variation on the old rule of gathering firewood: assume no revenue, factor in your fixed costs like rent, equipment, supplies, and every other variable you can think of—then double it. Work out a best-case scenario and a worst-case scenario. The truth is usually somewhere in between. But having that extra firewood will allow you to handle those problems you can't foresee and even the ones you should have seen but didn't.

THE BUSINESS PLAN

Your business plan is the most important factor in your start-up dreams. It tells you and potential investors exactly what this business is about. The business plan forces you to outline very carefully the details of your enterprise. Your market research and capital projections pay off here. A business plan makes you put down on paper all

AN INTERN:
They get invaluable experience; you get a job free of shit-work.

AN HONEST PARTNER:
If you can't trust the players, ditch the deal.

those ugly numbers you may not want to think about but need to if your business is ever to move beyond the dream phase. Without a solid business plan, you're asking for failure.

Of course, every business plan is different—they don't all need to be the size of *War and Peace* or as complex as an Einstein theorem. It depends on the type of business you're starting. Is it a relatively simple idea—maybe a recycling company for a town that has none? Or a biotechnology start-up built around a complicated new technology? Also, tailor it to your general target. A company that understands the market? Or a venture capitalist, who simply wants to know how he's going to make his money before getting out?

Remember that presentation is important: Word processing is a must, of course, and indexes, charts, and illustrations score points as well. If you lack expertise in certain areas—perhaps accounting, or technical history—hiring an expert to help write certain sections is not a bad idea. The business plan is an area where a little money often proves a good long-run investment.

Pay particular attention to your summary, because this is typically the first (and often the last) thing that a potential investor looks at. You've got two or three pages—no more—to grab your would-be investor's attention and convince him that your business deserves to be funded. Obviously this is more important if you plan on trying to reach outside sources of capital. But even rich Uncle Jack wants to know in detail how you plan to spend his money—and pay him back.

3:00 P.M. CUP OF COFFEE:
Beat the midafternoon blahs.

RAISING MONEY

So now you've got this smoking hot business plan to add to the mix. You're still missing the key ingredient: cash, or at least some equivalent like a loan or a credit line. If you've done your projections right, you know about how much you'll need to set up shop, purchase equipment, and keep yourself afloat for at least a year. As daunting as money-raising appears, there are many resources out there. You just have to work like hell to tap into them.

For most, commercial banks are simply not a realistic option. Generally, they won't give you the time of day until they see at least three years of successful business experience behind you. As obnoxious as that attitude is, most nascent first-time entrepreneurs turn to private investors, which indeed often translates into friends or family. The First National Bank of Dad, after all, is probably the only funding source willing to throw in some blind faith.

Individual venture capitalists are another option, and recently they've been proliferating like rabbits. Take note, however. This route is fraught with dangers: namely, how much control do you want to exchange for cash? If these investors are plowing money into your idea, it will generally come with a series of rules about how the cash will be spent. Venture capital is also a tough get without a track record. (One exception is if you come with a big reputation, perhaps a noted medical researcher who wants to start a company based on his breakthrough.) Second-timers might hit paydirt here, though.

So where does this leave first-time entrepreneurs who can't turn to Daddy for the big bucks? We'll call it creative financing. You'll probably call it maxing out the credit cards. Laugh if you must, but that credit card with the five-thousand-dollar limit is a plastic bank loan waiting to happen. Trust us. Gather ten of those beauties, and you are looking at fifty thousand dollars for your start-up. But be warned: you're paying a premium interest rate on all those cards.

GETTING STARTED

So now you're on your way. Get ready to work your ass off.

Get out there and sell. Sell like hell, baby. The initial goal is simply getting above your break-even point, which means that the business is paying for itself. Keep in mind that fast sales don't always equate to profits. Don't choke yourself by overhiring or by upgrading the office compter system prematurely.

A couple quick tips here: Don't try to do everything at the risk of doing nothing well. Always pay your payroll taxes, as tempting as it to let those payments to Uncle Sam slip. Rest assured that it has not gone unnoticed. He will come for it, and when he does, it will be ugly. And don't be afraid to get advice, from mentors, peers, or even pros. One group to contact is the Young Entrepreneurs Organization (703–527–4500)—they're in their twenties and thirties, and they all have started business with $1 million or more in sales.

Don't worry: it gets easier. With every year of business, your odds of staying in business increase. Eventually, you'll have to decide whether to keep sailing along, attempt to build an empire, or take the money and run. You should always keep an exit strategy in mind. But that's a problem for another time.

THE NEW YORK TIMES **OR THE** *WALL STREET JOURNAL:* **Start your day informed.**

OPENING YOUR OWN RESTAURANT

Wanna open a restaurant? Go back to bed. Go see a psychiatrist. Put all your money in a suitcase and take it to Las Vegas and throw it on a roulette table. When asked to offer advice for aspiring Wolfgang Pucks, industry experts have a concise answer: "Don't do it."

Of course, when was the last time you listened to the so-called experts? They also told you that O.J. was going down and people would dig New Coke. As entrepreneurial endeavors go, owning your own restaurant is exciting, even glamorous. Plus, you've barbecued a half-decent burger and eaten at 1,001 joints that screw it up yet nonetheless manage to stay in business. Whether it's chicken puttanesca à la Sirio Maccioni or chicken-fried steak à la Mel's Diner, you know you can do it better. So go for it. Money can be made. But it's important to know what you're up against.

Failure rates in restaurants are notoriously high. A 1992 study—the only long-term research on restaurant failure to date—from the hotel schools at Cornell and Michigan State universities found that 27 percent of new restaurants close within the first year, while half shut their doors by the end of three years. Of those that make it to three years, 62 percent will likely pass the decade mark.

Courtesy of the megaeateries creeping across the country—from Chili's and the Olive Garden to Planet Hollywood and the Spaghetti Factory—the competition is getting stiffer. Remember the local mom-and-pop hamburger joint? It's somewhere up in retail heaven alongside the independent bookshops and record stores. Today, national chains account for more than half of all restaurant sales in the country, a trend that shows no signs of reversal in the decades to come.

Still, restaurant ownership can be exhilarating, artistic, and a hell of a lot more fun than working in most offices. And despite all the naysayers, there are still those who defy the odds.

GETTING STARTED

Consider taking a job with the type of restaurant you plan to open or with a national chain, where the operating systems tend to be more efficient than elsewhere. Even if you've got a day job, a few nights or weekends will help you focus your plan.

FILEMAKER PRO 3.0:
A powerful database program with one significant advantage over your brain: Filemaker never forgets an associate's phone number.

AN ERGONOMIC WORK SPACE:
Get set up right now, and avoid those trips to the doctor later.

Bear in mind that a plain old Italian restaurant with Chianti and red tablecloths doesn't cut it with today's savvy diners. Gone, too, are traditional dinner houses with fifty-item menus offering everything from baked stuffed shrimp to T-bone steak. If all you have to offer is decent cooking, don't bother. Heightened competition means you have to be more innovative. Great chow is one thing (one vital thing), but a great concept that encompasses the entire dining experience is even better. Planet Hollywood and Hard Rock Café, after all, make buckets of money from food no better than the fare at your local diner.

While concepts are usually geared toward a specific sector of the population, such as college students or Florida retirees, a strong one can transcend its target audience. That doesn't mean you should open a beer-and-wings joint next to a nursing home. But have the vision, at least, to venture beyond your own palate.

Whether you're serving designer bagels or Italian-Japanese fusion cuisine, the most important thing to offer is good value. Nobody likes a rip-off, no matter how decadent the surroundings. A thirty-dollar steak is an easier sell in Dallas than Detroit, but it had better be good in either city.

CHOOSING THE RIGHT PARTNERS

When considering partners, don't just go with your best drinking buddy. Ask yourself: Does your potiential partner have a skill to bring to the table? Does he have a proven track record in the restaurant business? Can you trust him? Can he raise money? Is he a fugitive?

Another important trait in a partner is friends—lots of hungry ones.

GETTING THE CASH

While diners will eventually be your judge, the first people you have to woo are investors. Raising money for restaurants is difficult because of a vicious circle: they are a bad financial risk, so most banks don't want to lend to them, so new restaurants wind up going bankrupt because they are undercapitalized, and so on. It's no surprise that the most time-honored source for capital is family and friends.

Sometimes Uncle Sam is willing to lend a hand. Around six thousand new restaurants each year obtain loans of up to $750,000 guaranteed by the federal Small Business Administration (SBA). The loans are for borrowers who don't qualify for a commercial bank

OPTIMUS PRO 25 TITANIUM HEADPHONES: Guaranteed to block out the office riff-raff during those times when you actually need to get some work done.

loan but have good credit. Get information about SBA-backed loans at (www.sba.gov) or by calling 800–8ASKSBA. Another resource, available through Small Business Development Centers, is the Service Corps of Retired Executives (SCORE), which can provide free or almost-free technical and management consulting. Check out their Web site at (www.score.org).

Start-up expenses vary widely depending on a restaurant's size, location, extent of renovations, and type of food served, but $500,000 is as good a figure as any. For a better one, the National Restaurant Association in Washington (202–331–5965) sells publications including a guide to preparing a restaurant business plan. Another option is a restaurant consultant, who will charge a fee of 5 to 10 percent of start-up costs to guide you through the labyrinthine opening process.

Revenues are easier to project than expenses: count how many tables you intend to have, how many times they will turn on a given night, and multiply it by half an appetizer, an entrée, and a drink, for instance. Go back to your previous restaurant experience; if necessary, spy anew.

Start with enough money to cover all capital and operating expenses for three months to a year. Even if the eatery is a runaway hit, it will still take some time to make back the cash spent on furniture, equipment, contractors, lawyers, accountants, food, hired help, inventory, and labor.

GETTING A LOCATION

You know the old three-word magic formula in the real-estate business: location, location, location. Well, it's just as true about restaurants. To keep start-up costs down, retrofit a space that already houses a restaurant. It's less work and less money than starting from scratch. The downside is that problems that plagued the previous restaurant could dog yours as well. Be sure to investigate the space thoroughly, especially with regard to car and foot traffic, profit of adjacent businesses, and the demographics and lifestyle habits in the surrounding community. Remember when signing the lease that you're renting a space for a risky venture, not a place to grow old.

Once you have the spot, plan on allowing up to six months for renovations before opening. There are two ways to do the overhaul—on your own or with an architect, depending upon your ambitions. Some restaurant concepts lend themselves to do-it-yourself shabby chic; for a Southern country retro joint, Ground

WHITE OUT:
To err is human. . . .

REALISTIC BUDGETS:
Nothing's worse than having a deal fall apart in the middle because of faulty estimations.

Round–style bric-a-brac is easily obtained from garage sales or a restaurant-decor supplier. An airplane-hangar theme is harder to pull off without a hired gun.

An architect will run you anywhere from ten thousand dollars for a small restaurant in a small city to an easy fifty thousand and up for a high-caliber urban architect. While going it alone is cheaper, hiring an architect has its advantages. They know where to get deals on labor and supplies and understand the complex building codes that govern every element of restaurant design.

Construction is a good time to focus on applying for the seemingly interminable number of permits needed for building plans, plumbing, electrical wiring, and food service. If you want to legally change a hood on your stove, many places will require a permit to do so. For a fee of anywhere from two thousand to eight thousand dollars—well worth the savings in aggravation, some say—a seasoned bureaucracy expert called a "permit expediter" will shepherd the applications through the appropriate channels.

If you bought an existing restaurant, some permits may already be in place. Fees attached to new permits are incidental, except for the most important one. A liquor license can take four months to obtain and cost up to $120,000 on the open market in a town that isn't issuing new ones. (Thankfully, most cities are inclined to simply dole out more.) Research license availability in your jurisdiction before committing to a site—a microbrewery with no liquor license is a pretty sorry place.

STAFFING THE JOINT

Another headache for restaurant owners these days is staffing. Restaurateurs are grumbling that you just can't find good help anymore. Despite unbeatable cash in pocket, waiting tables is a less-appealing option when the employment market is on an upswing. Sweeten the pot with benefits like health insurance, which can run around two hundred dollars a month per person at an HMO.

Overall, expect to spend about a third of gross revenue on employees. The bulk of this goes to the chef, who is commonly found by raiding someone else's kitchen. Salaries for head chefs in major cities such as New York or San Francisco range from $75,000 at a small restaurant to $250,000 at a blockbuster; the range is about $50,000 to $150,000 in a smaller city.

Hiring a chef involves an inevitable catch-22. On the one hand,

AN EXTRA SHIRT: Just in case you don't make it home.

CIGARS: For that promotion just around the corner.

A BLACK TURTLENECK: Properly folded on the bottom of your desk drawer, it'll be ready when you aren't.

you want an artist who can come up with a killer menu. On the other, you don't want the menu to walk out with him in two years when he gets a better offer from someone else.

If you or your partner is an owner-chef, problem solved. If not, make sure you stay involved in menu planning.

GETTING OPEN

Don't wait until the grand opening to let people know about your restaurant. Send out flyers to local businesses and corporations. Become popular enough to fill the place with your friends. Consider promotional gimmicks.

Have a preopening party where you preview the menu and work out the kinks. While you're at it, have at least three: one for contractors and their families, and two sessions where you split the staff into two groups and allow them to serve each other as customers. Don't invite special guests and dignitaries until the operational shakeout is over.

When it comes to getting the word out, public relations is generally more effective than advertising. Community newspapers, trade magazines, travel publications, and fashion rags are all fair game. Some restaurants hire publicists to do the pitching for them.

UNIBALL PENS:
Nobody inks it better.

STAYING OPEN

It's not too hard to open with a bang. Surviving the honeymoon is another story. Diners are unforgiving and fickle. Trends change. The hippest new restaurants often croak the quickest, when the in-crowd leaves for the brand-new Vietnamese tapas cigar joint down the block.

Nobody knows for sure how to make a new restaurant stick, but certain things help. Maintain your marketing or advertising strategy even when business is good. Be open to events and parties. Keep the menu diverse in price and selection. Be willing to change. Remember that the life cycle of a restaurant is around a decade; even a popular spot needs some freshening up now and then.

Even if you do everything right, there are no guarantees. The worst thing that can happen is that you shut down after four months, lose all your money as well as your friends' and parents', and have to split town to flee creditors. Nobody said it was going to be easy. But it promises to be a wild ride.

CHAPTER 6

CASH CONCERNS

Q: HOW MUCH SHOULD I TIP?

The etiquette of modern tipping, if there is one, has become so vague and indistinct on this service-hungry cusp of the twenty-first century that consumers are routinely confused about what is expected—and why. Since the late 1970s, the going rate has been 15 percent. Although that's still the norm, there are subtle forces pushing the envelope toward 20 percent.

We've come a long way, baby. Consumers of yesteryear left no more than 10 percent on fountain counters. A decade ago, it was rare for tips to be brazenly solicited for counter service, but in today's coffeehouses and juice joints, with de rigueur "tipping brings good karma" signs, the going rate for donations to the tip jar is about 25 to 50 cents, with regular customers dropping an occasional buck for good measure.

The history of tipping is clouded in mystery. There is some evidence that tipping has its roots in the Roman Empire. One theory is that tipping—supposedly an acronym for "to insure promptitude"— became common in the "penny universities" (coffeehouses) of sixteenth-century England. Another explanation is that "tips" of gold were thrown by feudal lords on horseback to the unsavory peasants in the streets as payment for safe passage.

INVEST:
It's never too early. It's never too little. Compound interest, anyone?

The Motley Fool
www.fool.com
Here, the individual investor is king (or queen), and the Fools—two brothers, actually—dispense advice with much amusement. The Fools specialize in stock ideas, and you'll find lots of them here, whether in Boring Portfolio ("stocks that are low on gloss and high on potential") or Daily Double (one that doubled in the past year). Stock quotes, news, message boards. Wonderfully idiosyncratic.

Quote.com
www.quote.com
Quotes for stocks and bonds, of course, and a lot more: business news, a variety of stock charts, investment research reports, and links to on-line traders. Complex info, yet easy to view and access.

Financenter
www.financenter.com
Deciding whether to lease or buy a car? Looking to learn how exchange rates affect

At the turn of the century in America, practitioners of tipping had honed the custom to a kind of high art, carrying separate bill-folds full of purposely crisp bills and change purses full of coins expressly intended for service payment. A man wasn't a man who did not know how to secretively place a tip in the palm of a waiter.

Today the custom has degenerated to simple mathematical computations (twice the tax, rounded out), the result often left on the table in crumpled bills or artlessly added to the credit card bill.

Yes, tipping is expected. No, it is not obligatory. It is also not an antidote to rudeness. The key is to remember that waiters are not your dogs. They deserve to be treated with respect.

LONG-TERM INVESTING: THE REAL PATH TO RICHES

Exponential growth, even when explained, seems like a trick.

—BILL GATES

Unlike the Golden Rule and the Ten Commandments, investing's conventional wisdom does not apply equally to everyone. Most experts tend to talk about the investment outlook over 10 or 20 years—which requires more conservative short-term thinking and hedging. Older investors, after all, are more likely to cash in their stocks relatively soon—bad news if that need comes during a market correction. So they dump big chunks into bonds and T-bills, and counsel others to do that as well.

We're talking about a forty-year time frame, which is how you should be thinking if you're in your twenties or early thirties. When looking long-term, the real risk is the erosion of purchasing power caused by inflation. The way to eliminate this risk is to concentrate your capital in things that are growing fast enough to more than off-set inflation. And that, at this point in human history, means stocks. Nothing else.

This is retirement money—we're not counting on collecting anything from the pyramid scheme known as Social Security, and neither should you. And by starting early, you can rack up some big numbers: ten thousand dollars invested intelligently today can allow you to spend almost all of your paycheck for the rest of your life and still know that perpetual golf at Pebble Beach awaits whenever you're ready for it.

The key is aggressiveness. When you're looking at a forty-year time horizon, aggressiveness, leavened with a grasp of a few basic investment principles, isn't risky—it's prudent.

To see why, let's start with the most powerful and perhaps least understood concept in the world of money: compounding.

When something grows at a constant rate (i.e., exponentially), it doubles in a fixed number of years. For example, earning a steady 10.3 percent annually—or about what common stocks have returned since World War II—doubles your money in seven years.

Then the real fun begins, because each successive doubling is on a larger base: in twenty-one years, you've got eight times your original stake. In forty years $10,000 grows to more than $500,000.

That's not bad. But check out what happens when you replace 10.3 percent with the 12.4 percent that stocks from small companies (which have more upside potential) have historically generated. Your money now doubles in just under six years rather than in seven. A small difference in the short run, but over forty years it produces slightly more than one extra doubling. Instead of $500,000, your $10,000 nest egg becomes $1.1 million.

Now step up to a 15 percent annual return. The extra 2.6 percent adds yet another doubling, plus some extra, swelling your $10,000 into a net worth of around $2.8 million. And suddenly, thirty-year-old women are referring to you as "old but sexy."

Granted, $2.8 million won't be worth as much in 2037 as it is today. But with inflation running at just 2 percent a year, and your stock portfolio protecting you should it go any higher (stock prices tend to go up with inflation), you'll still be the king of the cabana. And that $2.8 million total assumes you never save another dime in your life. Which hopefully won't be the case.

Think about it: Bumping up your return by less than half, from 10.3 percent to 15 percent, yields more than five times as much money over an investing lifetime. That's the power of long-term compounding, and grasping it leads inescapably to two conclusions.

First, starting early (and then waiting as long as possible to raid the kitty) makes eminent sense, since fully half the total increase comes in the last five years. If you've cobbled together $10,000 when

your foreign stocks? With smart, question-based calculators, Financenter offers answers—plus charts and graphs—about credit cards, savings, and everything else about money.

Stock Master
www.stockmaster.com
What started as an MIT graduate student project now offers quotes and charts on almost all U.S. equities and mutual funds. Keep up with the beat of Wall Street, and get advice on top performing funds.

Morningstar.Net
www.morningstar.net
On-line home of the trusted Wall Street watchdog, packed with feature stories, stock quotes, and investment advice.

www.moneysearch.
com
Making sense of the many sites that deal with moolah on the Web. Reviews guide you to the top sites in categories such as banks, bonds, on-line brokers, and taxes.

you're twenty-eight and nonetheless wait until you're thirty-three to play our 15 percent return game, the difference is a cool million-three. Ouch.

Second, you need to reach for those extra few percentage points. It's doable, even through the next oil shock, presidential scandal, and unpopular war if you're armed with patience and an understanding of a few basic principles.

SMALL IS BEAUTIFUL

First—and exclusively while you're working with limited capital—you'll want mutual funds that invest in the stocks likeliest, in the aggregate, to win big. In the United States, these are generally called "microcap" funds. They buy the stocks of companies that the stock market values at less than $250 million. That, for perspective, is about 1/700th of General Electric's market value.

The theory behind microcaps is simple: the smaller the company, the farther it can run, in percentage terms, if successful. So microcap funds always buy a lot of really hot prospects, with the big winners offsetting the more numerous losers. Buy several such funds and you'll participate in the fastest-growing part of the American economy.

But limiting yourself to the United States is analogous to considering only Ford when buying a sports car. In fact, despite (or because of) the spectacular gains racked up by U.S. stocks in the 1990s, the real action in coming years could be overseas.

Brazil, China, Thailand, India—those aren't necessarily names that come to mind when you think of wealth creation. But because they're starting from a low base, they—and much of the rest of the developing world—are generating growth rates that dwarf those of mature economies like that of the United States. And growth, eventually, is reflected in stock prices. The Asian market collapse of 1998 just means more opportunity for the brave investor. Meanwhile, Japan and much of Europe have had weak economies—and therefore underperforming stocks—during the past few years. They'll recover eventually, and so will their markets.

Note that because foreign stock funds bet on both companies and currencies, they carry an extra layer of risk. So early on, at least, avoid funds that limit themselves to one country. Instead, stick with established, no-load international funds.

AN AIRLINE CREDIT CARD: There's a built-in rationale for every dollar spent.

HELP YOURSELF

Mutual funds are a great way to go for rookie investors, because they allow even the small-fry to hire the services of an expert. But once you've built up your nest egg—to twenty thousand dollars, perhaps—you should consider building your own portfolio of growth stocks. This is more fun than mutual funds, obviously, but it's also your best chance to find the one or two big winners that take your returns from good to great.

The legendary money manager Peter Lynch opens his book *One Up on Wall Street* with a discussion of what he calls "tenbaggers," stocks that go to ten or more times their original price. "In a small portfolio," he says, "even one of these remarkable performers can transform a lost cause into a profitable one."

How do you find tenbaggers? Not from reading the *Wall Street Journal* or *Business Week*, at least not consistently. Nor will you hear about them from your Merrill Lynch broker. The mainstream (read: national) investment community, simply because it is national, tends to focus on already established names. Even growth-stock newsletters, according to several studies, turn up little of value for their subscribers. Your only real alternative is to find a niche where you have superior information, i.e., information that has predictive value and is not yet widely disseminated.

That might be your field of expertise. If you're a salesman, you know who in your business has the hottest products, and therefore which stocks might do relatively well next year. If you're a parent, you know which toy companies are pushing your kids' buttons. And everyone has one natural advantage: proximity to the business activity taking place right down the street. Local companies are constantly emerging, restructuring, and dying. And they're doing much of it outside of Wall Street's gaze. Just by living where you do, in other words, you have access to information that can potentially help you beat the market.

An added attraction of this type of "Main Street investing" is that dozens of your neighbors are already doing it. They work for local brokerage houses, venture capital firms, the chamber of commerce, or simply for their own investment portfolios. And their ideas are available, if you know where to look and how to ask. Subscribe to the local business journal. You may be unaware that your city even has a business journal, since it's aimed primarily at executives in local companies. But it's there, and it's a gold mine of investment ideas,

CHECK CARD: Prevents you from spending money that's not yours.

including feature articles on small local companies, earnings reports, and, most important, the names of local people who know these companies intimately. Also, open an account with a local brokerage house. Being better connected to nearby companies is how local brokers differentiate themselves from their national competitors.

This doesn't, by the way, mean closing your existing brokerage account. Lots of people have more than one such account. And because local brokers tend to charge commissions in the "full service" range, a discount broker—especially one of the new on-line services—can still save you a lot of money.

FIRST PRINCIPLES

Finding the right stocks is half the battle, but only half. Where you keep them, how you add to them, and how long you hold them are, taken together, just as important. Here are some basic rules for making sure that compounding works for rather than against you.

401(K):
If you were a squirrel, you'd build a stash of nuts before winter. Consider this your stash for life.

DEFER TAXES. It's hard to be a successful investor if most of your money is in a taxable account. Period. That's because the IRS skims nearly a third of your profits, pushing a 15 percent return down to a why-bother 10 percent. Over forty years, as you know, that's a million-dollar difference.

Luckily, shielding a portfolio from taxes is fairly easy. At least one of the following tax-deferred accounts—in which profits aren't taxed until they're withdrawn—is available to all Americans.

An employer-sponsored 401(k) plan allows you to put aside a portion of each pretax paycheck. And most companies match some part of their employees' 401(k) contributions, thus adding a few percentage points up front, where they help most.

The one drawback of a 401(k) is that your investment options are limited to the mutual funds chosen for the plan. And microcrap funds—often called "emerging growth"—are often not on the list. But this is correctable. Most companies will add new fund choices when presented with a reasoned argument. Do some research. Compile a list of small-cap funds that have blown away the plan's current offerings, then take it to your benefits department and ask politely that one or more of these funds be considered. You'll be surprised how often this works.

An Individual Retirement Account (IRA) is available to most people not already covered by a corporate pension plan. Depending on your family circumstances, you can contribute between $2,000 and $4,000 annually. And if your income is below $35,000 ($50,000 for a family), part or all of the initial deposit is tax-deductible.

If you're self-employed, you can set up either an SEP-IRA or Keogh plan. Either will allow you to shield a large part of your earnings from taxes.

AVOID UP-FRONT FEES. The various "loads," "wraps," and commissions charged by investment advisors have the same effect as taxes. They drain off the few percentage points that separate OK from spectacular.

The best way to avoid them is to find good investments and hold them for years—decades, if possible. Also, remember again to stick with no-load mutual funds, which are sold over the phone rather than through commissioned reps and thus don't carry sales fees. No-loads are both abundant and of high quality, so try never to pay a load for any fund.

No-load variable annuities are mutual funds with a twist: Whatever you put into them grows free of taxes until it's withdrawn. And, unlike other tax-advantaged investments, there's no limit on how much you can contribute. The original variable annuities came with heavy surrender charges, or back-end loads, and exorbitant "insurance fees" that together made them uninteresting. But recently a few innovative companies have begun offering no-load, low-expense versions that are much better buys for the money. As with mutual funds, Morningstar is the bible of variable annuities.

MUTUAL FUNDS: Diversify, diversify, diversify.

If you do begin buying stock on your own, keep fees down by using deep discount brokers, including Ceres Securities (800–669–3900) and Brown & Co. (800–822–2021). Another option, if you're wired: on-line brokers. Two of the biggest are E. Schwab (800–327–4922), which charges $29 per trade, and E-Trade, at $19 per trade (800–786–2575).

STAY THE COURSE

One of the great fallacies of investing is that markets can be timed. They can't, at least not by the average investor. So trying to move in and out of growth stocks will cost you twice. First, you're virtually guaranteed to miss the lightning-fast run-ups that hit such stocks without warning. And second, whatever advantage you do gain by prescient timing will be frittered away on brokerage commissions and capital gains taxes. Better to just accept volatility as a fact of life.

The Dow Jones Industrial Average has fallen by 10 percent or more fifty times in this century, and by 25 percent fifteen times. And each time it's come back to hit new highs, stranding the easily spooked in bonds or cash. History teaches that for someone with forty—or even twenty—years to kill, a down market is a buying opportunity rather than a time to sell.

Volatility can even work in your favor if you invest regular amounts each month, regardless of what's happening out there. In so doing, you buy more when prices are down, less when they're up. This is called "dollar cost averaging," and in the long run it will beat most market-timing strategies.

Still nervous about staying the course? Check out the record of a mutual fund called Twentieth Century Giftrust. You can't buy into it—instead, it allows investors to gift money to, say, a child, while specifying when junior gets it. And once the money is in there, it can't be removed—this gives the fund's managers a stable capital base and a long-term horizon, and thus an opportunity to target the riskiest, most rewarding sectors of the economy. (Right now, about two-thirds of the fund is invested in technology stocks.)

There have been some stomach-churning peaks and valleys. The fund lost 17 percent in 1990, and then gained 85 percent in 1991. It fell 17.9 percent in July of 1996, but made it all back over the next two months. But the final result is pure gold: a ten-year average annual return of 23.6 percent—almost unheard of in the mutual fund world—versus 15 percent for the Standard and Poor's 500 and 13.3 percent for the NASDAQ index.

HOME BANKING SOFTWARE: Because paying bills is a pain in the ass.

DIVERSIFY OR DIE

Don't be lulled by all this talk about the power of compounding and the ephemerality of downturns. Many individual stocks go down—forever. That's why the crucial final piece of the 15 percent puzzle is proper diversification. Not diversification among asset classes like bonds and cash—we've already established that you're in stocks for the duration—but within the universe of growth stocks.

In 1992, Handex Environmental was cleaning up, literally and figuratively: record earnings, surging revenues, glowing reports from local brokerage houses, the whole package. Then its markets changed and its advantage evaporated. Its stock price melted.

This is not an indictment of Handex. It remains a viable company whose future is probably brighter than its recent past, and so might be a good buy today. But it does illustrate the point that even the best story can have an unhappy ending. So never put more than a tenth of your investment capital into any one stock.

So, there it is. You're now a citizen of the brave new world of (really) long-term investing, where aggressiveness is prudent, market timing is bunk, and time, if not gravity, is on your side. Follow our rules and you'll retire a millionaire; ignore them, and you're taking a much bigger—and more foolish—risk.

THE NUTS AND BOLTS OF ON-LINE INVESTING

You know the drill. Type "investing." Click enter: 140,000 matches. Type "funds." Click enter: 46,900 matches. Type "investment advisors." Click enter: 5,600 matches. Type "help." Click enter. Get noose.

There's a downside to living in this bountiful information age— sometimes there's too much of it. Nowhere is this postindustrial surfeit more evident than in on-line investing, an arena with enough data and resources to drive even the most devoted tech-head straight to his phone and the nearest broker. After all, the gent at Salomon Smith Barney has the exact information an investor is looking for; while the Internet offers an avalanche of information just waiting to bury you—unless, of course, you know how to sort though the bull and cut to the chase.

The key is ruling the information rather than being ruled by it. In this record-setting market, swiftness determines who will thrive— and who will merely survive. If you're ready to take control of the investment process, look no further than that too-often useless box on your desk: everything from research and recommendations to the ability to price and time your own trades is available on line. And it's remarkably easy once you know how.

DOING THE RESEARCH

Managing your money does matter, a point not lost on all the major on-line services (America Online, Prodigy, Microsoft Network, and so on) nor the countless newsgroups where like- and not so like-minded souls will gab in green for as long as you can stand it. (If you doubt us try misc.invest.stocks, one of the most active spots for chat.)

Still, if you don't want to be confined by the offerings at the on-line services or weed through the muck in newsgroups and chat rooms, the answer lies on the Web.

Start by creating a selective list of links with trustworthy, easy-to-navigate topography. Bookmarking a handful of active financial news sites creates a virtual resource room that can rival a business library's stacks. Some of these sites are virtual mirrors of their hard-copy progenitors, while others are unique siblings with novel ideas all their own, like fill-in-the-blank worksheets that the Web server can churn through its magic grinder to serve up answers to your question. Very cool stuff. Unfortunately (and unsurprisingly) more and more sites are starting to charge for access to the most interesting or most recently published parts of the site. For now, you can still access some of the best sites at no cost. Here are the best places to get knowledge, listed in order from general investment advice to more specific looks at various marketplaces.

COIN WRAPPERS: Rolling all your loose change sitting in that coffee can could end up sending you to Cancun.

♦ CNNfn.com: A one-stop shop for the daily financial planet, filled with news headlines as well as a comprehensive market watch. Keeping in tune with the daily pulse of regional and international markets may leave you crying in your cognac, but staying fully informed is one way to stay ahead of the herd.

♦ SmartMoney Interactive (www.smartmoney.com): A comprehensive financial planning and investing site that mirrors its hard-copy brethren—and then some. It's a must-click for anyone who wants to be in the know about how to make yourself a growth industry.

♦ The Motley Fool: Found at www.fool.com (where else?), this site is the Internet version of the America Online phenomenon that brought the investing world's attention to the Web. Fool creators the Gardner brothers can be credited with getting more people plugged in than GE—and now their cash commentary is available 24–7–365 via the Web. This site is packed with pithy picks and pans, as well as some basic investing guidelines. A bargain at any price, this free site will prove addictive.

♦ TheStreet.com: Jim Cramer's caffeinated site will cost you ($9.95 a month, to be exact), but TheStreet.com is trying to do what some fly-by-night online investment sites *aren't* doing—namely, provide deep and professional analysis of everything that trades on a daily basis—and do it with flair.

◆ Bloomberg.com: Wall Streeters pay roughly fifteen thousand dollars a year to rent one of Michael Bloomberg's proprietary information boxes. Now you can access a good chunk of that for free on the Web. A conventional but comprehensive medium for financial facts and an overall market view, with in-depth analysis, market quotes, and access to a range of market experts and money managers. You can also zip into a number of market and industry comparison charts that give you a snapshot of how your overall portfolio is faring.

◆ Morningstar.net & fundsinteractive.com: There's nothing new under the fund sun that these two sites don't know about first. Completely reversing the old way of gleaning fund info—waiting for a monthly magazine or newsletter—these sites offer you the ability to leapfrog ahead of the unplugged investor. Each site offers an informed and efficient way to judge the funds you're investing in and the funds you might want to check out—or check out of.

◆ StockSmart.com & dbc.com: If you track individual stocks, these sites offer real-time quotes, analysis, trends, and forecasts. But it's mutual-fund coverage where they shine. Whether you're looking for the top- and bottom-performing mutual funds, the best and worst fund managers, the largest funds, fund ownership of stocks, or sector-by-sector performance numbers, turn to StockSmart. If you want to look beyond a single rating system for funds and access more commentary on individual funds in relation to their peers, check out dbc.com's SuperStar Funds review. Together, StockSmart.com and dbc.com provide the most efficient, comprehensive sources for fund information on the Web.

◆ EIU.com (Economist Intelligence Unit): Probably the best site for following the international component (both stocks and funds) of your portfolio. EIU covers more than 180 countries, including emerging and newly emerging markets. EIU's core value is its consistent, objective analysis of trends across the world, with uniquely informed commentary from its five hundred analysts, consultants, and researchers.

AN ANTIQUE FROM YOUR GRANDFATHER: Don't have a grandfather? Then buy an antique. You should invest in one decent tchotchke to hand down to your kids.

MAKING THE TRADES

Once you've gathered your information, it's time to get in on the action. The Internet provides the most efficient way to invest—as well as the most cost-effective, since most Web traders do all of the work and thus receive substantial trading cost discounts. Sure, there are some misfires along the way (a busy day in the markets can leave you left out of the action, as many Schwab and Fidelity customers discovered during last October's one-day, 6.9 percent market slide), but the benefits far outnumber the occasional kink.

Several on-line brokers are geared toward the individual investor, and all of those allow for the trading of stocks, bonds, and funds, including Ameritrade (now merged with Ceres), Fidelity's Web Xpress, Schwab's e.Schwab, E★TRADE, SureTrade and DLJdirect. Each site offers different price structures for trades, as well as varying services you may or may not need. (See the above chart to assess which one is for you.) Generally speaking, Fidelity and Schwab currently offer the most comprehensive (and within the deep-discount universe, the most expensive) cyberfloors for all types of trades and analyses. If bare bones and low costs are what you're after (and you meet the account minimums) Ameritrade and E★TRADE may be your ticket. Eager to top the others, however, each of these deep discounters is moving toward more full-service benefits, such as bountiful research, trend analysis, and efficient, real-time quotes. The new kid on the block, SureTrade, already combines low costs with advice and analysis, as well as full stock, bond, and fund menus.

No matter which on-line broker you select, vigilantly check that they live up to what's promised. Ask whether there are any additional charges imposed, such as inactivity fees and postage-and-handling fees. Sites may not disclose all fees on the site, or may bury them.

KEEPING TRACK

Once you've identified investments to follow, go beyond simple bookmarks and enter the rapidly advancing world of "push" technology, where information is *delivered* to your desktop. Push technology's leader is PointCast (www.pointcast.com), which serves as a free customized news and business channel for your computer. You tell the program which stocks, industries, and topics you're interested in following (as well as specific sports scores, news headlines, and the like) and PointCast grabs the info off the Net and presents it on a flashing

ZERO-COUPON BONDS:
They're guaranteed, you can sell them at any time, and you get a better return than the old U.S. Savings bonds. You can't bet the *whole* farm on the aggressive growth stocks.

screen, much like a screen saver. Excite's My Excite at my.excite.com is another easy and elegant way to get personalized quotes and information.

On the Web, Yahoo!'s Yahoo! Finance (quote.yahoo.com) allows those who register (free) to get personalized quotes and the latest market news—and offers links galore to anything you might want to know about finance.

On-line investing remains a relatively new creature, still in its early stages of evolution. There's only one thing we can be sure of: its future revolves around *you*. If a service doesn't customize itself to meet all your financial needs, it won't last long in this competitive climate. This means full control over information—thus giving you most of the advantages of a full-service broker—with the cost savings that the Web has helped pioneer in this area. Not a bad combination, knowledge and savings—the kind, in fact, with which fortunes are made.

DONATIONS: Help your favorite charity—and get a tax break.

TWELVE TIPS TO REDUCING YOUR TAXES

Uncle Sam may sound like a friendly name, but if you're a young single guy, you're not his favorite relative. The tax laws are stacked against you and in favor of older, more established folks. You probably don't own your own home, so you don't get a mortgage credit. And single people generally have fewer deductions.

So basically to play it smart, you've got two choices. Hire an accountant, who should know all the tricks to minimize the government's take. Or buy a green eyeshade and utilize our handy-dandy guide through this singularly unpleasant chore.

1. ESTABLISH A RETIREMENT PLAN.

This one is an easy—and obvious—one. The more money you can defer from taxes, the more money you'll have compounding. If you're offered a 401(k) plan at work, take maximum advantage of it—always. This allows you to sock away money before it's taxed, which puts you somewhere around 30 percent ahead from the get-go. Many companies also make matching contributions. If you don't have a 401(k), establish an IRA and make the maximum allowable contributions—usually two thousand dollars. This gives you many of the same benefits. If you're self-employed, start an SEP-IRA or a KEOGH, which again defer taxes until the money is withdrawn.

2. CONTRIBUTE EARLY IN THE YEAR.

The sooner you start accumulating tax-deferred earnings, the better. So if you maintain an IRA or other retirement plan, contribute as early in the year as you possibly can. By contributing two thousand dollars on January 1 each year instead of waiting until April 15 of next year, over the course of thirty years, earning an average rate of 10 percent annually, you'll accumulate an additional $3,500 per year on that one contribution alone. Yes, you can still make an IRA contribution for 1996 even though it's 1997, as long as you do it before April 15. So if you aren't deferring taxes yet, you can get started today by knocking off 1996 and 1997 in one fell swoop.

3. DEFER INCOME WITH T-BILLS AND T-BONDS.

Another way to defer income is to buy Treasury bills that don't mature until next year. You won't be taxed on the interest this year, as you would if the cash were in a savings account. Interest on T-bills isn't taxed on the federal return until maturity, and they're tax-free on most state tax returns. Avoid Treasury notes, which pay taxable interest twice a year. With Treasury bonds, the purchaser is not required to declare interest until the bond matures. If the proceeds are ultimately used for college tuition, interest may not be taxable at all.

4. DEFER INCOME WITH PUT OPTIONS.

Think a stock you own is ready to top out? Let's say you bought a hundred shares of the Acme Widget Co. at $50 per share five years ago and it's shot up to $150. You fear the price will fall soon but haven't held your stock the requisite eighteen months to qualify for the lower capital gains tax. The solution? Defer capital gains income and tax until next year by buying an Acme Widget "put" option, and lock in your profit at today's level.

A put grants the investor the right to sell a specific number of shares at a specified price by a certain date. If, in August, you buy an Acme February $150 put, you have the right to sell a hundred shares at $150 at any time until the put contract expires in February. You've

LOTS OF CASH: You'll never be late because you have to swing by an ATM.

accomplished the same thing as selling the stock, and you've bumped the tax into the next year.

5. GENERATE LOSSES WITH TAX SWAPS.

Another way to minimize capital gains taxes is to offset them with losses. Of course, doing that means dumping a loser in your portfolio that you may well feel is ripe for a comeback. Fair enough. Try a "tax swap." In other words, sell the security and immediately buy a similar, but not identical, holding. This will generate a loss for tax purposes, but keep the composition of your portfolio intact. Caution: If you want to buy back the identical investment, wait thirty-one days, or the IRS will disallow the loss under its "wash sale" rule. Or better yet, buy it back for your retirement account—wash sale rules don't apply to IRAs and their kin. There's no limit on the amount of gains that can be offset with losses, but taxpayers may only declare three thousand dollars in losses in excess of gains. And no, Las Vegas gambling losses don't count.

6. BEFORE SELLING, CONSIDER THE "COST BASIS":

The "cost basis"—an asset's original price—is used to determine capital gains. Depending on your tax bracket, and what it will be next year, you may get more of a tax advantage by selling the highest- or lowest-cost-basis shares first. So before selling shares of a stock or mutual fund, consider the cost basis of the shares you want to sell.

Say you bought a hundred shares of a fund at $10, another hundred shares at $15, and hundred more at $20. Now that the stock is $30, you want to sell hundred shares—but which shares should you sell? Believe it or not, it matters which batch of shares you order sold. To produce the smallest gain (or sometimes, the greatest loss), review your records to identify the shares that have the highest cost basis, and sell them. If you're in the 15 percent tax bracket this year but just got a big raise that will soon shoot you into the 28 percent tax bracket, sell your lowest cost basis first. Selling those shares will generate the highest gain (or lowest loss), thus maximizing your taxes when it's most advantageous to pay them.

7. PREPAY STATE TAXES.

Prepay your estimated state taxes before year's end. The fourth-quarter estimated tax payment is not due until January 15 of the following year, but if you mail it prior to December 31, you can deduct it on that year's tax return. Be careful to pay close attention to the

TRIFOLD, BLACK LEATHER WALLET: Throw away that embarassing day-glo velcro job; this is the only wallet that can accommodate your cash, checks, and receipts.

amount due and not to overpay state taxes just to get the deduction. The IRS can penalize you for overpaying and deducting an unreasonable amount.

8. CONSIDER ANNUITIES.

Fixed annuities are investment contracts sold by insurance companies. Like a certificate of deposit (CD), they guarantee payments with a fixed rate of return for life or for a specified period, but the money is invested more aggressively, usually resulting in a greater return. There are also things called variable annuities—a life-insurance annuity contract whose value fluctuates with that of an underlying securities portfolio. The portfolio manager may invest in a variety of securities, just as a mutual fund manager does.

Annuities confer the same tax benefit that CDs do: you're taxed only on the interest when the annuities' term is done. Unlike mutual funds and some CDs, with an annuity you pay no capital-gains tax on your investment or dividends, so your money compounds tax-deferred as long as it's in the annuity. If you put money in an annuity at age thirty for retirement at sixty-five, you won't be taxed until you take it out.

9. DODGE THE BITE WITH GROWTH FUNDS.

Yet another reason to invest in growth funds. The earnings and dividends from mutual funds are taxable, even if you reinvest them. Growth funds bet on companies with lots of upside potential but little current earning power—thus little or no dividends. Thus little or no taxes. If you do choose a fund with hefty dividends, don't buy it at the wrong time. Many funds pay dividends on December 14 or 15. If you invest on December 13, though you've only been in for a day, you're taxed as if you were in all year.

10. LET THE IRS HELP PAY A FUND'S LOAD.

We feel strongly that investors should avoid all mutual funds with "loads" —that is, mutual funds that charge a sales commission and thus shrink your investment from the start. Some people, however, just have to have that fancy new Peruvian Emerging Growth Fund that comes with a fee and has no no-load peers. If you must, here's a nifty little trick to help minimize the damage: First, make sure the fund family doesn't charge a load for switching between funds. Then buy a money-market fund within the same fund family. Now switch the investment into the fund you really want. You'll realize a loss,

DIRECT-DEPOSIT SAVINGS ACCOUNT: Let the bank sock a few hundred away each month for you.

which is the load charged for the original purchase, when you sell the money-market fund. Report this transaction on your tax return as a loss equal to the amount of the load, and deduct the sales fee from your taxes.

11. DEDUCT YOUR STUDENT-LOAN INTEREST.

Now you can deduct up to a thousand dollars of the interest you pay on your student loans. Next year, the amount will go up to $1,500, and it will increase another $500 per year until 2001. Making this all the more attractive is that it's an "above-the-line" deduction— accountspeak for the fact that you don't have to itemize to benefit from it. This is a no-brainer, although you can use it for only five years, and those making between $40,000 and $55,000 can't deduct as much; those pulling in more than $55,000 are out of luck on this one.

12. DON'T GET HITCHED YET.

Congress talks endlessly about fixing it but they never do. Consequently, the so-called marriage penalty punishes those who say "I do." It works like this: say both you and your girlfriend make $25,000 in taxable income selling Ginsu knives door-to-door. Both of you will be in a 15 percent tax bracket for 1998. If you got married, your $50,000 combined taxable income would put you in a 28 percent tax bracket. (Married couples also get phased out earlier for the aforementioned student loan deduction.) Why the different tax treatment? The reasons are far too complicated to explain here, but as of right now, when you're trying to beat the IRS, it pays to live in sin.

A TRUSTED ACCOUNTANT: Loophole knowledge a plus.

CREDIT-CARD HOLDERS BEWARE

Been sweet-talked, then betrayed? Romanced, then ruthlessly cast aside with nary a shrug? Sure you have. But while you might expect such nefarious behavior from some of the women passing through your life, you don't expect it from our beloved system of capitalism.

You should.

When you're talking capitalism, you're talking credit, and for most of us that means bank credit cards. There are more than 500 million of them in use in the United States, almost all of them promising access to everything plastic can buy. Unfortunately, today such innocuous moves as paying your bill a day late, getting a credit card but hardly using it, or even calling the toll-free customer service number too often can land you in trouble.

That's right, make a mistake with a credit-card issuer and faster than you can say, "charge it," they can throw you into the land of bad credit. Once there, you get to fight your way through a thicket of fees, penalties, and attacks on your credit rating.

Don't be the next victim. Here's a tip sheet on the kinds of scams credit-card issuers can pull—legally—to trip you up.

◆ They hit you with new, disguised charges. Note the great U.S. economy, the record-low inflation; yet in the last five years, banks have doubled fees for late payments on credit card debt. Where banks used to let cardholders go fifteen to twenty days before slapping on late fees, large issuers such as Citibank will now tag you if you're just one day late. Banks also don't always post payments the day they receive them, so you can get docked for being late even when you aren't.

◆ The over-limit fee is another way of nailing you. If you miscalculate your limit and charge one extra buck, your card issuer will dock you twenty dollars or more. In the old days, if you exceeded your limit, your card would be refused; now, retailers put it through, and you get socked later.

◆ They raise your interest rate overnight. Capital One periodically pulls your credit, and if it sees plenty of accrued debt, it can suddenly sock you with a 24.99-percent rate, more than double its normal 11.87-percent rate. Likewise, depending on your credit status, Associates National Bank can slam interest up to 32.6 percent if you fail to pay on time twice in a row. Ouch!

◆ They harass you. Capital One sent notes to thousands of cardholders complaining that they were calling the toll-free customer service number too much. According to McKinley, other banks are so cheap that they are trying to abolish customer service altogether. First Premier Bank of Sioux Falls (South Dakota) charges many of its high-risk customers a flat dollar-a-month customer service fee. The message: "Don't bother us, we're busy." Indeed they are—busy raising your interest rate.

◆ They penalize you for being fiscally responsible. General Electric is among companies that charge a twenty-five dollar fee to people who routinely *pay off their balance each month,* even though those customers still generate GE income when they charge purchases. Advanta has introduced a fee for those who don't use its card for six consecutive months.

◆ They implement two-cycle billing. This is a sneak attack to watch for: it's a deliberate attempt to squeeze you. In the so-called two-cycle billing method, interest is applied on every new purchase from day one when the cardholder already carries a balance—even if that balance is a dollar.

So what can you do?

If you are absolutely certain that you can and will pay off your balance every month, get a card with the longest grace period and lowest annual fees. Those who clean their credit slate on a monthly basis are unlikely to get nailed. On the other hand, if you expect to carry a balance, or suspect you might, go for a low-interest charge from a company that doesn't monkey around with its rates.

WHOM TO AVOID.

Watch out for any of the national issuers who massively solicit business—Capital One, First USA, Advanta, and Associates National Bank are four examples—especially if they have really low introductory rates. Bigger is not necessarily better in the credit-card business.

WHOM TO CHOOSE.

There are about seven thousand issuers and altogether maybe twenty-five thousand card variations, including all the standard, gold, and platinum cards. To know your options, call CardTrak at 800–344–7714 to order their five-dollar list of credit-card issuers. They're listed by their interest rates, whether they charge annual fees, and service area (some only offer cards to residents of certain states). You can also see which really have low interest rates, and which ones

LONG-TERM PLANNING: Social Security will be gone by the time you get old.

are pulling you in with introductory teaser rates. Caveat: some of the low-rate outfits require a flawless credit history and low debt and limit their credit lines. Perennial favorites—straight-up, decent outfits with good rates and no baloney—include Wachovia Bank (800–842–3262), Simmons First National Bank (800–636–5151), and Pullman Bank and Trust (800–785–5626).

JOIN A CREDIT UNION.

Credit unions offer credit cards with an average interest rate of 13 percent—about five points below the average for banks. And they're "plain vanilla," meaning their rates aren't just temporary "teasers." They often don't charge annual fees, and they rarely hit you with service charges or sudden increases. Downside: credit limits tend to be lower, and some don't offer twenty-four-hour phone access. Credit unions are affiliated with specific professions, military service, churches, and other organizations. To find out about one that might work for you, call the Credit Union National Association: 800–358–5710.

TRY YOUR NEIGHBORS.

Go to a local bank, which is far more likely to treat you well than the national "junk-food" card issuers. The local guys have to live in their communities. If you open an account there, that often helps you get a credit card.

ASK QUESTIONS.

Before you sign up for a card, call the issuer's toll-free number and ask for someone who can answer detailed questions about its policies. Then hit 'em with these:

◆ How long is the grace period?
◆ Is the interest rate fixed or at least tied to the prime interest rate? Or can you raise it at any time?
◆ Do you have a punitive rate that can go into effect if I pay late several times? How many late payments are allowed before the interest rate is increased?
◆ What is considered a late payment? How many days beyond the stated due date do you wait before slapping on a late payment fee?

◆ Does the bank review my credit report, using it to make adjustments to my interest rate, and how often? If I currently have high balances with other issuers, will you use that as a reason to raise rates?
◆ Are there any additional fees other than late fees? What are they?
◆ Will I be penalized or have my account canceled for inactivity?
◆ Do you approve purchases that cause me to go over my credit limit, then charge an over-limit fee?

Of course, there is one foolproof way to beat the credit card hustlers.

Pay cash.

FINANCING YOUR POSTGRADUATE DREAM

In college you had plans—big plans. You were going to start your own grade school, lead an archaeological dig, write the great American novel. Today, that may all seem worlds away.

Well, don't give up hope, Renaissance man. There are thousands of institutions across the country with the goodwill—and good cash—to fund your fantasy. Grants and fellowships are not just for graduate students; many foundations and federal programs earmark money for young professionals and struggling artists looking for a break.

So how do you tap into this largesse? Start by doing your homework. Too many grant-seekers pitch proposals blindly, without researching the programs offered. Most grants are also awarded under exact terms, so it's important to tailor your idea to their specifications.

The career planning center at your alma mater is a good place to start. Many schools also have Web sites providing information on grants and fellowships that anyone, regardless of alumni status, can access. If you were a member of a fraternity as an undergrad or were affiliated with any organization that has a national presence, find out whether the group provides funds for the postgraduate pursuits of former members.

BIG TIPS:
Nothing says class like a man not afraid to spread the wealth quietly.

COME 'N' GET IT:
TOP GRANTMAKING FOUNDATIONS

John D. and Catherine T. MacArthur Foundation

140 S. Dearborn Street, Suite 1100
Chicago, IL 60603–5285
(312) 726–8000
(www.macfdn.org)
Two major grant categories: human and community development and global security and sustainability. The foundation also gives the famous "genius grants"—no-strings money awarded to people with exceptional creative ability. Approximately 2,000 total grants awarded each year totaling $140 million.

John Simon Guggenheim Memorial Foundation
90 Park Avenue
New York, NY 10016
(212) 687–4470
(www.gf.org)
For arts and sciences and the humanities, except for performance artists. (They'll fund the choreographer, but not the dancer.) Out of 2,876 U.S. applicants last year, 164 were given an average of $28,700 each.

Soros Foundations Network Open Society Institute
888 Seventh Avenue
New York, NY 10106
(212) 757–2323
(www.soros.org)
Supports research projects that promote an "open society." Operates offices in 24 countries. Awarded $362 million in grants worldwide in 1996.

The Ford Foundation
320 East 43rd Street
New York, NY 10017
(212) 573–5000
(www.fordfound.org)
Supports activities that "strengthen democratic values, reduce poverty and injustice, promote international cooperation and advance human achievement." Approved $367 million in grants in 1996.

The Rockefeller Foundation
420 Fifth Avenue
New York, NY 10018–2702
(212) 869–8500
(www.rockfound.org)
Subject areas include arts and the humanities, equal opportunity and school reform, and international science-based development. Strong international interests, including a special African initiative. Projected figures for 1996: $107 million in grants and fellowships.

Russell Sage Foundation
112 East 64th Street
New York, NY 10021
(212) 750–6000
(www.epn.org/sage.html)
Grants an average of $50,000 to individuals researching the social sciences, including work, immigration, intergroup relations and literacy.

The Pollock-Krasner Foundation
725 Park Avenue
New York, NY 10021
(212) 517–5400
(www.pkf.org)
International grants to visual artists, from $1,000 to $30,000 each.

National Endowment for the Humanities
1100 Pennsylvania Avenue, NW
Room 402
Washington, DC 20506
(202) 606–8400
(www.neh.fed.us)
Uncle Sam will pay for you to explore history, literature, philosophy and other humanities through education, documentary films and more.

Since congressional offices serve as liaisons between private citizens and the federal government, they're another good place to learn about federal grants and fellowships. A helpful congressional aide should be able to tap into two congressional databases: Pre-Awarded Grants and Post-Awarded Grants, which include data from the *Catalog of Federal Domestic Assistance* and information on current government grant recipients from the *Federal Register*. Congressional offices can also help you find grants awarded on a regional basis. (More than 70 percent of foundations limit giving to their own area of the country.)

The money's out there. A bit of homework, some creative salesmanship and a well-honed pitch might just bring it into your pocket.

CASHING IN YOUR YOUTH

While you didn't know it at the time, you spent your prepubescent years making thousands of smart investments, thirty-five cents at a time. We're talking baseball cards here. What red-blooded American boy didn't go through a *Rain Man*–like collectibles phase? And unlike your dad, you were probably smart enough to keep your trove of Pete Roses and Robin Younts away from Mom—and the dumpster.

So what are those cards worth today? If visions of a week in Bali, a new set of Pings or even a down payment on a house are dancing in your head, you're probably not too far from the truth—provided your collection is heavy on cards from the sixties and seventies, as opposed to the eighties.

In 1981, you see, Donruss and Fleer entered the baseball card market, challenging the monopoly that Topps had held in the business for decades. Several other companies soon followed. The result was a glut on the market that pushed the value of post-1980 cards far lower than their predecessors—generally 300 percent less for your average card.

So, basically, your newer cards aren't worth squat. But if your collection was amassed during the bad-clothes decades, you could indeed have a little nest egg in your possession; a random thousand-card collection from the sixties and seventies, in pristine condition,

GOOD CREDIT:
It doesn't matter till one day when it does.

WILD CARDS

To help you separate the Mickey Mantles from the Mario Mendozas, we've listed the most valuable sets and cards from the decades of your youth. But remember: Prices denote the market range for cards in near-mint to mint condition, so don't start sleeping with them under your pillow.

1970

Complete Set: Topps ($1,000–$1,800)
Hot Card: Topps Nolan Ryan ($275–$375)
Chatter: If one player's cards from this era are worth more than all others, they're Ryan's.

1971

Complete Set: Topps ($1,400–$2,000)
Hot Card: Topps Willie Mays ($50–$90)
Chatter: Say hey! Even from the twilight of his career, a legend's card is worth major-league ducats today.

1972

Complete Set: Topps ($1,000–$1,700)
Hot Card: Topps Carlton Fisk/Cecil Cooper ($35–$60)
Chatter: Two rookies on one card make for a valuable piece of cardboard.

1973

Complete Set: Topps ($500–$750)
Hot Card: Topps Mike Schmidt ($200–$300)
Chatter: Lifetime Phillies' rookie card may be worth even more if it's centered and the border colors are true.

1974

Complete Set: Topps ($325–$600)
Hot Card: Topps Dave Winfield ($75–$125)
Chatter: Wait until Winfield makes The Hall to sell his rookie card; if he doesn't make it, another seagull dies.

1975

Complete Set: Topps ($500–$800)
Hot Card: Topps George Brett ($125–$200)
Chatter: If you can't get $150 for this rookie card, permission to go pine-tar wild on someone.

1976

Complete Set: Topps ($250–$400)
Hot Card: Topps George Brett ($30–$60)
Chatter: Note the deflation from the previous year; second-year cards can't touch rookie gold.

1977

Complete Set: Topps ($225–$375)
Hot Card: Topps Andre Dawson ($25–$50)
Chatter: If the Hawk hadn't toiled all those years in Montreal, his rookie card might be worth even more.

1978

Complete Set: Topps ($150–$275)
Hot Card: Topps Eddie Murray ($75–$125)
Chatter: The Quiet One is still tallying dingers; wait till The Hall calls before selling his rookie card.

1979

Complete Set: Topps ($100–$200)
Hot Card: Topps Ozzie Smith ($60–$100)
Chatter: The Wizard's glove magic, plus his recent stint hosting *This Week in Baseball,* keep his rookie card hot.

1980

Complete Set: Topps ($75–$150)
Hot Card: Topps Rickey Henderson ($25–$40)
Chatter: Despite a slew of records, Rickster the Trickster's surly rep reduces the value of his rookie card.

1981

Complete Set: Topps ($25–$50)
Hot Card: Topps Nolan Ryan ($3–$8)
Chatter: Note the deflation: Fleer and Donruss enter the market, driving prices down; no good rookie cards in '81.

1982

Complete Set: Topps ($75–$125)
Hot Card: Topps Cal Ripken ($45–$75)
Chatter: A blue-chip rookie card. If you must sell your collection, this might be a good one to hold on to.

1983

Complete Set: Topps ($75–$125)
Hot Card: Topps Tony Gwynn ($30–$50)
Chatter: Another batting title, five more dollars in your pocket. Gwynn's rookie card is only increasing in value.

1984

Complete Set: Donruss ($110–$220)
Hot Card: Donruss Don Mattingly ($20–$50)
Chatter: Since fewer were produced, Donruss's Donnie Baseball rookie card is worth six times its '84 Topps counterpart.

1985

Complete Set: Fleer ($60–$120)
Hot Card: Fleer Roger Clemens ($15–$25)
Chatter: Fourth Cy Young will up the value of this rookie card; note: Fleer and Donruss cards from this era worth twice as much as Topps.

1986

Complete Set: Donruss ($25–$50)
Hot Card: Donruss Jose Canseco ($6–$12)
Chatter: Canseco's continuing injuries and domestic troubles make the best card of '86 one to unload.

1987

Complete Set: Fleer ($25–$50)
Hot Card: Fleer Barry Bonds ($12–$20)
Chatter: Bonds's rookie card is worth twice the *entire* '87 Topps set; Topps flooded the market, rendering its cards uncollectible.

1988

Complete Set: Fleer ($8–$20)
Hot Card: Fleer Greg Maddux ($1–$2.50)
Chatter: You're not going to get that new stereo by selling '88 cards. Too many were made by too many different companies.

1989

Complete Set: Upper Deck ($75–$110)
Hot Card: Upper Deck Ken Griffey, Jr. ($60–$90)
Chatter: Upper Deck's rookie year and the only true Jr. rookie card— worth nine times the entire '89 Topps set.

1990

Complete Set: Leaf ($110–$200)
Hot Card: Topps (unnamed) Frank Thomas ($1,000–$1,500)
Chatter: A very rare error card; counterfeits exist, albeit doubtfully in your attic. A normal version fetches four bucks.
Source: Beckett Baseball Card Monthly

could net you anywhere between $2,500 and $5,000. By far the best way for you to determine their accurate value, though, is to grab your cards, grab a spare weekend and grab the latest issue of *Beckett Baseball Card Monthly,* the bible of baseball cards; a perusal of its price lists will allow you to quickly determine the worth, or lack thereof, of your wasted youth.

When doing so, bear in mind that most baseball cards are like dollar bills—common, functional, and worth, well, about a buck. There are quirks, however, that can up the value of seemingly worthless cards. For example, through 1973, Topps issued their cards throughout the season in numerical batches, meaning that far fewer of the late-numbered series were produced. So while your average 1972 card numbered 1–132 will fetch you only sixty cents, a typical one numbered in the 700s will pocket you twelve dollars—something to consider when you run across that number 752 Joe Morgan from 1972 (worth up to forty-five dollars).

The card's condition is a huge factor, no matter the year. One dog ear or tape mark sends the value plummeting. Also keep in mind that any player's first card—the mythic "rookie" card—will invariably be his most valuable.

Once you've carefully determined your collection's market value, you have a much harder decision to make: should you sell them, or keep them ensconced in a safety deposit box for posterity . . . or at least your son?

Ultimately, this choice relies more upon who you are than who's on your baseball cards. If you're a mushy sentimentalist who gets teary-eyed at the end of *Citizen Kane* because you, too, miss your boyhood sled, then you should probably hold onto your cards, no matter what. After all, we're talking about baseball *and* your childhood—a lethal combination of nostalgia.

But if you're a bottom-line kind of guy looking for net annual returns, there's absolutely no question: unload 'em. Card collecting is not an investment. It's a hobby. It's for somebody who is a baseball fan or a fan of collecting. For investing, you're better off selling, taking the money, and buying mutual funds.

Indeed, even the highest-value cards—mint-condition Hall of Famers or can't-miss inductees—only increase in value annually by 10 to 12 percent, a rate matched by many stock mutual funds. If you toss in the loss you'll take on the cards of whining, prima-donna stars like Rickey Henderson, you've got a very unreliable investment. (Henderson's rookie card, once priced at more than two hundred dollars, is now worth only forty.) Not to mention that returns on all cards have been notably lower in the past few years, given the public's disgust with strikes, greed, and the game's general loss of innocence.

Still, if you're going to sell your oldest investment, you'd better make sure you get a good deal on it. And to do that, all collectors advise the same general strategy: Take the book value of your collection, as determined by *Beckett,* set a price you're willing to meet (generally 50 percent of book is considered a fair deal), visit several local baseball-card shows (the dates and locations of which can be found in the weekly *Sports Collectors Digest*), shop your cards from table to table until you get the best offer, and then sell the whole lot of them.

Then turn around, leave. and don't look back. You just cashed in your youth.

CHAPTER 7

AT HOME

Q: WHAT'S THE DEAL WITH RENTER'S INSURANCE?

RENTER'S INSURANCE: One little payment erases that prowler's power.

Just because you rent your house or apartment doesn't mean you're free from all the hassles of ownership. Not when people sue—and win—when they spill a cup of coffee on their own lap. Renter's insurance is a decent idea to protect your belongings, but it's the liability coverage that makes it a clincher for most people.

Liability insurance can be a lifesaver if you get sued by an injured guest who trips on your loose rug or slips on your icy front porch. If you have pets, any damage they cause to others (such as dog bites) is also covered. And if you live in a condo and start a grease fire that guts a few floors, you can bet the owner will expect you to pay for repairs not only to your unit, but also to the entire building.

Some renters mistakenly assume that the landlord carries insurance for such mishaps. But if you are at fault for putting someone in the hospital or causing serious structural damage, your future wages can be garnished, and your assets can be wiped away.

Here are some smart buying tips to help you make the most of renter's insurance:

1. DOCUMENT IT.

There's no sense insuring your stuff only to get shortchanged should disaster strike. Make an inventory of your belongings, and keep it in a secure place away from home, such as a bank safe-deposit box. Update your list annually to include any new purchases, and attach a file with sales receipts, appraisals, or other documentation proving what you paid. This should result in a fast, fair, hassle-free claim settlement.

2. KNOW YOUR REPLACEMENT COST.

While most renter's policies will reimburse you for the full current value of lost or stolen items, some inferior policies pay only the depreciated value. For example, if you bought your bed for five hundred dollars four years ago, it might be worth only two hundred dollars. But if a fire gutted your apartment, it would cost seven hundred dollars to replace it with one of comparable quality. A "replacement cost" policy would pay out seven hundred dollars; an "actual-cost value" policy would kick out just two hundred. Make sure your contract guarantees your replacement cost. Also make sure you have enough coverage to cover your inventory.

3. KNOW YOUR LIMITATIONS.

Avoid renter's policies that cover only "named perils" such as fire, theft, and vandalism. This leaves you vulnerable to any loss caused by something not named on your policy. The best policies are called "all-risk" because they cover every imaginable peril except for specific exclusions listed on the policy—notably earthquakes and floods, which require separate policies. Another danger sign is if your policy covers only theft but not "mysterious disappearance." Also be wary of policies that impose limits as low as a thousand dollars for valuables like jewelry and silverware. You may need to buy a rider or endorsement that provides additional coverage for such valuable items.

If you run a business out of your home, your computers and other items that are used to operate your business are probably excluded.

4. ASK THE RIGHT QUESTIONS.

Among them:

◆ Are claims handled by a local office? Or do you deal with a faraway agent who isn't familiar with this neighborhood?

◆ What is the typical turnaround time for adjusting a claim and issuing payment? (Some insurance companies set service standards and boast of their efficient, responsive work.)

Realtor.com
www.realtor.com
One-stop real estate shop offering access to a national database of realtors and homes for sale. Find homes or condos for sale in your specific price range. Use the mover's toolkit to compare salary, crime, and insurance rates between your current city and your prospective city.

Rent Net
www.rentnet.com
Comprehensive apartment rental guide. Search for an apartment anywhere in the country by price range and preferred number of bedrooms. Also has listings for Australia, France, Hong Kong, Italy, Portugal, Spain, Sweden, and the United Kingdom.

LivingHome
www.livinghome.com
Home-improvement answers, whether you're interested in gardening, remodeling, or decorating.

HomePath
www.homepath.com
For help buying or refinancing a home.

• Does the policy include "loss of use" coverage that pays for you to temporarily live somewhere else if your home is destroyed?

• Does the insurance company have a twenty-four-hour phone line to handle emergency claims?

5. CHECK FOR DISCOUNTS.

Most standard renter's policies cost between $150 and $500 a year, depending on the amount of coverage you want and the deductible you choose. You can save money by opting for low limits (say, $20,000 or $30,000) and high deductibles ($500 or $1000). Shop around and compare quotes, because premiums can vary widely from company to company (unless you live in a high-risk state such as California, Florida, or Hawaii, where your choices are limited). Also ask your agent if you can get a "dual-policy" discount if you use the same company to insure your car and your personal property. Other discounts may be offered if your rental has a security system, smoke alarms, a fire extinguisher, or other features. As a rule, never agree to a final amount until you ask your agent, "Are there any other discounts that I qualify for that will lower my premium?"

A REAL BED:
Stop kidding yourself—a futon is *not* comfortable.

A PULL-OUT COUCH:
When guests say the floor is fine, they're lying.

DECORATING YOUR DIGS

Fact: Guys generally don't know squat about how to decorate a place.

Also fact: You don't particularly pretend to care.

Big mistake, considering that a nice space has as much to do as a nice face with whether she'll spend the night. It's a selling point—as important as the way you look, smell, or tell a joke. So suck it up, buddy. Throw away the beer-company posters, return the supermarket milk crates, and get to work.

STEP ONE: THE SPACE PLAN

Think about how furniture is arranged in relation to the structure of each room. Take note of architectural elements—a fireplace, windows, built-in bookshelves, and so on. Then take inventory of what stuff you have, room by room. At this point, make a list of any additional pieces you want to buy.

Such planning is a pain in the ass, but it's crucial. You need to think about the purpose of each room—this functionality question will in turn drive the layout and the contents. For example, if your bedroom is also your home office, a big bed that takes up 85 percent of the room isn't a good idea. A better (if not really cool) plan is placing a single (yeah, as in twin-size) bed on one wall, so you'll have room for a desk or large table. If you're dealing with a small space, such as a one-room studio or aptly named "efficiency," you need to select pieces that can serve a dual purpose.

Indeed, function takes many forms. In the living room, dining room, or any other common area, the arrangement of furniture should be conducive to conversation. (The bedroom is the exception, since you're presumably skipping the small talk there.)

Once you've established function (i.e., "This will be the living room, where I hang out with friends"), you've shopped for the stuff and you're ready to set up, you have to decide how it all fits best. Lesson one: don't shove everything up against the walls. Guess what? Even a small space seems bigger when furniture floats. Conversations flow, things come together. Factor in walkways as well. A good rule of thumb is to leave three feet wherever possible, as in between the couch and the wall.

Aim for a focal point. Remember the architectural elements you looked for? Pick your favorite and work around it. Arrange your furniture so that if people are sitting, they can enjoy looking out the windows at the pretty view or gaze into the fire you've been nice enough to kindle.

STEP TWO: COLOR

Don't get caught up thinking of color as a silly ol' decorating thing. It can actually help enlarge a room and make up for a lack of interesting furniture. When you're talking color, you're talking walls, fabric, and floors.

Here's the professionals' trick: if you use lighter and darker shades of the same color throughout, your place will look bigger. The easiest way to choose paint, for example, is to pick a color you like and select lighter and darker shades of the same hue.

A good, safe, neutral color like gray is the best way to go, and the best trick is to use the same trim color throughout. She suggests

BLINDS:
Or curtains, or shades. Keep the voyeurs at bay.

PICTURES ON THE WALL:
Follow us—posters are for dorm rooms, pictures are for apartments.

GOOD LIGHTING:
You'll be surprised what a difference it makes.

PAINT:
One coat makes all the difference.

white: it's clean, goes with everything, and enhances the appearance of moldings in older apartments.

But stay away from white walls unless you have special pieces of art or furniture. White becomes what's called "the invisible background," and what's in front of it suddenly becomes more important, which means it's going to draw a big bull's-eye around your mom's hand-me-down sofa, if that's what you're working with. If you don't have interesting pieces, the color emerges as the focus. A standard-issue halogen lamp is not interesting; a cool table lamp you picked up at an estate sale is.

Floor coverings can help enhance the look of your apartment, as well as provide warmth and drown out noise. If you'd like to make an investment (and have some time to talk with experienced dealers), Oriental rugs are a popular option. The rug can be the most expensive piece of furniture you buy, so make sure you love it and are likely to love it for a long time. Even if you're not ready to spend big bucks, however, don't opt for bare floors. Stores like Pier 1 Imports and Ikea carry all kinds of inexpensive sisal rugs and straw mats; Urban Outfitters also offers a nice throw rug for about sixty dollars.

STEP THREE: THE SMALL STUFF

This is the category that most guys ignore even more than color. It includes bedding, window treatments, lamps, books, candlesticks, and picture frames. It's the stuff that really makes a place feel like home.

A good rule of thumb: pick things that reflect your interests. If you smoke cigars, a nice humidor is something of interest to have on the coffee table. The most inexpensive way to achieve a "lived-in" look is to frame photographs and display them on shelves or tables.

This is also a good way to get love interests to spend more time at your place. Trust us. Women want to know more than what you tell them. By being able to wander through your place and look at your stuff, they get a better understanding of who you are. Those neat framed photos of you and your buddies on your last ski outing tell us just as much about you as your blathering at the local pub.

Then there's lighting. Incandescent or halogen lighting is always preferable to fluorescent: it creates a warmer ambience. Dimmers are great, because you can adjust levels of lighting according to moods. If you don't have overhead lighting, make sure you have an end table or two for lamps.

Nobody expects (or wants) you to become Martha Stewart—

CLEAN UP:
Trust us: getting rid of those dust bunnies *will* make you feel better.

VACUUM CLEANER:
Particularly for the space between your couch and coffee table.

that's not the point. But there's no reason your place should look like a college dorm; it isn't one. Stick to the basics, invest in one or two nice things, and put it together so it makes basic sense. In interior decorating, a little knowledge is a good thing.

SCAVENGING FOR FURNITURE

You've heard about life's two inevitable scourges—death and taxes. Now it's time to cash in. Every weekend, in every corner of the country, antique furniture, generations-old jewelry, and household relics of every kind are being sold at bargain prices. The deals are being struck at estate sales.

An estate sale is a macabre version of a yard sale, where the entire contents of a recently dead person's house go on the market. Every last item must be sold for cash and hauled away so relatives, lawyers, and creditors can settle the estate. By the end of the weekend, a lifetime's worth of possessions will be sold at bargain prices.

While estimating the savings available at such sales is an inexact and anecdotal science, they're potential gold mines for careful and patient shoppers. The goods are typically undamaged, functional, and often in wonderful condition. Merchandise can run the gamut from grandfather clocks to geriatric toilets. Many items are sold for half of what they would cost new in stores. (In fact, antique dealers use the sales to stock their shops, marking the prices up another 50 percent to make their profit.)

Although the choicest items often fly out the door in the first frantic hour of a sale, sometimes the best strategy is to come back on Sunday afternoon for the final hours. By that time, liquidators are willing to slash prices just to move leftovers.

Furnishing your new pad? Looking to upgrade? Consider the following estate-sale strategies, and you might just come away with a steal.

◆ Sales are listed in the classifieds section of your local newspaper, typically on Fridays. They can be listed as "estate sales," "house sales,"

A SET OF WINE GLASSES:
It's time to trade in your beer mugs.

SLEEPLESS IN SEATTLE:
In case she just stops by.

COMMANDO:
For when she leaves.

or sometimes "moving sales," but scan through the yard and garage sale listings in case they're listed there. The *Chicago Tribune* distinguishes such sales from run-of-the-mill yard sales by listing them as "Conducted House Sales." Smaller suburban papers will often have display ads with a detailed listing of contents.

◆ The neighborhood and the company running the sale often offer clues as to what you'll find. Many families choose liquidators by word-of-mouth, so people in the same social and economic circles often choose the same company. Liquidators also develop an expertise in certain items.

◆ Don't buy antique items as an investment unless you know what you're doing. Many items at estate sales appear old and valuable, but it's often hard to make a snap judgment on their worth.

◆ Browse a few sales before making any major purchases. Checking out what the market prices are can save you from overpaying. Find out in advance what type of payment the liquidator will accept. Most will take a check or credit card, but some sales are cash only.

◆ Getting your purchases home is your problem. Liquidators rarely deliver.

◆ Purchases are final and as is. There are no warranties and no returns. Buyer beware.

◆ Be prepared to wait in line. Most sales have a long line when they open, so you'll either have to get in line early and wait for an opening or arrive later and wait with other customers. Lines will dissipate over the course of the day, but the choice items could be gone.

◆ Get a number to reserve your place in line as soon as you arrive. The liquidators will let in a few people at a time and will call out your number when it's your turn.

◆ Check opening times carefully if you're going to hit several sales in the same area. You can often pick up numbers reserving your place in line at several sales and, if you hurry through each house, can get from one to another before your number is called.

SOMETHING GROWING IN YOUR HOUSE (BESIDES THAT STUFF IN THE SHOWER): Plants add oxygen to the environment, are relaxing to look at and low-maintenance, and best of all, chicks will think you're sensitive. Remember to replace them when they turn brown.

◆ Don't expect to find everything you want all at once. Part of the tradeoff for reduced prices is having to invest your time attending several sales before you find just the right piece. On the other hand, you may end up buying items you never even thought of before.

STANDING UP TO YOUR LANDLORD

If you're an apartment dweller, we'll bet your landlord is a bit like your appendix—you never think much about him until something goes wrong.

Most landlords are generally OK types, willing to fix problems even if they do it with the kind of consternation more commonly associated with undergoing major surgery. But what happens when you wake up to an apartment overrun by roaches and missing something like, let's say, hot water, and the Big Guy Downstairs (or, more likely, Anywhere but This Building) simply doesn't care? Fear not—despite the terminology in your lease that promises everything but burning at the stake if you cause trouble, you do have options.

1. WRITE A LETTER THREATENING FORMAL ACTION.

The slightest whiff of the words "court" or "lawyer" will usually cause the negligent shyster in question to stand at attention and fix your damn garbage disposal or unclog your toilet. Letter writing is the easiest, most basic step, and it's rare that you'll have to go further. Simply and politely state the nature of the problem, request that adequate repairs be made as promptly as possible, and send it to your landlord via *certified* mail (preventing the old "I never got it" excuse). If your landlord fails to respond within ten days, proceed directly to step two.

2. REQUEST AN INSPECTION.

Contact your local health department or city inspection service. Have the inspector carefully detail all violations; if he certifies any as dangerous or impairing your well-being, you can take additional

A FAN:
The kind that circulates air, not the fair-weather Dallas Cowboys type.

A BLENDER:
Come off like a smoothie.

AN IRON:
No matter what the department stores want you to believe, wrinkle-free clothing is not fashion-forward.

A SEWING KIT:
So you don't have to throw it away when you lose a button.

action. If nothing else, having your place inspected gives you some official heft and lets your landlord know you mean business. Often, you can seek the help of the local courts and file a preliminary petition to make your landlord adhere to the state sanitary code.

3. REPAIR AND DEDUCT.

This is a nifty little dodge to use if your landlord has failed to respond to written requests. Often, you can have the repairs done yourself (or literally do it yourself if you're the handy type) and then deduct the cost from your rent. Always take before-and-after photographs to bolster your case. Be forewarned, though: some municipalities are more tenant-friendly than others; it always helps to know whether the law is on your side, so do some advance research to make sure you won't get stuck with a hefty renovation bill.

4. TAKE THE BASTARD TO COURT.

This is where the writ hits the fan. Often, this is a reactive step on your part, since landlords sometimes invoke the law in an effort to make you pay any rent you're withholding. Generally, you can sue for documented losses (rent and repair costs) if your landlord and his inaction have interfered with the "quiet enjoyment"—regardless if "quiet enjoyment" means ten friends and a game of Nude Crisco Twister—of your pad. If a day in front of a judge still doesn't mollify you, you can wearily proceed to the final step.

5. PLEAD "CONSTRUCTIVE EVICTION."

This is *not* a terribly pleasant option, but for the most part it's a fail-safe escape hatch if things just get intolerable. If you can readily assert that conditions in your apartment have deteriorated to the point where it's uninhabitable and that your landlord has been seriously negligent, you can plead "constructive eviction" and move out, *sans* obligation on the remaining rent.

Thankfully, most landlords, even ones for whom gross negligence is a congenital defect, will be sufficiently moved by a firm, vaguely threatening letter or phone call and will act promptly. Which will, of course, leave you free to deal with other, more pressing problems—like trying to convince that same landlord that the burn mark on the living room carpet and the crack in the bedroom wall were there *before* you signed the lease.

SHOE TREES:
Don't let your Bruno Magli's get kicked around the bottom of the closet.

MAKING THE MOST OF YOUR MORTGAGE

The only thing that can match being your own boss is being your own landlord. There's a reason owning a house or condo has always been considered the American Dream. The space is yours, and the monthly check you write suddenly becomes an investment rather than a loss. Plus, the government subsidizes your purchase through tax deductions.

Making the dream a reality, alas, is not quite as simple as strolling into the neighborhood savings and loan, signing a piece of paper, and having George Bailey hand you a tidy check for a hundred grand. But with a little education, some patience, and, well, some money, getting your first mortgage can prove as painless as an ATM withdrawal.

1. KNOW WHAT YOU CAN AFFORD.

Don't open the real-estate section of the Sunday paper until you know your price limit. Add up, to the penny, what you can reasonably spend on housing each month. A rule of thumb: 28 percent of your monthly income should go to housing. Most banks, when offering a loan, will allow you to spend up to 33 percent of W-2 wages. Don't. It's no use owning a house if you can't afford to furnish it, host people in it, or park a car in its garage.

Also know your own financial history: your credit report is going to be examined with a fine-tooth comb; make sure you're all paid up on your debts. It's OK to still have student loans—as long as you haven't defaulted on them.

2. LET THE BANKS EDUCATE YOU—FOR FREE.

Many banks offer free seminars for first-time home buyers. Becoming familiar with the head-spinning array of mortgage and real-estate terms reduces any chance you'll get taken in what's likely to be the biggest purchase of your life. At many of these programs, you can even get preapproved: fill out a nonbinding loan application, and the bank will issue a letter of financial commitment, giving you the ability to make a quick decision at crunch time. That makes you a more attractive buyer.

DIGITAL KITCHEN TIMER: Great for keeping quick naps from going the distance, keeps you from forgetting to pick up your girlfriend at the airport, when your laundry is done, when your dinner is about to combust in the oven.

3. LET A MORTGAGE BROKER DO YOUR WORK FOR YOU.

You can call thirty banks to shop for the best mortgage, or you can consult a broker who knows what dozens of lenders have to offer and works for none in particular. A broker is aware of special deals, including some that aren't publicized, such as cut-rate mortgages for first-time buyers. And a broker can help you with tricks your bank won't, including how to deduct your closing costs on your taxes. This matchmaking service is personal, gives you an array of options, and is almost always free—the bank where you eventually get your mortgage often covers the broker's fee.

4. SKIP THE INSURANCE.

If you put 20 percent down on your new home, you can skip mandatory-mortgage insurance, which can add fifty to sixty dollars a month to payments on a hundred-thousand-dollar loan. Insurance payments are not tax-deductible, either: they're money down the drain. Hoard as much cash as you can for the down payment— besides saving the pointless insurance costs, you'll have less interest to shell out on your loan. Try not to cash in your 401(k), however, because the tax man will sock you with a huge penalty for early withdrawal.

5. ALWAYS GO FOR THE ADJUSTABLE-RATE LOAN.

You're young and moving up in the world—40 percent of first-time buyers sell their first homes within five years. Don't lock into a thirty-year rate; you can get an adjustable-rate mortgage, which is a good bit lower than comparable fixed offerings for the first five to seven years and then switches to fluctuating, presumably higher rates. Which is fine by you: by then, most likely, you'll have already moved.

Getting your first mortgage will probably be the biggest investment of your life to date, and it can be a nerve-racking one. But playing a heads-up game when landing a mortgage could leave you with more house than you bargained for.

FULL-LENGTH MIRROR:
Never tuck in a shirt without one.

BOOK IN THE BATHROOM:
It may double your productivity.

CASHING IN ON CAPITAL-GAINS TAX

Psst . . . Hey buddy . . . Want a simple, *legal* way to earn up to five hundred thousand dollars every two years without paying a penny of taxes?

No kidding, and it's no scam; it's all there in plain (well, we'll *make* it plain for you) English—in the 1997 changes to the U.S. Tax Code. It's Tax Code 121 to be exact, and it's courtesy of our friends in Congress, who, most likely, didn't realize exactly what a goody they were giving us.

The deal is this: Before last year, you had to be fifty-five or older to get a tax exemption on profits from selling your house; now the age limit has been revoked, so anyone can get it. It also used to be that you could only use this break once; now you can bask in it every two years for the rest of your life. What's more, the old cap of $125,000 tax-free gain per married couple has been upped to $500,000 (and a cool $250,000 if you're single).

Enter you, the cat waiting to pounce on such a tasty opportunity. Here's what you do: buy a home, nothing too modern, and fix it up while you live in it for at least two years. Refurbishing can be painstaking, but it's almost guaranteed to be profitable.

Start with landscaping, which immediately ups that cuddly intangible known as curb appeal. Manicure the overgrown shrubs. Pour a bit of mulch around the perimeter. Touch up the outside paint. You're already increasing your returns.

Then update the kitchen, install a family room, and create a master bedroom suite—renovations that will net you a 25 percent profit come selling time. And consider yourself lucky if your new home has but one bathroom; adding a second, which will run you between five thousand and twenty thousand dollars, is more guaranteed profit.

Now the fun part: sell that puppy for up to $500,000 more than what you paid and put into renovations ($250,000 if you're single) and *pay no taxes on the profit*. Repeat the whole process until you don't like making easy, tax-free money anymore.

The break went into effect in May 1997, so it will be a couple of years before anyone gets the opportunity to cash in on it twice, but according to Thompson and other tax experts, there is no catch, and no reason you can't do this for a living.

PHOTO ALBUM:
For that box of pictures you break out once in a while.

MAGNETIC PICTURE FRAME:
For the fridge.

CHAPTER 8

COMPUTING

Q: HOW DO I GET FREE E-MAIL?

Several companies offer free E-mail accounts in exchange for a little marketing information and a daily flood of spam in your in-box. Considering that most Internet Service Providers (ISPs) charge about twenty dollars monthly for E-mail accounts, it's not a bad trade.

Hotmail (www.hotmail.com) works through your Internet browser, so you have to have Web access (i.e., an ISP) prior to signing up for an account. It's ideal for employees who are hooked to the Web but don't want their boss snooping around their in-box; it's also convenient for people sharing one E-mail account within a household who are tired of sifting through other people's messages. Signing up is easy. Just log onto Hotmail's Web site, and follow the instructions. Bonus: You can check your E-mail from any computer, anywhere, so long as there's a browser and a connection.

If you aren't already on the Web and don't have any interest in surfing, Juno offers free E-mail accounts, software, and dial-up access for Windows users. If you have a friend with Internet access, you can download it off of Juno's Web site (www.juno.com). Otherwise, call 800–378-JUNO for a copy (shipping and handling will cost you a one-time fee of $8.82).

CONTROL+S/ APPLE+S: Insurance against those maudlin, unexplained computer crashes.

Once you have an E-mail address, iName will help you customize it. No more: johndoe@company.com or jimdoe@university.edu. The iName Web site (www.iname.com) gives you access to a whole new Web identity. Possibilities range from earthling.net to cyberdude.com. The name before the @ is yours to create. The company will forward all mail from your more creative address to your real one, allowing you to send E-mail without identifying yourself with a company, school, or ISP.

Interested in creating a home page? Whether you're out to promote a cause, display your artwork, or just post pictures for far-flung friends and family to view, GeoCities is a great (and free) place to get started. They offer 3Mb of free space as long as you allow them to display ads on your page. Plus, there are a few restrictions: you're not allowed to sell anything, present pornography, or use hate speech. If you can handle that, GeoCities will provide help with building your Web page and even link you to volunteer tutors for assistance. To sign up, go to (www.geocities.com), and follow the instructions.

GETTING WIRED ON A SHOESTRING BUDGET

Two years ago, technology magazines were raving over 486 computers and 14.4 modems. Today they claim that stuff is as relevant as a fountain pen. Don't believe the hype. You'll survive the information revolution even if you're not maxed out on baud and RAM. Consider these tips for a bare-boned but solid system.

1. BUY A USED COMPUTER.

A random (er, highly selective) Web search dug up some great bargains—386SX40 Mini-Tower with a 200MB hard drive, 4MB RAM, 1 MB video card, keyboard and serial mouse for $375. Add a fourteen-inch Color VGA Monitor for another $125. Another site proffered a Compaq Prolinea laptop with 20MB RAM and 200MB hard drive for $700. Type in the stats on what you're looking for and the search engines yield thousands of spots like Alpine (www.alpinecom.com)

The Computer Network
www.cnet.com
A techno-rich site that's fun, friendly—and for the computer laymen among us. You don't need to know Java, C++, or any other computer language to understand C/NET. With its comparative reviews and "digital life" stories, C/NET helps you make sense of cyberspace.

ZD Net
www.zdnet.com
An authoritative source for computer news, with useful features (such as 201 hot tips for home computing) from various Ziff-Davis publications (*Computer Life, PC Computing*), along with a software library and a trade-show calendar. For power users, wannabes, and even the computer-phobic.

whatis.com
An easy way to learn the latest technobuzzwords, with definitions of everything from ActiveX to WAIS. Browse the site's

that offer used options. The classifieds section of your local paper should also do the trick.

A word of caution, however. Just as though you were shopping for a used car, you should know what you're buying. Take along a techie friend when you go to look at the merchandise. If ordering by phone or through the mail, make sure you get some sort of warranty so you can get it checked out.

2. FIND SOME FREEWARE.

There are thousands of programs that will perform any task you will ever need and won't cost you a dime. Amateur code crunchers like to throw out their wares for testing, while software companies offer scaled-down versions of popular software to try to seduce you back for the "real thing." Some of the best programs are the E-mail software Eudora Light (www.eudora.com), WinZip compression software, and LView graphic viewer software. Whole lists of programs including those above can be found at the Freeware Publishing Site (194.197.188.25/cgi-bin/search.pl) and Jumbo! (www.jumbo.com). Also take a look at the freeware that might already be included with an older operating system. Telnet is a perfectly good way to get connected to the Internet, while Windows 3.1 Notepad is more than adequate for basic word processing functions.

One caveat—the slower the modem, the longer the download will take. Downloading can be a lot like watching a trickle fill the sink. So go to a cybercafe or library with Net access, and download the software onto a floppy and bring it home.

3. SHOP SELECTIVELY.

Just because there are 24X speed CD-ROM drives on the market doesn't mean you need to revamp your system. Of course, the manufacturers won't tell you that. They would rather have you buy into a vicious cycle: in order to run the new drive you need the latest thirty-two-bit software, which means a newer operating system, which means a whole new computer.

4. RELAX.

Let the technology get a little ahead of you so when it does become necessary to upgrade, you won't be left with a lot of expensive, underused equipment.

5. SEARCH, SAVE, AND SALVAGE YOUR OLD TOOLS.

Once you do start to collect an inventory of computer dinosaurs, don't chuck them. You never know when you might need them—say, for spare parts or to maintain a backup.

FIVE TIPS FOR TELECOMMUTERS

God bless the new economy. Business is booming. And suddenly, in the information age, you're a wanted man. Best part is, since more and more gainful contributors to the GNP are punching in from home, your employer might not even want to see you. Some 50 million Americans now work at least part of the time from their abodes, and that number is growing fast. So when your time comes to get up and go nowhere, you'll want to be prepared.

1. GET UP. GET OUT OF BED. DRAG A COMB ACROSS YOUR HEAD.

While one of the beauties of working at home means that you're the only one at the bar who doesn't panic because it's 2:00 A.M. and you've got a breakfast meeting with the boss, don't abuse the situation. Get up at a reasonable hour, have some coffee as you're logging on, and please, take a shower—you never know who might pop in.

Do things to quell the inevitable stir-crazy factor. Get to know your neighborhood merchants; befriend at least one person at Kinko's. And get a beeper so you won't feel chained to your desk and can indeed run all those errands your workplace freedom is supposed to allow.

2. SET UP A PSYCHOLOGICAL WORK SPACE.

Draw clear boundaries: this is my office, this is my home, and never the two shall meet. No reason to accidentally eye that report you're working on when you've called it quits for the day and are enjoying a cold beverage in the company of Kramer. It's simply bad karma. Conversely, repeat after me: I am not going to log on to ESPN.SportsZone.com between the hours of nine and five. If you

Excite
www.excite.com
The most intuitive and option-packed of the search sites, with lots of extras: live chat, free E-mail, news, and weather info.

www.search.com
All sorts of search sites on every topic imaginable, gathered within an elegant, easy-to-use interface. Use it when you're searching for something specialized (a used car, say, or a new job).

can successfully set your work and play boundaries—and stick to them—you'll feel more liberated. There's nothing worse than turning your home into the office you can never escape.

3. SET UP A PHYSICAL WORK SPACE.

Don't drive yourself crazy trying to do your job without the proper tools. Take the time to create an office environment that mirrors what those poor commuting saps have. Install an extra phone line to avoid messages like, "I'm either out of the office, on the other line, or on the Net; if you want to send a fax, call back and press star 83." Such messages spell Big Loser to potential clients. Better still, push the boss to pony up for an ISDN line. These babies can carry four channels, so you can talk on the phone, surf the Net, and receive a fax—just like you would be doing if you went into the office.

Ditto for mirroring an ergonomic environment. Don't work from bed, the kitchen table, in the bathtub or hanging from the ceiling fan, or you'll spend all your time in a doctor's office.

4. E-MAIL IS EVERYTHING.

Woody Allen once said, "Eighty percent of success is showing up." His words couldn't be more relevant for you, the virtual commuter. Even if you're spending most of your day working on a freelance project, flirting on-line, and catching up on all those *Rhoda* reruns, stay in constant touch with your boss and coworkers via E-mail, creating the illusion that you are immersed in work even when you're not. And a few times a week, zap them a quick note around 10:00 P.M. (just before you hit the bars). It'll remind them you're *always* at the office.

5. RETHINK, REFOCUS.

Recalculate the concept of an eight-hour day and focus on results. Figure that most of the world spends one to two hours a day commuting, an hour on smoking breaks and/or coffee breaks, about an hour at lunch, a cumulative hour engaged in senseless conversation with coworkers, and thirty minutes as the "computer expert." Use your time at home wisely. Be more productive than your coworkers. Pick up side gigs that expand your horizons. Learn to play the guitar. Just don't end up on the couch, scratching yourself and eating Cheetos—you've got all night and all weekend to do that.

Set goals for yourself, visit the office every few weeks, make and meet deadlines, and don't get so tied down you're loath to take a meeting out of the house when it's raining. Finally, write guidelines for yourself and stick to them—i.e., "I will finish that report by 5:00 P.M."; "I will not sleep with the retiree next door." You'll be glad you stuck to the program.

JUNK E-MAIL EVASION

Like the junk snail mail that has become an inevitable fact of life, spam too appears here to stay. Maybe you can't totally eliminate spam, but here are some ways to minimize junk E-mail hell.

◆ Be aware of and activate any filters your Internet service providers may have in place. In AOL, for example, go to Mail Controls and Preferred Mail to make sure the available filters are turned on.

◆ Get a filtering program of your own. Windows users can download Spam Hater at (www.download.com.) You can also use Eudora at (www.cs.nwu.edu/~beim/eudora/index/html).

◆ Be aware where spammers get your screen name. Basically, if your screen name can be seen, it can be collected. Create a "public" screen name to use in chat rooms, newsgroups, and other public spaces, and a "private" screen name for E-mail.

◆ Be wary of giving out information on Web pages where you might be asked to register your screen name or other information.

◆ If you are on AOL, delete your profile.

◆ Visit the site for the Internet E-mail Marketing Council (www.iemmc.org), and put your name on the "global remove" list.

◆ Write your congresspeople and senators (don't E-mail them!) and let them know you support the Netizen Protection Act of 1997 (H.R. 1748).

AN INTERNET HOME PAGE:
Duh.

The following Web sites are excellent starting points for information on spam—and what you can do to stop it.

◆ The Coalition Against Unsolicited Commercial E-mail (www.cauce.org)

◆ The Junk E-mail Page (www.junkE-mail.org)

◆ Stop Spam FAQ (www.mall-net.com/spamfaq.html)

◆ Doug's SPAM Filter Page (www.erols.com/dtoombs/spam.htm)

ERGONOMIC SPLIT KEYBOARD:
It hurts to think—it shouldn't hurt to type.

BUILD YOUR OWN WEB SITE

Creating Web sites isn't rocket science. In fact, it's not even sanitary maintenance engineering. The truth is, anyone who can turn on a computer can build a Web site. You don't need a degree in computer science, years of hacking experience, or even a steady diet of Cheetos and Jolt. All you need is a computer, a Net account, and a brain. And the brain's the most important part of the mix.

While the Web may seem vast and unwieldy, its history is relatively straightforward. In the late eighties, the Web was created by a nice man in Switzerland named Timothy Berners-Lee as a way for academics and others to share information. Soon, the masses realized the powers of this new medium's ability to put text, hypertext, and graphics into an easily navigable on-line interface. By the early nineties, with the development of Mosaic, the first graphical "browser" (which would in turn spawn Netscape and Internet Explorer), Web sites started popping up all over the place. Mr. Berners-Lee is now working his magic at MIT's renowned Lab for Computer Science while the rest of us are left to deal with the amazing aftermath.

According to the research firm Cyber Dialogue, there are 41.5 million users on the Internet, with projections of some 50.5 million users by the end of 1998. The total value of on-line consumer purchases was more than $3 billion last year, a number expected to grow to $10 billion in 2000.

The Web remains a wide-open field where loads of people are making big bucks with very little investment. There's no reason you can't get in on the booty by starting your own Web site, or at the very least getting familiar with this rich terrain. Like the Wild West, it's a frontier with no boundaries, almost no laws, and unlimited opportunities. Whether you want to start a business, be a goof or a gadfly, or just make a place for people to find out about your many talents, the Web's the place to be. You just need to know how to get there. You're about to find out how.

STEP 1: HARDWARE

Besides a brain, having a computer available to you is helpful if you want to get started. You don't need an expensive computer—anything with a color monitor will do. You'll also need an extra phone line hooked up to your house (unless you want your friends to get busy signals every time you're on line). Finally, you need a modem (prices keep plummeting—get at least a 28.8 bps, preferably more).

STEP 2: SOFTWARE

In the early days of the Net, software for making Web pages was hard to come by. Today, it's spilling out of every orifice on the Internet. There are WYSIWYG (What You See Is What You Get) "editors" (basically, the program that translates your content for the Internet) for Web sites that cost anywhere from nothing up to a thousand dollars. But keep reading and you won't need them.

Essentially, you want to procure just three things: a text editor (NotePad for Windows or SimpleText for Mac), an FTP (file transfer protocol) program for uploading your files to the Internet, and a Web browser, either Netscape Communicator (www.netscape.com) or Microsoft Internet Explorer (www.microsoft.com) so you can view your work.

Later, once you know the basics of HTML (the predominant and simple layout language of the Web), you can move up to a fancy editor if you want to spend the money. You can find a whole selection for either Macs or Windows at Tucows (www.tucows.com).

You also need somewhere to put your home page. Most com-

QUARKXPRESS:
Learn a little layout—and watch your documents sing.

mercial Internet service providers (ISPs) are now providing space for their users to place their home pages. EarthLink, America Online and CompuServe all provide user Web space. If your ISP doesn't offer a place for your site (or wants to charge you extra for it), don't despair—more and more spots offer free Web hosting (see www.povmag.com for a list).

To get your Web-page files up to your site, you're going to need an FTP program. These programs allow you to transfer files from one place on the Internet to the other. If you're using Windows, check out CuteFTP, a simple file-transfer program (available at www.cuteftp.com). If you're using a Macintosh, try Fetch (www.dartmouth.edu/pages/softdev/fetch.html).

STEP 3: LAYING THE FOUNDATION

Once you've got your gear, you've got to decide what it is that you want to put on the Web. Do you want a personal site with pictures of your friends and your dog? A site with your résumé and references? How about a business site that lets Web-surfing customers know what your company does?

No matter where you want to take your site, as you prepare to lay the first brick, you'll want to be organized. For starters, make sure all the copy you want to put on your site is in electronic format. If you've got photos, you need to scan them and turn them into graphic files. If you don't have a scanner (or digital camera), look in the Yellow Pages for a high-end photo lab or printer. Many of them will scan pictures for a fee. If you've got a roll of film that you want put into the computer, you may want to try a Photo CD. Any film lab that has Photo CD capabilities can put your film on a CD-ROM.

Now that you've got your structure set and your content all ready to go, it's time to roll up your sleeves and actually put your page together.

The first thing you should understand is that a page is a collection of *tags* that tells your browser what to display on the screen. It's just like what goes on behind the scenes in your word processor. If you've ever mistakenly opened a word processor document in a text editor like the Windows NotePad, you've probably seen a whole load of gobbledygook surrounding the text you typed in. That garbage is the formatting commands inserted by your word processor to make your text look like it does on paper. HTML works the same way. Surround a sentence with bold tags (<B>) and the sentence

EIGHT MORE MEGS OF RAM:
Speed kills.

turns bold when viewed in your browser. Put a paragraph mark in (<P>) and you get a paragraph break. Simple, huh?

Computers are stupid. They do what they're told to do. And Web browsers are even more stupid. They don't understand multiple spaces. They don't understand the line break you get after you hit the "return" key. They only understand HTML commands. You can hit "return" all day long when you're making your page and your browser will still display your lines as a jumbled mess unless you explicitly tell it otherwise with an HTML command. Remember: only use HTML to format your text. Repeat: *only use HTML to format your text.*

Begin by starting a new file in your favorite text editor. If you use Windows or Windows 95, NotePad works fine. If you use a Mac, use SimpleText. Don't use a word processor because the formatting commands will muck things up.

Let's enter the basic commands you need for your page. Type in:

```
<HTML>
<HEAD>
<TITLE>My Home page</TITLE>
</HEAD>
<BODY>
</BODY>
</HTML>
```

That's it! Really—that's a basic Web page. A really boring one, but still a page.

Let's pick it apart.

First, the <HTML> tag tells the browser that yes, this really is a Web page. You can also see another tag at the bottom of the page that looks pretty similar: </HTML>. This is an *end* tag, indicating that everything in between the beginning <HTML> and the ending </HTML> is indeed HTML.

Next, the <HEAD> tag indicates that you're going to be setting up the header of the document. The header can include lots of important information—programming commands, comments, messages to search engines, and, in our case, a <TITLE> command. Nothing in the header shows up in the main body of your page.

The <TITLE> command tells the browser what to display in the title bar of the window your page is displayed in. Here, it's called "My Home Page," but you can call it whatever you want. The closing </TITLE> tag goes at the end of the title.

IOMEGA ZIP DRIVE: Like having a whole new hard drive—and almost indestructible.

End the header section with a </HEAD> tag (starting to see a pattern here?), and set up the section that will constitute the bulk of your page by entering a <BODY> tag. This tells your browser that you're about to start the main body of your page. Since you're only putting up the foundation now, you're not going to enter body info, so end the empty body section with a </BODY> tag, and end the whole shebang by closing our original <HTML> tag by entering </HTML>.

That's it! Save the file and call it "home.htm." Pat yourself on the back, hoss—you've just put your stake in the ground on the frontier of cyberspace. To see what your stunning achievement looks like, use your browser to open your file by selecting "Open File" from the "File" menu. You should see a blank gray document with a title that matches the title you entered in. If you see anything else, go back and check for typing errors.

STEP 4: INTERIOR DECORATING

Now that you've got the basic stuff in place for your page, let's start making it look nicer. The first thing we've got to do is get rid of that ugly gray color. It might be fine for battleships and aliens, but for Web pages it screams "Loser!"

Color values are represented by three combined numbers standing for red, green, and blue values. Sounds easy enough, right? Here's the rub—you have to specify your color values as hexadecimal (base-16) numbers. Hexa-what? Well, if you don't remember the torture of your high school precalculus class experiments into different number bases, don't worry—there are a few programs that will let you choose your colors and then give you the numbers to use. Mac users should check out Pixel Spy (www2.trincoll.edu/~bhorling/pixelspy/), and Windows folks should visit Tucows' HTML color picker's page (tucows.ameritel.net/tucows/color95.html).

Start off by changing the background color of the page. In this case, choose the green color that happens to have a value of #379969.

Go back to your file and find the <BODY> tag. Insert BGCOLOR="#379969" into the <BODY> tag so that it looks like this:

```
<BODY BGCOLOR="#379969">
```

REAL PLAYER:
Turn your computer into the world's clearest, most powerful radio.

Save your file and look at it again. Bingo! Green background.

Graphics. Everyone loves graphics. And, sad but true, our home page is pretty boring right now without any images to gaze at. Luckily, inserting pictures is really easy.

First, you need a picture to put on your page. Teaching you how to scan pictures or create graphics is way beyond the scope of this lesson. Let's just assume that you've got some pictures already in your computer.

Any graphic will do, but it must adhere to these specs:

1. 72 dpi resolution
2. GIF or JPEG (jpg) format
3. Not be a picture of anything that will get you arrested

OK. Say you've got a picture of yourself that you want to use on your home page, and it's called me.jpg. Make sure that you put the picture in the same place on your hard drive as your home.htm file and insert the following code after the <BODY BGCOLOR= "#379969"> tag you just created:

```
<IMG SRC="me.jpg">
<BR>
<BR>
```

The <IMG SRC=> tag tells your browser to "insert an image here." The SRC= part tells your browser what image to use—in this case the "me.jpg" file. The two <BR> tags following the picture tell the browser to insert two blank lines so that the text you're going to add later doesn't bump up against the picture. You don't want to crowd yourself.

Save your file and take a look. Not bad, eh? There you are in all your glory. If you want your picture centered on the page, just enclose the <IMG SRC="me.jpg"> tag with <CENTER> commands like so:

```
<CENTER> <IMG SRC="me.jpg"> </CENTER>
```

. . . but you don't have to, it's your desig

STEP 5: TYPE IN, FIRE UP, FRAME OUT

It's time to add some content to your page. Sure, you've got a picture, but people might consider you more than a bit narcissistic if that's all your home page contains. A warning though—as you've probably

KEYBOARD WRISTPAD: You protect your mouse—why not protect your arms from carpal tunnel syndrome?

figured out, your source code doesn't look much like your finished page. Open your text editor and your browser at the same time so you can see your changes as you make them.

First add a header for your page. Something like "Welcome to My Home Page" might work. Open your home.htm file, move down just after the <BODY BGCOLOR="#379969"> tag and the <IMG SRC="me.jpg"> tag, and type:

```
<H1>Welcome to My Home Page!</H1>
```

Your file should now look like this:

```
<HTML>
<HEAD>
<TITLE> My Home Page </TITLE>
</HEAD>
<BODY BGCOLOR="#379969">
<H1> Welcome to My Home Page! </H1>
<IMG SRC="me.jpg">
<BR>
<BR>
</BODY>
</HTML>
```

BACKUP DISKS:
Saving
everything will
someday save
you.

Save the file, and open it in your browser. Look! You've got a page with a whole line of text.

You'll notice that what you typed in is in big, bold type. That's from the <H1> command, a command that stands for "header level one," the biggest and the boldest text. <H1> is designed for making headers, so it also automatically puts a line break at the end of the line.

Next add a welcoming message underneath your picture so folks know what they're getting into. Type the following after the two <BR> tags:

```
<H3> Check my latest photos of friends
and family. Got a great job? See my on-
line résumé and HIRE ME!</H3>
```

Save your file. Open it in your browser, and take a look. You'll notice that this line is a little smaller than the first line. That's because you used <H3>, or header level three, which shows up smaller than <H1>. There are actually six levels of headers, one being the largest and six being the smallest. If you think that higher numbers should mean bigger, welcome to the club—just blame it on computer geeks and move on.

That first welcome line looks a little boring flush left, doesn't it? It should be in the center. How do we center something? Use the <CENTER> tag. Complicated, right?

Go back and put <CENTER> tags around your first line so that it looks like this:

```
<CENTER><H1>Welcome to My Home
Page!</H1></CENTER>
```

Save the file, and take a look. Centered!

Centered, yes. Boring? Yes. You need some more text. How about giving people a menu so they can choose where to go next on your page? To do so use the <MENU> tag. Open your source code in your text editor, go to the line below the one you just added, (the one with the <H3> tags) and type:

```
<B>Photos of my friends:</B> <BR>
<MENU>
<LI> Amy
<LI> John and Keith
<LI> Chris (my girlfriend) and me
<LI> Climbing the peak in NM
<LI> My dog, Jake
</MENU>
```

The <B> tags make the title of the menu bold, the <MENU> tags tell the browser you're making a list of stuff to use as a menu, and the <LI> tags mean "list item" and tell the browser that what you type after them is an element of your menu. Save your file.

Believe it or not, you've now got a Web page. Not an incredibly ornate Web page, but you've shown that you are not a wimp when the going gets tough. You've got the basic structure. You've got the basic format. You're the Man.

T1 WEB CONNECTION: Anything less is Neanderthal.

STEP 6: FIREPOWER TO THE LINKS

That's the simple skinny as far as making a page is concerned. In fact, at this point you could put up your home page and be perfectly happy. But the Web's all about links. And a page without links is a lonely page indeed.

A basic link looks like this:

```
<A HREF="page.html">something to indicate
link</A>
```

The <A HREF="page.html"> part tells the browser what page you want your link to go to. After the > bracket is the thing on the page that indicates a link. It can be a simple "click here" or a graphic. You need something. If you don't, your users will have no idea what to click on for the link. Finally, the </A> tag indicates the end of the whole link tag.

Go back to the example. Say that you created a simple page to show a picture of your friend Amy. It could be a simple page like this:

```
<HTML>
<HEAD>
<TITLE>My friend Amy</TITLE>
</HEAD>
<BODY BGCOLOR="#000000">
<IMG SRC="amy.jpg">
</BODY>
</HTML>
```

YOU DON'T KNOW JACK: A CD-Rom for those with a *Jeopardy!* jones.

Just a black background with a picture of Amy. Save it with the name amy.htm in the same place you've saved all your other files so far.

If you look at our original example, Amy is on our list of pictures:

```
<B>Photos of my friends:</B> <BR>
<MENU>
<LI>Amy
<LI>John and Keith
<LI>Chris (my girlfriend) and me
```

```
<LI>Climbing the peak in NM
<LI>My dog, Jake
</MENU>
```

However, at this point there's no way to get to the Amy page. Change the <LI>Amy line to read:

```
<LI> <A HREF="amy.htm">Amy</A>
```

This line says make the word "Amy" a link to the page amy.htm. When you save and look at your page again, you'll notice that Amy has an attractive blue line under it, showing you that you've made a link to the amy.htm file. Click the link and watch Amy appear.

A link like this is a local link, and it only links to files in the same directory as your home.htm file. What if you want to link to another Web site? Easy! Just include the whole Web site address:

```
<A HREF="http://ESPN.SportsZone.com">
Click here to go to ESPN</A>
```

This link would show up as *Click here to go to ESPN,* and anyone clicking the link would go to the ESPN SportsZone Web site at ESPN.SportsZone.com.

Finally, you can even use links to send E-mail. Use the format:

```
<A HREF="mailto:email@email.com">
Click here to send E-mail</A>
```

and substitute your actual E-mail address for email@E-mail.com.

Voilà! We're done.

STEP 7: THE ULTIMATE GLOBAL HOUSE-WARMING PARTY

So now you've got a home page living happily on your hard drive. Unfortunately, it isn't going to do you much good unless it's up on the Web for others to see.

Depending on your ISP, the exact answer as to how to get it up will be different, but the principles are all the same. You have to FTP your files to your ISP (see www.povmag.com for details).

GLARE GUARD FOR YOUR MONITOR: Go easy on the eyes.

Now it's time to get the word out.

First thing you do is send everyone you know E-mail announcing the birth of your site. If you are going to use your page for your business, make sure that you get the URL printed on everything—print ads, business cards, letterhead, stationery, hats, T-shirts, bumper stickers, bar glasses, coasters—whatever people see.

Next, tell the world about your new page by registering it at all the search engines. You can go to every major search engine and register your page. A better idea: go to Submit-It! (www.submitit. com), a service that lets you register your page at about twenty search engines for free, and at more than four hundred for sixty dollars.

Now sit back and wait for the world to come to you. You're on the Web.

INTELLIGENT NET LIFE

If you're looking to "get connected" with someone on the Net, as they say on MSNBC, there's no shortage of ways to do it. You could trot into The Flirts Nook on America Online and chat until your fingers turn as numb as your brain. You could pop on over to livecenterfolds.com on the Web and converse, as it were, with an authentic naked Net chick for only $5.99 a minute. You could wander into the Usenet newsgroup alt.fan.rush-limbaugh and pick a fight with a horde of dittoheads, or you could poke your head into alt.conspiracy to argue the finer points of the single-bullet theory with a gang of raving lunatics.

All these things might be stimulating, in their own ways, but few of them are likely to engage any part of the brain higher than the cerebellum. The relative anonymity of the Net turns many discussions into virtual drive-by shootings: sitting seemingly invulnerable in the blue glow of their video monitor, nameless malcontents feel free to dump the contents of their id onto the Net, spreading wild rumors and crafting elaborately nasty flames. And live chat? Forget it. There's something about chat on the Net that transforms even the most erudite Netizens into doddering, sex-obsessed imbeciles.

But intelligent conversation isn't impossible on the Net; you just have to look a little for it. If you want mass, try Forum One (www.ForumOne.com), which offers a search page of on-line forums. If you want class, here are a few places to start.

Perhaps the most famous outpost of reasonably civilized discussion on the Net is the virtual community known as The Well (www.well.com), the Rosie O'Donnell of on-line communication. At the heart of The Well are its on-line conferences—electronic bulletin boards where members can post their thoughts on everything from fiction writing to their favorite sexual positions—if they can figure out how to navigate the system's less-than-elegant architecture.

The Well (the name stands for "Whole Earth 'Lectronic Link") is based in the Bay Area and still has a whiff of the sixties about it. The system emerged from the counterculture institution known as the *Whole Earth Catalog*, and even today, long after the death of Jerry Garcia, the system is still dotted with a score of Grateful Dead–related conferences for Deadheads to talk about—well, whatever it is exactly Deadheads talk about. But it has also attracted a wide assortment of Net-savvy folk from the Bay Area and elsewhere; you'll find everyone from smart sexpert Susie Bright to cyberpunky sci-fi writer Bruce Sterling poking around in The Well's various conferences, which range from the relatively highbrow (the Books con-

QUICK TIPS FOR WEB MONKEYS

KEEP YOUR PICTURES SMALL, with file sizes no larger than 30K per picture.

USE LINKS. Don't put all your information on one page. Each page should really be a "chunk" of information.

BE CLEAR AND CONCISE. Be funny. Don't be boring.

CHECK YOUR SPELLING. Nothing screams "lame!" more than misspelled Web pages.

AVOID CLIP ART IF POSSIBLE. No matter what the ad for the clip art disk says, clip art always looks like clip art. And that ain't art.

CREATIVELY STEAL. If you like someone's Web site design, use the "View Document Source" button in your browser to look at their code and see how they did it—everyone does. Use their design as inspiration.

STAY AWAY FROM IMAGES that may be copyrighted. Really.

HAVE FUN.

ference, cohosted by John Seabrook of *The New Yorker*) to the low (the Weird conference, whose host, Gerard Van Der Leun of *Penthouse*, describes himself as "a rabid crackpot").

The Well's East Coast equivalent, so to speak, is New York's Echo(www.echonyc.com). Echo skews to a younger demographic than The Well, or so it seems; the tone of the discussions is distinctly more sarcastic, and conversations are less likely to be interrupted by someone's memories of life on a commune in 1973. Echo topics cover the waterfront, as its Web site notes, "from Angst to Zines"; in the interstices you'll discover Echoids discoursing on everything from sex and shopping to movies and TV (not necessarily at the same time). The tone is often irreverent, but at their best, discussions on Echo rise above mere glibness. (Of course, on the Net as elsewhere, the best things in life aren't always free: access to the conferences on The Well will run you $10.00 a month, and Echo's will cost you $19.95 a month.)

Meanwhile, the man who has done the most to popularize the notion of the "virtual community," writer Howard Reingold, has started up one of his own: the Electric Minds site (www.minds.com), host to an array of "Conversations" with topics ranging from on-line community to electronically "Altered Minds." The system is relatively easy to use: Howard himself greets you at the door (that's him with the hat, the crazy grin, and the even crazier shirt); after registering, you're free to post your own thoughts.

Hoping to encourage a kind of interactivity with their readers that goes far beyond that allowed by the traditional letters-to-the-editor page, a number of on-line magazines have incorporated elaborate conferencing systems into their Web sites, and some of these have begun to metamorphose into real on-line communities. The *Utne Reader* magazine, something of a *Reader's Digest* for the alternative set, has long promoted local face-to-face "salons," where readers can gather to discuss articles in the magazine and anything else that pops into their head. So it's not surprising that they've brought a similar approach to the Web, with something called Café Utne (www.utne.com). Other on-line magazines have done the same: HotWired (www.hotwired.com), the on-line sibling of *Wired* magazine, has its "Threads"; Salon (www.salonmagazine.com), which presents an eclectic mix of literate commentary on pop culture and politics, has "Table Talk"; and Feed (www.feedmag.com), a New York journal of cultural criticism, has its "Feedbag."

For the most part, these on-line salons mirror the publications from which they've emerged: Café Utne, like the *Utne Reader* itself,

E-MAIL AIRFARE DEALS: Because you need *something* to look forward to on Wednesday.

PURGING YOUR E-MAIL: Delete those personal and potentially career-damaging messages before they come back to haunt you.

exudes a certain soft, vaguely new-agey sense of political correctness. HotWired's "Threads" encourages rants, and debates on topics as arcane as Schopenhauer have been known to inspire vitriolic flame wars. *Salon* offers up a menu of discussion topics ranging from art and literature to sex; the only discussion area that hasn't taken off, at least not yet, is sports.

Not all smart on-line discussions are quite as highbrow, even at the most self-consciously literary of sites: Salon's Table Talkers have earnestly (and less than earnestly) discussed such topics as comparative orgasmology (who has the best ones—men or women?) and the glory that is ABBA.

Most on-line conference participants, whether they're Echoids or Café Utne regulars, agree that a moderator, or host, is crucial for keeping on-line forums running smoothly; in many ways he or she can be the difference between an on-line community and sheer chaos.

AUTO-SAVE: Because the crash always comes.

TALK THE TALK

Stay or Bail Moment. That first moment when a visitor to your site decides whether or not to click into the site or click onto another.

Third-Generation Web Site. Coined by David Siegel in his book, *Creating Killer Web Sites*, a third-generation Web site "uses typographic and visual layout principles to describe a page in two dimensions. Third-generation site designers carefully specify the position and relationships of all elements on the page, retaining fine control of the layout."

Fish Food. Contests, quizzes, puzzles and other interactive tricks put on a Web site in order to get people to the site and to keep them coming back.

Dancing Baloney. Wacky graphics, gratuitous animations, and other eye candy designed to spiff up an otherwise lame Web page.

CobWeb. A site that hasn't been updated in a long time, often sporting lots of dead links and "Under Construction" signs.

Kilroy Page. A single-page Web site constructed by a person or company just so they can say that they're on the Web.

World Wide Wait. The true meaning of WWW.

CHAPTER 9

TOYS

Q: SHOULD I BUY A NEW TELEVISION SET?

That's a trickier question now than it was a year ago, courtesy of the Federal Communications Commission, which recently mandated that all television broadcasters pipe out their signals digitally by 2006. On the surface, this means that your current television—which, even if it's brand new, still socks *Seinfeld* to you in a strictly analog fashion—will eventually morph into an interesting-looking coffee table.

MINI-SATELLITE DISH:

Channel-surf in a *much* larger ocean.

There are some upsides. Specifically, digital television will offer enhanced picture quality—it will be comparable to motion pictures. Digital TV will also give you enhanced audio vibrancy. Also on the upside will be the new tubes' price tags—initially two thousand to five thousand dollars.

So you have to ask yourself: *How badly do I need a new box?* If you're stuck watching the big games on a cruddy ten-year-old, thirteen-inch tube, please go buy a midrange set and enjoy (you've earned it). But if you're looking for some serious screenage, *caveat emptor*. Do you really want to buy the television of a lifetime when that lifetime is your dog's?

This teledilemma is eased by the fact that people owning a "dino set" will be able to purchase a converter box to let the old guy go digital. But who knows how much these converters will cost, or how much you'll be missing versus the television of tomorrow?

As is the case with fashion fads, gang violence and other trends, the ten biggest cities will get the first look. These markets will all be digital by spring 1999; Boston, New York, and Los Angeles by fall 1998. Gearheads in these towns can plunk down the big bucks for prototype digital sets and gaze into the future. The rest of us, however, should just enjoy our mortal tubes and wait it out a few years, when digital becomes mandatory and the prices drop accordingly. (Remember what VCRs and CD players cost when they first came out?) That's when it's time to strike. Just imagine what'll be on pay-per-view by then.

ESSENTIALS FOR YOUR JAZZ COLLECTION

If you're looking to build a jazz collection, where should you start? We asked Wynton Marsalis, and based on his picks and those of few key jazz historians, here's a pretty good list:

THE CLASSICS

LOUIS ARMSTRONG:
The Hot Fives and Hot Sevens (Columbia) or *Louis Armstrong, Portrait of the Artist as a Young Man* (4 CDs, Columbia)

COUNT BASIE:
The Standards (Verve)

CLIFFORD BROWN, WITH MAX ROACH:
Alone Together (2 CDs, Verve)

ORNETTE COLEMAN:
The Shape of Jazz to Come (Atlantic)

PlaySite
www.playsite.com
Nothing new about chess, checkers, or backgammon, except when you're playing a game with a gal (or geek) from halfway around the globe. Chat with your newfound pals as you play. The future of gaming, now.

Hotgames
www.hotgames.com
A snazzy gaming publication, with reviews and demos of games like Total Soccer ("play against Britain's best") and Cobra Gunship ("a choplifter clone oozing with gameplay").

Rocktropolis
www.rocktropolis.com
Everything for the rock fan, from news and gossip to a music store and chat rooms.

REI Online
www.rei.com
Pacific Northwest outfitter brings its store on line. Order gear. Learn about upcoming adventures. Find a nearby store.

JOHN COLTRANE:
Crescent and *Ballads* (Impulse!); *A Love Supreme, Giant Steps,* and *My Favorite Things* (Atlantic); *The Last Giant: Anthology* (2 CDs, Rhino)

MILES DAVIS:
Kind of Blue, 'Round About Midnight, Sketches of Spain, and *Miles Ahead* (Columbia); *Birth of the Cool* (Capitol)

DUKE ELLINGTON:
Blanton-Webster Band (3 CDs) and *Black, Brown, and Beige* (3 CDs, Bluebird); *Ellington at Newport* and *Uptown* (Columbia); *Beyond Category* (2 CDs, Smithsonian)

DIZZY GILLESPIE:
Dizzy's Diamonds (2 CDs, Verve)

BENNY GOODMAN:
Live at Carnegie Hall (2 CDs, Columbia)

DVD PLAYER:
Will make your VCR look like the dinosaur it will soon become.

HERBIE HANCOCK:
Maiden Voyage (Blue Note)

FREDDIE HUBBARD:
Hub-Tones (Blue Note)

WYNTON MARSALIS:
In This House, On This Morning (2 CDs, Columbia)

CHARLES MINGUS:
Thirteen Pictures (3 CDs, Rhino)

THELONIUS MONK:
Genius of Modern Music, Volumes 1 and 2 (Blue Note)

CHARLIE PARKER:
Yardbird Suite (2 CDs Rhino) or *Confirmation* (2 CDs, Verve)

BUD POWELL:
Jazz Giant (Verve)

SONNY ROLLINS:
A Night at the Village Vanguard, Volumes 1 and 2 (Blue Note)

WAYNE SHORTER:
Speak No Evil (Blue Note)

ART TATUM:
The Complete Capitol Recordings, Volume 1 (Capitol Jazz)

BEN WEBSTER:
Coleman Hawkins and Ben Webster or *The Soul of Ben Webster* (2 CDs, Verve)

VOCALISTS

ELLA FITZGERALD:
The Songbooks or *The Duke Ellington Songbook* (3 CDs, Verve)

BILLIE HOLIDAY:
Lady in Satin or *Lady Sings the Blues* (Verve)

SHIRLEY HORN:
Close Enough for Love (Verve)

ABBEY LINCOLN WITH STAN GETZ:
You Gotta Pay the Band (Verve)

SARAH VAUGHAN:
The Divine Sarah Vaughan: The Columbia Years 1949–1953 (2 CDs, Columbia)

JOE WILLIAMS:
Count Basie Swings, Joe Williams Sings (Verve)

MAKEOUT ALBUMS

DAVE BRUBECK:
Time Out (Columbia)

RAY CHARLES AND BETTY CARTER:
Ray Charles and Betty Carter (Dunhill)

AA BATTERIES:
Because they're never around when you need them.

MILES DAVIS:
Some Day My Prince Will Come (Columbia)

JOHN COLTRANE:
The Complete Africa/Brass Sessions (2 Cds) and *John Coltrane and Johnny Hartman* (Impulse!); *Coltrane Plays the Blues* (Atlantic)

DEXTER GORDON:
Ballads (Blue Note)

JOE HENDERSON:
Lush Life (Verve)

WYNTON MARSALIS:
Standard Time Volume 2–Intimacy Calling or *Standard Time Volume 3–The Resolution of Romance* (Columbia)

ANYTHING BY BEN WEBSTER

UP-AND-COMERS TO CATCH

TRUMPET:
Nicholas Payton, Terence Blanchard, Jon Faddis, Marcus Printup, Ryan Kisor, Roy Hargrove

SAX:
James Carter, Joshua Redman, Jesse Davis, Joe Lovano

PIANO:
Eric Reed, Jacky Terrasson, Benny Green, Marcus Roberts, Stephen Scott

BASS:
Reginald Veal, Christian McBride

VOCALIST:
Cassandra Wilson

THE JAZZ AT LINCOLN CENTER ORCHESTRA:
Wynton Marsalis, conductor.

A GOOD TURNTABLE:
So you can remember what seventies originals sounded like before Puff Daddy got to them.

A UNIVERSAL REMOTE:
Control the entire world from your comfy chair—just like Captain Kirk.

LIVING LEGENDS YOU CAN STILL SEE

Sonny Rollins (sax); Wayne Shorter (sax); Joe Henderson (sax); Freddie Hubbard (trumpet); McCoy Tyner (piano); Elvin Jones (drums); Ron Carter (bass); Ray Charles (piano, vocals); Joe Williams (vocals); Betty Carter (vocals); Shirley Horn (vocals)

CLOSEST THING TO SEEING BILLIE HOLIDAY LIVE

Abbey Lincoln

ART COLLECTION ON A BUDGET

A FRENCH PRESS: How real men make coffee.

Art museum? You've got the drill down. Pay the admission, admire the handiwork, buy the poster.

Art gallery? That's another story. Artists with names you've heard about only fleetingly. Paintings with price tags. Saleswomen coming up to you with the dreaded question, "What are you looking for?"

Well, there's no reason you shouldn't have an answer, even if the only thing you've ever painted is a ceiling. Art, after all, is a most intriguing purchase: something that can instantly brand you tasteful or twisted, that has no intrinsic value, yet potentially may yield you a vacation home. But how can you tell a Rubens from a ruse?

Before you commit cold cash, understand that when it comes to art, value is in the eye of the beholder. Above all, know your own mind—and eyes.

1. START SMALL.

While billboard-sized paintings with world-famous signatures inspire awe, they exact a high price (and are a bitch to get up the stairs). Smaller-scale prints, on the other hand, are more often reasonably priced and provide an attractive entry point for collecting. An original oil by Chagall, for example, fetches an average three hundred thousand dollars today; an original signed lithograph by the celebrated Russian-turned-Frenchman will set you back only about two thousand dollars.

Etchings can be bought on the cheap and are the strongest candidates for appreciation. (They will also make an honest man out of you when you invite her back to your pad to "show her your . . .") Etchings and lithographs (each begins as an image on stone, metal, or glass) typically are offered in limited editions of at least fifty, signed originals being the top of the line. The numbers "4/300" on a print denote the fourth copy in an edition of three hundred, but that's just a bookkeeping notation—a low number is not more valuable, nor does a smaller print run necessarily mean a pricier edition.

2. FIND A REPUTABLE GALLERY.

To ensure that what you're getting is the real deal—and for legal recourse, in case you discover that Keith Haring original you bought for five thousand dollars was, in fact, painted by some talented art student—only do business with established galleries. A dealer who has been in business more than a decade and who has membership in professional organizations, such as the Art Dealers Association of America, is a good bet.

3. SHOP SMART.

Buying art is not like buying a Buick—price haggling isn't the norm. However, one way to lower the ante is to seek out an artist directly and make your bid. Large galleries, though, generally take an artist's work on consignment—the price is the price.

Dealers tend to show work *they* like, so be critical when trying to discern whether a new artist is being featured because he's a genuine comer or because he's the owner's boyfriend. Trust your instincts. Ask the dealer a lot of questions—the more honest and objective the answers, the better the buy.

4. INVEST IN A DECENT FRAME.

Don't cheap out by spending a fortune on a piece of art and then ruining it with some awful frame from Kmart. A really sharp frame can salvage a mediocre painting. Avoid frames whose seams are noticeable. Never cover an oil with a glass pane, but do so for watercolors (prevents fading) and prints (adds body).

A frame should complement—not dominate—a picture. Don't pair contemporary art with gold-lead curlicues. Beware the too large and the too fancy.

A PERSONAL GLOBAL-POSITIONING SYSTEM: You'll never get lost again.

5. ART ISN'T REAL ESTATE.

Forget buying art as an investment—unless you're the scion of some Swiss banking family, chances are you haven't got the kind of serious loot necessary to turn art collecting into commerce. "Be guided by your interest—have a feeling for [the art]," says Walter Newman of Philadelphia's prestigious Newman Galleries. "You can ask dealers whether it will be more valuable ten years from now . . . but we can be wrong." Never base a purchase solely upon an artist's reputation. The future value of a piece of artwork is determined by market trends and the overall perception of its quality—both as elusive as van Gogh's sanity. As with advice and IPOs, it's almost impossible to judge whether a piece of art will increase in value over time. Make sure that you'd be happy enough just to look at it.

HOME BARTENDING SUPPLIES

First question: Did any guests bring booze to your last party?

Second question: Did those gracious guests quickly find you were equipped to serve only beer and wine and then leave the aforementioned booze on top of your fridge as an 80-proof reminder that you fail as a home bartender?

Presentation counts when throwing a party. Ice cubes should be kept in an ice bucket, not in a salad bowl; a gin and tonic should be sipped from a highball glass, not from a coffee mug or a plastic cup. It's the difference between entertaining guests in a semidignified manner and presiding over a scene that would be staged more appropriately in a dorm room.

Third question: Did someone at your last party try to start a game of Twister?

Don't answer. It doesn't have to happen that way. Assembling an impressive home bar is neither difficult, nor cost-prohibitive—smart shopping can help you do the job for around three hundred dollars.

Begin with the WMF Bar-set Impulse ($69.98; Macy's), a seven-piece stainless-steel bar kit. The bar set's round, tapered container

A NERF BASKETBALL HOOP:
At home or the office, it's as much fun as when you were a kid.

A NICE SAND WEDGE:
Other than the putter, it may be the most important club in your golf bag.

holds a minirack of six implements, including a corkscrew, a stirring rod, a coil-rimmed strainer, and a jigger/pony combo; lift the minirack from the container, and boom—instant ice bucket.

For mixing certain drinks, a simple stirring rod will suffice. But for drinks that contain juices, sugar, or cream, a shaker is essential. (Besides, shaking drinks is fun and makes you look like a pro.) Pottery Barn's stainless-steel, two-piece Cocktail Shaker ($39) takes a certain degree of cluelessness for granted: recipes are engraved on the shaker. The unit consists of the shaker itself and a container with a series of small, diagonally aligned squares cut out of the side. Together, they work like a dial: placing the shaker inside and aligning a drink name with the arrow at the container's top reveals the ingredients.

Frozen drinks will require a blender; don't skimp in this area. Make a long-term investment with the heavy-duty Waring Blendor ($119; Williams-Sonoma). Forget putting in crushed ice; this bad boy can pulverize whole cubes. Equally important, it looks cool—the fifties-style, chrome-based Blendor is a model of retro chic.

CD CHANGER:
When you have a party, spend time with the ladies, not your stereo.

On to the vessels. Purists assert that using the proper glass enhances the drink. But some types are more crucial than others. Drinking a martini from anything but a martini glass is damn near unthinkable, which is why you should have some in stock. Pottery Barn's Platinum Martini glass ($10 a piece) is fine choice from a cost/quality standpoint. It holds more than seven ounces, has a lot of heft, and is stylishly designed.

Those big red plastic cups were great for the Old Milwaukee of your college frat party days, but those don't cut the muster with the microbrews you're now serving up. A tasty beer deserves an appealing presentation like that of the Direction Pilsner glass from Crate & Barrel ($7.95 apiece). Shorter and slightly rounder than the traditional pilsner, this seventeen-ounce, handblown glass brings a touch of class to beer drinking.

Finally, you should always have two items at the ready: a bartender's guide and a chilled bottle of good champagne. References such as Mr. Boston Official Bartender's and Party Guide ($9.99; Warner Books) are filled with recipes and tips and prove a good defense against the wise-ass guest who always requests a drinks no one's heard of. And the champagne? Hey—you never know when you'll have an occasion to celebrate.

Now you have the basics of a bar setup your guests will envy. The only thing you need is booze. How's the stock on top of your refrigerator? (See "The Hard Stuff" on page 76.)

HANDCRAFTING YOUR HUMIDOR

Appropriate housing is the lifestyle component most likely to frustrate the seeker of both upward mobility and a balanced budget. More than a few fast-track careers have been derailed by the gaudy imperatives of an uptown address—or the shoddy look of a starter apartment.

That same dynamic holds sway for cigars. Stogies, you see, crave a "humidostatic" (70 percent humidity is about right) domicile to make their best impression on your lips. Which means that you can't stick them in a pickle jar or leave them under a sofa pad and expect consistently rich redolence when you light up.

Enter the humidor. Part furniture, part ecosystem, it is both the cigar smoker's cachet and the cultivator of his smokes. In its climate-controlled recesses lurk the promise of eternal mellowness.

Unfortunately, mellowness has its price—about two thousand dollars for high-end humidors of lacquered, burled tree trunk and with exotic, inlaid patterns. Of course, that's the extreme. But we challenge you to find anything decent for much less than three hundred dollars, most of which is going toward aesthetics. There is one other option on the market: inexpensive glass or plastic canisters, the cheap one-night stands on the humidor continuum.

We have an alternative route: Build your own, a three-step process that requires a little art, a little science, and fifty to a hundred dollars.

Start with a wood box. It can be an old plywood cigar box, a rosewood jewelry box, a particleboard knickknack box—whatever, just as long as there's an airtight seal. This requires, in addition to a flawless fit between lid and base, hardware (hinges, or perhaps a "catch") that permits no wiggle room. If you tap on one side of a humidor lid and there's even a hint of movement on the other side, rescue your cigars.

Next comes the humidor's core—unscented Spanish cedar, a tropical wood that makes those compressed cigar leaves feel right at home. Until recently, acquiring suitable cedar was a daunting challenge, while creating a lining for your box from a block of this wood required the day rental of Bob Vila. Not anymore—woodworking catalogs featuring humidor supplies are, well, coming out of the woodwork. Just

HOTRONICS SKI BOOT HEATERS: No more cold toes to bring you down on the mountain.

make sure you know what you're ordering. The cedar should come from Central, not South, America. Beall Tool (800–331–4718) offers cedar lining of a quarter-inch thickness for a "large" box (12 in. x 18 in. x 6 in.) for between twenty to thirty-two dollars.

Now, for the science—a chunk of floral foam functions as a humidity regulator. Usually encased in perforated plastic, this spongy puck can be purchased at most cigar specialty stores for anywhere from ten to fifty dollars, depending on size and bells and whistles. To make sure it's functioning correctly, add a hydrometer—a thirteen-dollar brass analog for looks, a three-dollar plastic digital if just for accuracy. Suddenly, you've re-created tenth-century Guatemala, where the resourceful Mayans puffed on their first sik'ars.

Kept at room temperature, your cozy, ecologically correct humidor will provide home and hearth for your cigars. There's even a small business here: if you do it right, you can sell your finished box for triple its cost. Selling three-hundred-dollar humidors, after all, beats buying them any day.

POINT-AND-SHOOT CAMERA: Always have one loaded and handy, just in case.

PORTABLE PUTTING GREEN: Because your short game needs all the help it can get.

FINALLY, YOUR OWN PINBALL MACHINE

Pinball has been around, in one form or another, since the 1920s. In the earliest versions, you just shot marbles into randomly placed holes and added the scores in your head. Fun, fun, fun. Bumpers, targets, automatic scoring, and the infamous tilt mechanism improved matters, but it wasn't until flippers were added in 1947 that skill entered the equation. After that, the game got faster, the designs got wilder, women with plunging necklines were added to the artwork on the back glass, and business boomed.

Then video happened—not that there's any real comparison. Video games are, after all, just blips on a screen. Pinball, on the other flipper, is physical. Sensual. Real. If you bump the machine, you alter the roll of the ball. If you change the timing of your flip by just a fraction of a second, you've transformed the game.

But in the battle for the nation's quarters, pinball lost big time.

The upswing, however, was that the aftermarket burgeoned, giving people like you the chance to fulfill your childhood dream of having all the free games you want—in our own home or office.

New pinball machines cost upwards of four thousand dollars, but after two years on the street, the price can drop to half that. If you find one that has been played longer, you can get a steal. By diligently scanning your local shopper's guide, you may find a used one for as little as $150—the same price as a mediocre video-game console—though you'll have little control over selection or condition.

So why not go hunting? It's half the fun, after all: break out a roll of quarters, go to an arcade, start playing, and see what game features you like.

Once you've played the field, hit the phone book—game sellers are usually listed under "amusement devices." When you start hearing price quotes, remember that each used pinball machine, like each used car, has a unique history. Go out to the warehouse or showroom and play the machine you are interested in. Or just go and browse—hey, it's a free afternoon of pinball.

As you play, keep these warning signs in mind:

♦ Don't necessarily settle on a dated machine just because it's cheap. Kitschy vintage images can be charming, but you'd better make sure you're happy looking at Jimmy "J.J." Walker or Evel Knievel every single day.

♦ If the machine is going to be set up in a public place, like your office lobby, consider whether the artwork is going to attract a complaint of sexual harassment. Remember that these games are designed to appeal to young boys hanging out in arcades—and older boys hanging out in bars.

♦ Look for signs of fire damage on the cabinet and cigarette burns—common problems with machines that spent part of their lives in saloons.

♦ Make sure that every bulb is working. Don't think you can just replace or do without one—a single burnout can be indicative of a larger problem, like a blown transistor.

♦ While perusing the playing field, check for chipped or peeled paint near the targets. Too much wear and tear can affect your game.

A PROPER CIGAR CUTTER:
Let your grandpa tooth it.

◆ Don't assume that older, simpler machines will be easier to get fixed. A tinkerer with a lot of common sense might be able to handle the job, but in general, computer boards can be replaced much more easily than the relays on vintage machines. Any reliable seller will have a service staff, but make sure you know what house calls and replacement parts costs. Push for a strong warranty.

In the end, the machine you buy should be one you won't easily tire of playing. Here are some of the best:

◆ Captain Fantastic (Bally, 1976). Rare is the film that inspires more than one machine; Captain Fantastic is the second, and better, of two games based on the Who's pinball-themed movie *Tommy*. The first, Wizard, was produced in 1975.

◆ Comet (Williams, 1985) and Cyclone (Williams, 1988) are a pair of carnival-themed games with high-speed chutes, perfect for those who like the action fast but understandable.

NHL '99:
You're never too old to make Gretzky's head bleed.

◆ Eight Ball DeLuxe (Bally, 1982) is one of many pins with a poolroom theme, taunting hesitant players by booming, "Quit talking and start chalking!"

◆ Haunted House (Gottlieb, 1982) has eight flippers that help you move the ball through three different levels. The musical accompaniment to your steel orb's wild ride is Bach's "Toccata and Fugue."

◆ Star Trek (Bally, 1979) highlights the prepaunch crew of the original Enterprise, who helped turn this machine into a best-seller—although purists might quibble with the appearance of the physically enhanced Lieutenant Uhura.

BOARD GAME STRATEGY

She visits your apartment for the first time. Things have been going well enough that you actually care what she thinks about you. So you've cleaned up the place. You've stocked the fridge. You've hidden Kathy, the doll with the perpetual yawn.

While you're in the rest room, uh, resting, she opens a couple drawers, peeks into your closet, where she discovers . . . your games. This, friend, is a crucial moment. Your games are a direct reflection of you—a glimpse at your inner game-boy—and they speak volumes to her about what type of bloke you'll turn out to be. Playing board games may have been uncool in college, but owning a select collection at subsequent stages in your life flags you as a man of smarts and whimsy, as well as someone who doesn't necessarily need copious amounts of booze or particularly bad movies to have a good time.

Whether you are putting together a game collection or deciding which ones to liberate from your parents' attic, start with chess, backgammon, and Parcheesi. These foolproof, no-need-for-apologies classics show whoever stumbles upon them that, despite your eccentricities, you have a solid core. Make sure your chess set is neither plastic, indicating cheapness, nor gimmicky (i.e., Civil War generals instead of the traditional pieces), indicating overt nerdiness.

Next, grab a copy of Scrabble. Only those who can compete at Scrabble actually own Scrabble, so she'll think you have some brains—at least until that fateful day when she challenges you. Then plan on spending most of the time whining, "Why can't I get any good letters?" while she's spelling *quagmire* and *vestibule.*

Monopoly is another respectable choice, but be prepared for it to reveal more than you might want to know. In other words, if you're a free spirit who likes putting five hundred dollars on Free Parking but your lady friend is a stickler who pays 15 percent extra to get a property unmortgaged (as, she reminds you, is *clearly* stated in the rules), ultimately, nothing good will come of the evening.

She probably won't want to play Risk, but this Cold War classic deserves a place of honor anyway. A precursor to all those far-too-obsessive war games, Risk has been around since 195, but went through an unpopular stretch the next decade when global domination was a tricky subject matter. Couple it with Stratego or Battleship, and the right woman will appreciate that you still have a bit of the little warmonger in you.

At this point, you might be tempted to give in to childhood memories and add The Game of Life to your collection. Listen to Nancy and just say no: the fun game you fondly remember has undergone a disturbing political-correction process. What used to be a contest about becoming a millionaire is now about being nice; you now get extra points for doing things like recycling and learning CPR. Boring.

YOUR OWN POOL CUE:
Only if you know how to use it.

THE MOTORIZED TIE RACK:
It makes choosing a tie an adventure.

Instead, try to find the deeply stupid Mad Magazine Game (no longer available in stores, but infesting the garage sales of America), which announces that you've embraced your inner Alfred E. Neuman—and should remain in the closet until you are both very, very drunk.

Beyond that, follow these basic rules:

◆ Avoid anything with a recognizable person on the box, especially the cast of any television show.

◆ Spurn anything with a spinner. Dice rule.

◆ Ditto for anything requiring you to put together cardboard pieces.

◆ Any game that requires batteries could be problematic. If you've gone through med school, you can explain that someone bought you Operation, but it would be pretty difficult to explain Don't Wake Daddy so easily.

◆ All role-playing games in the Dungeons & Dragons realm should be relegated, along with your Haircut 100 and A Flock of Seagulls records, to a part of your past that you simply don't talk about.

Finally, keep in mind that you should never, ever play any of these games one-on-one in the early days of a relationship. She'll either trounce you or you'll trounce her. Or, in the case of chess, you'll be up all night playing. In every case, you lose.

REVO SUNGLASSES: Expensive—and worth it. You'll never see the world the same way again.

GEARING UP FOR SLEEPING OUT

If you venture into a sporting-goods store in search of camping gear, chances are you'll quit backpacking before you ever reach your first happy trail. There are just too damn many choices—not to mention the salespeople, whose outdoor experience often goes no further than a backcountry trek to the far end of the parking lot.

Thankfully, the hike to the store is one path you'll never have to take. If you strap these all-purpose essentials on your back, you'll instantly transform into a Mountain Man—or at least look like one.

SLEEPING BAG

The great "sleeping-bag debate" is no debate at all. Down filling vs. synthetic filling? Get over it, and get down. It's lighter, more compactible, and delicious to sleep in. As for the major knock—that a wet down bag is a deadly bag—that's moot. Get a down bag that's constructed with highly water-resistant outer fabric, like Marmot's Pinnacle ($429), and you can sleep in the rain. Granted, it's not cheap, but it's the only bag you'll ever need: warm, well built, lightweight, roomy, and stuffed with the finest goosedown money can buy—707–544–4590.

TENT

Some stores will try to sell you their so-called no-hitch tents—those pop-up jobs that pitch perfectly in the store . . . and almost nowhere else. Believe me, there's *always* a hitch. Instead, buy the Sierra Designs Clip Flashlight CD ($185). It's extraordinarily light (three pounds, ten ounces), easy enough to set up and has room (though not a lot of it) for two—800–635–0461.

SLEEPING PAD

A good night's sleep is often the difference between an enjoyable camping trip and a lousy one. Skip the foam pad, carry a few extra ounces, and make sure you sleep soundly. Purchase the Therm-a-Rest Staytek Standard Long camping mattress ($64)—not the three-quarter length—and you're sleeping like a soccer mom on Prozac—800–531–9531.

BACKPACK

The debate here is "internal frame" vs. "external frame." Externals (those packs with the metal bars on them) hold your gear more efficiently, but they're heavier, less compact, and far less comfortable. Better to go internal, with the Dana Design Glacier ($339), a 5,500-cubic-inch bad boy that packs a financial punch—but will last longer than you—888–357–3262.

TWO-PART KEY CHAIN:
Put your house and car keys on one side, and everything else on the other.

STOVE

There's a heap of choices, but again let's make this simple: purchase the MSR RapidFire ($42.50). It's an IsoButane stove, and you'll need IsoButane canisters ($4 each) to use it, but the RapidFire is the most reliable, user-friendly, and maintenance-free stove available. Period. 800–877–9677.

FLASHLIGHT

Actually, don't get a flashlight; get a Petzl Zoom headlamp ($37.80). Yes, they look dorky. But fashion doesn't exist in the woods, and what a joy it is to have both hands free when you're doing something at night—like cooking, gathering firewood, or reading a book— 800–282–7673.

KNIFE

Swiss Army knives are fine for Boy Scouts, but 90 percent of those silly gizmos go unused. Get a *real* knife. Consider the Buck Knives Folding Hunter ($57), a hefty, four-inch, straight-edge blade that's as useful for spreading peanut butter as skinning deer—800–326–2825.

MISCELLANY

Water filters, all of them, are pains in the ass—they're slow and need constant maintenance. Instead, take Potable Aqua iodine pills ($6.99), and add some Kool-Aid crystals to mask the flavor. Also needed: two Nalgene wide-mouthed water bottles ($6.50 each); MSR Alpine Cookset ($32.75); T-Mos One Cup Brewer coffee maker ($2.99); Coghlan's waterproof Fire Sticks ($1.99); Sawyer Products Travel Soap ($1.59); and maps, compass, first-aid kit, mugs, and bowls. All of these can be purchased from Campmor—800-CAMP-MOR. Finally, bring a Frisbee ($7). It's great fun—and doubles as a dinner plate.

Note: Most gear listed can be ordered through "GearFinder" at Backpacker *magazine's Web site (www.bpbasecamp.com).*

HAMMACHER SCHLEMMER CATALOG:
Even if you can't afford to buy the personal submarine, it's fun to find out it exists.

THE WIDE-SLOT TOASTER:
Because by the year 2010 a bagel will bigger than the human head.

CHAPTER 10

BEHIND THE WHEEL

Q. DO I REALLY HAVE TO PAY MY PARKING TICKETS?

Parking tickets are the runty stepchildren of the traffic-violation family: no one gives them even an iota of respect. Any rapscallion who receives one is just as apt to shred it as to remit. Is this sensible? Can an unpaid parking ticket result in huge fines, brusque impoundment or even . . . prison?

The good news is you'll be spared hard time on the rock pile. What's more, you can ignore the threats from collection agencies—unless your fines hit Willie Nelson/IRS levels, your credit rating won't be affected. Still, the parking ticket is no pseudoinfraction that's useful only when the Charmin runs out. There are several issues to consider if you have a congenital inability to get back to the meter on time.

1. Parking ticket enforcement has become a pretty thorough science. Lockheed Martin IMS, a subsidiary of the defense industry behemoth, assists dozens of large cities in tracking down scofflaws. They've set up a network with roughly fifty DMVs around the

A DECENT CAR STEREO:
A must for any decent road trip.

country to access driver information. One of those cities, no doubt, is near you.

Whether or not one particular municipality will follow up at all depends on where you were ticketed. If the ticket was in-state, the state could withhold your registration renewal until it's paid—but if it's your own vehicle, with out-of-state plates, it's not often you'll be chased down.

2. Don't dump it on Hertz. Rental car companies know who had what car, when. Not to mention the fact that they have your credit card number. The rental company will sometimes pay the ticket and simply charge your card. No muss, no fuss—but you're stuck with the bill.

3. Das Boot? Nein. The Denver Boot—that hideous yellow contraption that renders a car impossible to drive—is scary but rarely employed. The fact is, the Boot exposes cities to liability. What if the ticket's been paid or improperly recorded? What if they put it on the wrong car? Not too keen a PR tactic.

The bottom line? If you're close to home, start writing the check. If you're afar, the circular file just might beckon.

WINNING AT THE NEW CAR DEALERSHIP

If you've ever shopped for a new car, you know the dealer's act—the one where he'd have you believe that the fair price of that shiny baby is some sort of enigma that you need a doctorate in Car Sales to unravel. It ain't so. With just a little homework, you can save a ton of cash as well as all that god-awful haggling time that makes you feel like a scumball.

1. EDUCATE YOURSELF.
Start by arming yourself with three pieces of information:

◆ the invoice price of the model car you covet

◆ the "destination charge" (a glorified delivery fee) of that car

◆ both the wholesale and retail costs of all the options you desire

These figures will tell you exactly what the dealer paid for the vehicle (by adding the invoice, destination, and wholesale costs of options) and can be obtained by mail or fax from many services, including Consumer Reports (800–269–1139) and on-line companies such as PriceCostco Auto Program (www.pricecostcoautoprogram.com), CarSmart (www.carsmart.com) and Kelley Blue Book (www.kbb.com). Another option is IntelliChoice — the Complete Car Cost Guide, which can be ordered at 800–227–2665 or accessed on the Web at (http://www.intellichoice.com). IntelliChoice compares ownership value for cars and trucks based on the cost to own over five years versus the purchase price.

2. REMOVE ALL EMOTION.

Easier said than done, but you really must go to the dealership with your game face on. Remember, you don't have to buy a car today. Make sure the salesperson understands this. Absolutely refuse to start discussing financing or your trade-in (these are merely diversionary tactics to confuse you).

After a test drive in something you like, it's tough to get back into the rolling rust bucket that served you through college. You'll want to sign away your first born right then and there. Don't do it! A salesperson's easiest prey is a buyer who has fallen in love with the car. Half of the negotiating process is psychology, so appear disinterested, and make them dance for you rather than the other way around.

3. KNOW WHAT YOU CAN AFFORD.

Even after you've found what you're looking for, the salesperson always seems to show you another model with a few more goodies that's only a thousand dollars more. While it seems easy to justify over the loan period, all of that money adds up while the car is depreciating. Have a limit in mind on the most you are willing to part with, and be sure things such as tax, title, and other add-ons are included.

Avoid items such as paint sealant, snazzy wheels, pinstriping, and the like. Remember that the dealer has to make a profit on each of these: paint sealant, for instance, is nothing more than a good coat of wax, and many cars have a rust warranty anyway. There is nothing a dealer can add to the car that you can't do later and probably for less money. Avoid cars that are billed as "anniversary" or "limited edition." These vehicles are often dolled up with special paint, wheels, and badging, which do nothing but stroke your ego. And whatever you do, don't let the dealer talk you down from the sticker price—talk up from the bottom line you've calculated.

The dealer's quote—and your negotiation range—should be the difference between the wholesale and retail costs of your options. Tell him that all you want to know is the lowest markup over invoice he will accept, write down the figure, and leave. In and out. Repeat this process at a couple of other dealerships, and go with the best offer. A fair markup is from two to five percent of invoice, depending on how popular your vehicle is.

4. USE A REPUTABLE DEALERSHIP.

There are salespeople who still say, "What will it take to sell you the car right now?" That's your first sign to make tracks. Ask your friends about their car-purchase experiences, or call the Attorney General's office or Better Business Bureau to find out if any complaints have been filed. Some salespeople are wizards at producing a convincing-looking deal, and you end up paying more than you think somewhere down the road. Keep the old saying in mind: If it seems too good to be true, it is.

5. WATCH THOSE TRADE-IN PRICES.

When it's time to trade in Ol' Bessie, most people expect to get the retail price for their trade and the new car for a couple bucks over invoice. Not gonna happen. The dealer needs to make money on your trade as well as the new vehicle they are going to sell you—that's how they stay in business. If you're really concerned about getting the most for your old car, stick a "for sale" sign in the window, and park it in your front yard.

ASKING DIRECTIONS:
Face it, you don't always know where you're going.

LOOK BEFORE LEASING

She whispers your name each time you go by. There are several weeks of sidelong glances. Then, one day, you stop. You have to get closer. See her for yourself. See just what it is you might be missing.

"Just looking," you tell yourself as you inspect the shiny black sport utility vehicle. With a $38,000 sticker price, you could never afford the down payment. But while you're lamenting, the guy standing next to you might be driving away with her, and he might not even have enough money in the bank to buy a tank of gas. He might be leasing.

About 30 percent of all new cars sold in the United States are now leased, nearly twice as many as five years ago. And experts predict the number will keep growing as cars become more expensive to buy. While leasing isn't for everyone, if you lust for new cars, drive less than fifteen thousand miles a year, and are well versed in the fine art of smooth talk, it can prove a smart option.

It sounds basic, but the most important part of leasing a car is doing your homework. If you're not careful, you could wind up paying thousands more than you should for the privilege of driving a new car; know what you're doing and you could be driving down Easy Street.

While financing a car purchase will allow you to own it in three or four years, leasing is basically like renting an apartment on wheels. You pay your monthly fee, and in a couple of years you return the keys and move out. The most appealing part of leasing is that often

AAA CARD:
About fifty dollars yields you free maps, jumps on demand, and all the tows they can eat.

NITTY GRITTY INFO

Look Before You Lease
A pamphlet from the Federal Trade Commission, available by calling 202–326–3224 or on the commission's Web page at http://www.ftc.gov

Expert Lease Pro
Software that compares leasing and buying. Available from Chart Software at 800–418–8450. Analyses and evaluations of all manufacturer-offered leases. From IntelliChoice on the Internet at www.intellichoice.com.

The Reality Checklist for Vehicle Leasing
Developed by the Consumer Task Force for Automotive Issues. Write to: The Reality Checklist Project, P.O. Box 7648, Atlanta, GA 30357–0648. Also available from the Missouri attorney general's consumer hotline at 800–392–8222.

Federal Reserve Board Vehicle Leasing Worksheet
Available by calling the Fed's public information office at 202–452–3000.

you get to drive a car that you could probably never afford to buy. Because car dealers are eager to lease (people who lease are guaranteed return customers—they have to come back to the showroom eventually to return the car, and will likely need another one), they typically offer attractive incentives.

So how do you find the best lease? Easy. The ones that give the most bang for your buck are typically those with an interest rate below the amount you'd pay if you were to finance a purchase. The best deals often are available at the end of the quarter.

Ready to drive that Explorer off the lot? Watch out for speed traps: the biggest problems with leases are those dreaded "hidden costs" that are buried in the fine print and can balloon your monthly payment way beyond what the advertised price suggests. Example: Most leases restrict driving to twelve thousand or fifteen thousand miles per year. That might sound fine when you're sitting behind the wheel in the showroom, but if you get a new job that's twenty miles farther away or you drive halfway way across the country to see your baby nephew, you may find yourself quickly over the limit—and taking it in the shorts for as much as twenty-five cents for each extra mile.

Another trap is additional charges for "excess wear and tear," a term that is rarely spelled out in the contract and that may include anything from worn tires to a scratch in the paint. And there also can be unexpected down payments, penalties for early termination of the lease, and even restrictions on driving in a foreign country. Most of these hidden costs are not calculated until the lease expires—on purpose, so you can blissfully tool along and not realize you're going broke.

For those without the stomach for hardball games at the auto dealership, the government is stepping in to make things easier. The Federal Reserve Board recently proposed revising the U.S. Consumer Leasing Act to require that dealers disclose and itemize certain information to consumers. Although the rules aren't effective until October, the Fed has designed a worksheet for consumers to use as they go lease shopping, and some dealerships already are ponying up additional information.

The new rules require dealers to disclose key aspects of a lease, including the total amount the consumer will pay over the lifetime of the lease, down payments, monthly payment calculations, and potential extra charges. The government is also cracking down on TV ads that tout "no down payment" or "only a penny down" when, in fact, drivers are most times required to pay other fees before they can drive away in their new car or truck. The problem is that those "other fees"

NAPKINS IN THE GLOVEBOX:
For sticky fingers, long-range sneezes, or her angry tears.

scroll at the bottom of the television screen in miniscule print that looks like hieroglyphics and are accompanied by a voiceover that sounds like an art auctioneer. Under pressure from the Federal Trade Commission (FTC), several carmakers have agreed to stop providing critical lease information in tiny, unreadable print deals.

Be prepared—there's a ton of information out there on car leases. Advice, statistics, financial analyses, and consumer booklets are widely available through local consumer-affairs offices, the FTC, and on the Interet. Still not sure leasing is right for you? Then turn to your computer, and let it do the work. Leasing software can plug in the numbers and let your computer steer you to the best deal around.

So the next time you hear the siren song of your dream car, make sure you listen closely. You just might be able to get behind the wheel, turn up the radio, and hum along.

AUTO INSURANCE: HIGHWAY ROBBERY

Guys between the ages of eighteen and twenty-five are marked men with the automobile insurance industry. According to Insurance Information Institute statistics, they have nearly 35 percent of all accidents and are involved in almost 70 percent more accidents than women of the same age. They cost the insurance companies a lot of money—and they pay for it. Follow these five tips to minimize the bite.

1. SYMBOLISM.
Forget about the six-speaker Bose CD system for a second, and find out the "symbol" of the car that you're looking at. Every car has one—it's a classification for the estimated replacement cost of a car. Although every state has its own standards, 1995 models range in symbol from a Saturn SL (3), through a VW Jetta (10), up to Porsche 928 (a whopping 27). Submit a short list of cars to your insurance agent before you purchase—they can plug in numbers to help you make the best buy.

2. DISCOUNT SHOPPING.

Every state requires insurance companies to offer discounts for various items and situations. The problem is that you're not guaranteed to get them unless you ask. Antilock brakes, passive restraints, and airbags bring automatic discounts in most states; alarms, tracking devices, steering-wheel "clubs," and window "etching" can shave from 5 to 35 percent off your comprehensive coverage. Other potential discounts: proof of public transportation use, insuring two cars from the same household, low annual mileage, no traffic incidents over three years, and even good grades in school.

3. CHOOSING COVERAGE.

Nearly every state has compulsory insurance, which often includes damage that you do to someone else, his or her property, or to your own car if it's financed. Beyond that, there's a lot of flexibility. Use this to your advantage. If you have good health and/or disability insurance, consider minimal coverage and/or higher deductions on personal injury protection. Examine optional coverage—medical payments, collision, limited collision, and comprehensive—to see where you can afford to take a greater risk for lower premiums. Forget towing and labor coverage if you've got AAA or another roadside plan. But one place never to skimp in these litigious times: bodily injury to others or damage to their property.

A FOOTBALL IN YOUR TRUNK: You just never know when a game'll break out.

4. PARK IT.

Where you keep your car has a substantial impact on the bottom line. City, bad; suburbs, good; rural, better. If you must live in the city but use your car infrequently, find out if there is a friend's or family member's place in the suburbs where you can leave it the rest of the time. Don't overdo it, though, because insurance companies can and will reject claims if they determine fraud.

5. DOUBLE TROUBLE.

Don't get lazy when it comes to moving violations and accidents. If you are wrongfully ticketed, go to court and challenge it. Similarly, if you are not at fault in an accident, or if bad weather was a factor, you should not be assessed points on your insurance rating. Of course, the biggest way to save, ultimately, is to keep your bumper clean and ticket-free.

TALK YOUR WAY OUT OF A TICKET

It's not some freak accident (no pun intended) that car-insurance rates are generally higher for young men than any other single group of drivers. Young men have many important places to be, such as the beach or softball games, and are constantly running late, coming from other beaches and softball games. Who wouldn't understand, then, why guys are such flagrant speeders behind the wheel? The police, that's who.

The obvious solution to this quandary—obeying the law and staying out of trouble—is something only your mother would tell you. The reality is that you'll soon be blazing down the blacktop one sunny Saturday, and some Officer Friendly will want to have a little talk with you. When that happens, unless you're the officer's grandmother, there's no guaranteed way to talk your way out of it. But there *are* certain ways to improve your odds.

1. MAKE THE OFFICER FEEL SAFE AND CUSHY.

Have you seen that dashboard-camera footage of a Texas state trooper getting dragged to the roadside and killed with his own gun by three people he stopped for a traffic violation? Every police officer in the country has seen it. And it's guaranteed that this scene is playing somewhere in his mind as he's walking up to your car.

You know you're harmless; he doesn't. So you must prove this to him. Pull over quickly, turn off the car, put the keys on the dash, put your hazard lights on, and rest your hands on the top of the steering wheel. At night, turn on your interior light as well. Finally, remember that tinted windows are a nightmare for the police—they don't know if that's a sleeping infant in the backseat or Hannibal Lecter. Roll them down without being asked to. A comfortable cop is an agreeable cop.

2. DON'T FEED THE COP A LINE.

Every lame excuse you can think of has already been foisted on your officer. Everyone is late for work or picking up his mother to take her to an overdue dialysis session. Yes, it's true that as long as officers meet their summons quotas—intended to ensure they're doing their jobs instead of sleeping behind billboards—officers *are* allowed to use

USING YOUR HORN:
To remind drivers talking on their cell phones that they're actually *driving*.

their discretion in issuing tickets. But know this: your lame-ass line isn't going to do the trick.

3. MAKE LIKE GANDHI.

The fastest way to immediately get a ticket is to argue with the police officer or display any type of attitude—an approach that always strikes cops as bizarre. *You* have done something wrong and are relying only on *their* benevolence to escape a citation, yet you curse at *them*. There is no point to this, and you will always lose. Police officers report to work and are given sticks to hit people with—they have no problem putting you in your place.

4. GET TO KNOW A COP.

Dating a police officer or becoming close friends with one merely to get out of tickets might seem a little mercenary, but it works—particularly if you can use your relationship to score the little-known "courtesy card." Essentially, this is the cop equivalent of knowing the secret Masonic handshake, and it works like a Monopoly "Get Out of Jail Free" card. In New York City and elsewhere, every police officer gets several courtesy cards from the police union with the officer's shield number on them and strict instructions not to give them to some mope like their crack-addicted uncle. The unwritten rule is to let a person with one of these cards go, since they are the relative or good friend of a police officer. When you present a card like this, place it behind your license and registration, and hand it to the police officer. Don't flash it or present it right away—that's tacky.

5. DON'T TRY TO GREASE ANYONE'S PALM.

If you like being in jail, try to bribe the police officer—you'll get to go right away. Ever since internal affairs units began conducting highway sting operations to snag wayward cops, the days of the folded-up Jackson or two behind the license are gone. A cop will get more credit from his boss—and money in overtime processing your bribery arrest—than your measly twenty or forty bucks could offer him. So if you're on a date and you get pulled over, follow the tips above, and save the palm greasing for the maître d'.

A PICTURE OF AUDREY HEPBURN TAPED TO YOUR DASHBOARD: Angels bring you luck. (Keep Betty Page in your glove box for when you feel naughty.)

ROAD RULES

Buy a car, and you don't just get a car, you get a mystifying headache of epidemic proportions over which, if you're lucky, you'll spend the next decade obsessing. To help lead you through this dark tunnel of automotive ignorance, we've culled experts from across the country—people who devote lifetimes studying the minutiae of these machines—to guide you through the most troubling and nagging of car questions. Oil changes and speed traps? Strange, green, viscous fluids and flying tissue boxes? We've got your answer right here, baby.

Let's start with my brakes—they're squeaking. Does that mean they need to be replaced?
Absolutely not. While most people tend to freak out at even the slightest noise from their brakes, Bill Sauer, the founder of Automotive Information Systems in St. Paul, Minnesota, assures us that in "85 to 90 percent" of all cases, the squeaking from your brakes is not a reason to have them replaced. However, such signs should not be ignored. "You should definitely get your car inspected," Sauer advises. The squeaking is probably the result of a problem with the friction material in your brakes, a problem which can be solved by adding a pad or applying goop.

That's a relief. I also got this small dent when a local street punk threw his football into my hood. Can I knock this out myself, or will I just end up doing more damage?
That depends. A tiny ding in a rounded area—the curved top of a fender, say—can be thwacked out quite nicely if you place a broom handle or dowel rod against the dent and, using a rubber mallet, gently pound the handle or rod from the underside. Generally, though, the paint will crack and need refinishing.

How about a dent with a sharp crease in the metal and cracked paint on the surface?
Those are tougher. For this job, auto-parts stores sell (for about ten dollars) the brilliantly named "dent puller"—a rod with an expandable fixture on one end and a heavy weight on the other. After drilling a hole in the center of the blemish, you can use this tool to cajole a big dent back to its original shape. A caveat, though: the hole

TWO DOLLARS IN CHANGE:
With tolls, as with heavy dates and final exams, it pays to be prepared.

then has to be welded, ground down and painted—all of which is better left to the body-shop boys.

Well, what about the big stuff? How can I tell if my mechanic is ripping me off?
Unfortunately, not very easily. According to Donna Wagner, the director of operations for the Car Care Council, "There's really no pat answer. It's a 'buyer beware' market, and the customer has the responsibility to ask the right questions."

Isn't there a Better Business Bureau (BBB) for mechanics?
No.

That doesn't seem right, does it?
Nope. Of course, you can always give your local BBB a call and see if the mechanic-to-be is on the up-and-up. Or, as Joe Albanese, Jr., owner of Joe's Service Station in Garfield, New Jersey, advises, shop around and be cynical: "You want to always see the old parts . . . the ones that were actually pulled from the car."

What does it mean if my car starts leaking green fluid?
You mean those growing puddles of green liquid you sometimes see beneath a parked car's front end that look an awful lot like what you threw up that one night after playing "Vermouth or Dare" at the fraternity house?

Yeah, that.
That's antifreeze, and that innocent puddle is a major hazard. You should see an auto specialist as soon as possible. According to David Solomon, publisher of *Nutz & Boltz*, an automotive/consumer newsletter from Baltimore, "It could be a bad radiator cap or a cracked recovery container, which would cause a leak. Or perhaps it's a bad hose, a head gasket, or the radiator itself—it could be any of the above."

Isn't that green juice bad for the environment, too?
You betcha. That stuff washes down sewers and contaminates groundwater. Not to mention, says Solomon, that it's decidedly Fido-unfriendly: "The smell of antifreeze is sweet and attracts animals. All it takes is a couple laps of the stuff, and you've got a dead animal."

ONE SMALL CAN OF NU-CAR SPRAY:
Get that "new car" scent, without that "new car" price tag.

Speaking of viscous liquids, how often should I change my oil?
Change your oil every three thousand miles. That's easy to remember because it's the length of our country. If you wait any longer, you'll have dirty oil coursing through your engine, and its parts will become dirty and age faster than Keith Richards.

Should I take it to one of those ten-minute, $19.95 oil-change chains, or am I better off at a "real" mechanic or a dealer?
Jiffy Lube is probably safer, just because all they want to do is change your oil. An enterprising dealership or mechanic may tell you that your seventh fetzer valve needs to be replaced when, in fact, there's no such thing.

Do you think I should just learn to change my own oil?
Definitely. Watch closely at the beginning of Billy Joel's "Uptown Girl" video, and keep an eye out for the moment when Christie Brinkley realizes that she's in love with Billy. Strangely, it isn't love at first sight for the leggy model and the lemuresque crooner. The cover girl falls for the grease monkey once she realizes he knows how to change the oil in a car. Moral of the video: something perverse about beautiful women, oil, and the most important car-maintenance skill you'll ever learn.

Cool. So how do I do it?
Easy. First, drive to a gas station somewhere near you. (Some composite driveway surfaces can be seriously damaged by oil, and it's always helpful to have a trained professional nearby.) It also helps to run your engine for a few minutes to warm the oil before draining it. After removing (in this order) the oil cap, oil filter, and oil plug, make sure that the oil drains completely; old oil that remains in the tank can make the clean oil much less efficient. As the oil pours luxuriously from your car, put some of it on your finger. If it's really gritty, that means you need to change your oil more frequently.

From there, the process is fairly simple. Just pour the new bottle in. (Your car will thank you if you use new drain-plug washers.) Once you think the tank is full, run the engine for a minute, and then check again to make sure. And remember, when the entire operation is complete, wipe your hand on your forehead. While the obsidian streaks may seem aesthetically repulsive to you, they are a badge of manliness.

All right, let's shift gears here. . . . Hey, stop that. No automotive puns.

MANUAL TRANSMISSION: Automatic is for grannies and wussies.

Sorry. Anyway, is it true that a tissue box placed on the rear window sill can kill me if I make a sudden stop and it flies forward?
No. Along with crop circles and alien-abduction ephemera, the legend of the "Snot Rags of Death" is one of those urban myths that has been recycled through the generations. "The problem isn't Kleenex boxes, it's anything with real mass—stereo speakers, or a pet," says Solomon. "With a pet back there, it's guaranteed death or severe injury to the animal. I've witnessed situations where the pet became a serious projectile—[killing] the pet and [injuring] the driver." He adds frostily, "And, for heaven's sake, don't put the pet in your lap. It's a good way to crush it."

Eech. Speaking of which, should I put a seat belt on my dog?
Yeah, and maybe you can have him read the map for you, too. . . . No, seat belts don't work on pups. The solution is a pet harness, available for about seventeen dollars for discerning drivers looking to keep the family mutt from meeting an untimely end. "They're very similar to the harnesses you see on dogs being led on a leash," says Amanda Bevers, a salesperson at Pet Expo, an on-line pet-supply emporium. "You slip the harness around your dog and then slide the seat belt through the loop on the back." Be aware that harnesses of any size are impractical for the family feline, which is just as well, says Bevers: "I can't imagine any cat tolerating one."

A SPILL-PROOF COFFEE MUG WITH AN ENORMOUS BASE: Useful and funky.

Speaking of accidents, I've heard that certain-colored cars are involved in more accidents than others. Is this true?
In a sense, yes. Insurance companies have determined that light yellow cars are the most visible and therefore the safest, while a deep, midlife-crisis red is the hardest to see and thus the most dangerous. But really, it's all about demographics.

How should I deal with speed traps?
Forget your fuzzbuster. It's essentially good at telling you when you just got nailed. Better to be armed with information from Andy Warner's WWW Speedtrap Registry (www.speedtrap.com/speedtrap/), an Internet site that logs the worst traps in the country.

OK, I'll slow down. Then how about downshifting—is it bad for my transmission?
No. Actually, a driver should downshift, according to Miriam Schottland, director of the Driving Company in Washington, D.C.,

as long as it's done properly. "Downshifting is necessary to keep your engine in the proper power band so your car can continue to be gas-efficient. If you're in too high a gear, you don't burn fuel properly."

So what's the right way to downshift?
"The trick is to hit the throttle when the clutch is engaged so the rpm's rise, and then the transition down is smooth."

What does it mean if my car keeps pulling to one side on flat roads?
According to noted car designer/entrepreneur John DeLorean (yes, *that* John DeLorean), when your car is pulling to a side like that it means one of two things: gross misinflation of the tire, or more likely, really bad wheel alignment. If it *is* the wheel alignment, DeLorean tells *P.O.V.* reassuringly that "most tire shops can fix that in about an hour." Thanks, John!

How about starting my car in cold weather? Is there a right way?
Yes. The first thing you should do is turn off all electrically powered equipment like the radio and lights. If the temperature is below ten degrees Fahrenheit, press the accelerator pedal down twice; push it once if it's warmer. Then, keeping your foot off the accelerator, start your baby up. If the engine doesn't catch within fifteen seconds or so, turn off the ignition. Wait about thirty seconds. Once again, push the accelerator to the floor. (Never pump it; you'll flood the engine.) After the engine is started, allow it to warm up for thirty seconds, and then give the accelerator a quick stomp and you're off.

What about idling? Is it more gas-efficient to let a car idle for fifteen minutes while I'm waiting for someone, or should I turn it off instead?
You should leave the tardy asshole behind, is what you should do. But assuming you're willing to wait, it's best to turn that baby off, says Doug Crowhurst, vice president of Northern California Diagnostic Laboratories, a licensed emissions-testing lab that also studies alternative fuel sources. "Let's say you're driving to a friend's house, and the car is already warm," he says. "Turn it off. If, on the other hand, the car has been cold for more than an hour or so, leave it going to warm up the engine," as it's a bad idea to shut off the ignition before the engine has had a chance to purr. The best bet, of course, is to trim your circle of friends to those who are punctual.

How about breaking in a new car?

Don't sweat it. Back in the bad old days, when engine tolerances varied by model, cars had a specific "break-in period," during which they could not be driven above certain speeds for a certain number of miles. These days, though, most cars come to the dealer preconditioned. Bearing that in mind, it is still suggested that you take it easy on your car for a few hundred miles by varying speeds and not doing anything radical with the brakes or accelerator. Also, it is vital to change your oil after the first two thousand miles or so. Otherwise, just sit back and enjoy the drive.

I don't want to buy chains. What else can I do, inexpensively, to give my car better traction during an icy winter?

Snow tires, baby. That's the advice offered by Mark Cox, director of the Bridgestone Winter Driving School in Steamboat Springs, Colorado. Cox agrees that chains are pointless (unless you're already stuck in a gully), and all-season tires are merely a marketing ploy. But by using a set of snows four months out of the year, you can have your summer tires last 33 percent longer.

Other tips that won't cost you a penny: Make no sudden turning or braking movements—in other words, slow everything down, and drive like you're in a David Lynch movie. And when braking in a hurry, the best method, according to Cox, is "threshold braking," where you press the suckers until the moment just prior to lockup, then ease off slightly and hold as the car gradually slows. And from the "debunking myths" file: while sand or kitty litter is good to spread under your tires for traction, toting its weight can be dangerous when turning and braking; next time you're stuck, try sticking your floor mats beneath the tires.

Is there really any difference between 89, 91, and 93 octane? Does it make any difference to my car?

The definitive answer: maybe. Some high-powered engines will knock and pang and spit and spew other onomatopoeia with anything less than 93 octane gas. But unless your car makes such noises, there's no reason to use anything but the lowest-octane gas available, according to Ignacio Mas, owner of Mas Automotive in Moorpark, California. "Play it by ear," Mas says. "My wife has a '96 Honda and uses the regular stuff with no problem. But there are some cars—we see a lot of Dodge Caravans with V-6s in them—that need to use a high octane." It varies throughout the country, too, Mas says, as hot and hilly environments require more power from a car's gasoline. Another nugget of advice: before upping the ante with higher-octane gas, try using a different brand.

Is it bad for my car to give someone else a jump?

No. Nothing bad can happen to your car or battery by being the jumper. In fact, according to Kenny Morse, known to Los Angeles–area radio and television audiences as Mr. Traffic, it's bad karma *not* to stop and share your juice with a distressed fellow driver. "If you see someone broken down and don't give them a jump," Morse says, "you're going to come back in your next life as a Hyundai."

Well then, how do I use jumper cables without electrocuting myself?

If you want to jump a car and not come out looking like Don King, it helps to wear rubber gloves. Put *something* rubber on your fingers, anyway. (Perhaps you've got some latex in your wallet?) Then turn on the jumper's engine, and check which battery ends are positive and which are negative; don't guess. Connect the clamps to the dead battery first, and lay the other two clamps on the ground *separately* (italics in this case meaning, "very important"). Connect negative to negative and positive to positive—the order in which you do this makes no difference—and turn the key in the dead car. Everything should work just fine, but if you happen to see flames, run.

I bought the Club last month. Did I just waste my money, or does it really work?

You didn't exactly waste your forty dollars. According to Police Sergeant Derek Glenn of Newark, New Jersey—a city widely recognized for the dubious honor of Car Theft Capital of the World—"The Club is effective in helping to stop someone who is not serious about his car theft." He says you're best off incorporating two or three antitheft devices to add precious seconds to the car thief's "get-the-hell-outta-here" time—something every thief relies on.

You mean other devices like that LoJack thing?

Yeah, although the basic system costs $595, that LoJack thing's actually pretty effective. With regards to LoJack, the onboard tracking device that allows police to track down stolen cars, Sergeant Glenn sounds like a paid advertisement: "In 1989 Newark had fifteen thousand cars stolen. Today that number is half of that, because of devices

YOUR OWN SQUEEGEE: For a couple bucks, you will always be the master of your car's domain.

like the LoJack system. With LoJack we can find and track the vehicles with a much higher recovery rate."

Couldn't I just pull the spark plugs instead?
Well, you could, but actually getting under the hood of your car and pulling the spark plugs might be more trouble than it's worth, especially because spark plugs tend to break in half when they're not pulled properly. Then it's like trying to take the bottom half of a broken bolt out of a greasy piece of metal. No fun. Instead, try a kill switch, which you can get at a local auto parts store for less than fifty dollars; any mechanic can rig it up for you. The switch, which can be hidden almost anywhere in the car, will cut off all its electrical systems, make it impossible to start, and is a pain in the ass for any thief.

Well then, how about I just buy a car that I don't care about being stolen, like one those three-hundred-dollar Army Jeeps.
The U.S. military has many fine traditions. Jabbing a pin into the chest of rookie officers is one. Another is paying a lot of money for cheap hardware. Morse sums it up: "Those cars are pieces of shit." What he means is they're OK as long as you're not going to be driving on surfaces like, say, pavement. "They're meant to transport troops," Morse says of the surplus vehicles, "not survive a rotary circle."

FIRST-AID KIT:
Toss in the trunk
and hope you
never see it
again.

CHAPTER 11

HEADING OUT

Q: HOW DOES AN UNCOUTH ANIMAL SURVIVE A FANCY DATE?

This one's for guys who ball up their cloth napkins and place them in the middle of their plates after eating. You guys, the ones who hold their soup spoons with grips better suited to tennis racquets, we're talking to you, too. Your date probably read *Table Manners for Teenagers* back in junior high. It's time you learn that proper table etiquette is more than just using the correct fork.

MODERATION: Postcollege drinking 'til you drop is *so* unattractive.

FIRST IMPRESSIONS

What works at Sigma Chi may not fly at Le Cirque. If you're a beer drinker, drink from a glass, not the bottle. Sit up straight, don't tip back in your chair, and (yes, your grandmother was right) keep your elbows off the table. Leave the cellular phone at home. And amateur dental hygienists take note: no toothpicks at the table.

SILVERWARE 101

When your place is set with more than one fork and knife, begin with the piece on the outside and work your way in. Hold the knife or fork with the thumb and three fingers, keeping the index finger extended on the handle. When cutting meat, the prongs of the fork should point down, not up like a shovel or scoop. And if you're old enough to cut your own meat, you're old enough to know that you should cut one piece at a time rather than dice your steak into bite-size pieces all at once. The same policy applies to dinner rolls. You're not making a sandwich here, so break off and butter one small piece of bread at a time.

THE SEMIOTICS OF CUTLERY

Being a good waiter means never having to ask, "Are you still working on that?" Imagine your plate as the face of a clock. While you are eating, don't rest your silverware on the tablecloth. Instead, rest the fork and knife handles at seven and five o'clock, respectively, placing the fork over the knife, prongs down. Waiters will recognize this as the "rest" position. When you are finished eating, place the knife and fork, prongs down, side by side on the plate with the handles at four o'clock, a.k.a. the "I am finished" position.

RELAX

Dating veterans will tell you that a superlative dinner partner is someone who sustains eye contact, doesn't flirt with the waitress, and is a good conversationalist, i.e., doesn't just talk about himself but asks open-ended questions and listens to your responses. If you've got those three down, your date will most likely forgive a lapse in proper fork usage. Just try not to drink out of the finger bowl.

SCORING PRIME STADIUM SEATS

Unfortunately, not all of us know someone who is a corporate tool for Don Kirschner. Why would we want to? Because people who work inside the ticket industry are the surest bet for getting the best available ticket to a U2 concert or Major League playoff game. If you know one of these blessed souls, stop reading and go buy them a burger (read: kiss up). Otherwise, here are some ways to increase your odds of landing in the front row.

1. CONSIDER A BROKER.

While not legal in every state, ticket brokers can be the best way to land prime eats, and they're guaranteed. Brokers deal with both pro-moters and venues to nap up the choicest seats and then resell them to the public for face value plus a "service" fee, which can range anywhere from $7.50 to a whopping $200, depending upon whether you're looking to see a ballet in Seattle or the Super Bowl. If price isn't an object, it's the way to go: most brokers will even fax you a seating chart to show you in advance exactly where you'll be sitting.

2. TIMING IS EVERYTHING.

Finding out the exact moment tickets go on sale is the key to getting good ones. First, find out dates for the concert, play, or sporting event you want to see. One great source for this is *Pollstar*, a trade magazine with a handy Web site (http://www.pollstar.com) that contains reg-ular updates on tours. Then call your local venue every day, and ask them when tickets go on sale. Here's a little-known secret: when you first call, operators will tell you in a friendly voice that they do not know when the tickets are going on sale. But one day you will call, and the operator will be clipped and short, and curtly assert, "We don't have any information!" *Bingo*. You know that they have just been told the tickets go on sale the next morning. It never fails. In the case of a play, keep in mind that theaters usually keep a certain number of prime tickets, called house seats, in reserve (in case Barry Diller calls and wants to get in to see *Rent*, for example). But almost all house tickets that aren't claimed by the body celebrity hours in advance are dumped back into the ticket pool via computer—mean-

your request, and seconds later you've got your map, complete with points of interest. Zoom in, zoom out, and print. There are even driving directions. Toss out your frayed Rand McNally.

The Weather Channel
www.weather.com
Enter a city, any city, and you've got your forecast, plus extras—weather maps, travel conditions, pollen counts, and a glossary with definitions of weather terms, from "absolute zero" to "wind shear," that you've heard lots of times but never understood.

www.sidewalk.com
Boston, Chicago, Denver, Houston, New York, San Diego, San Francisco, Seattle, Sydney, Twin Cities, Washington. . . . movies, restaurants, events, arts & music, sports, places to go.

www.boulevards.com
If your looking for the best spots for late-night grub in the city (or other survival tips for today's urban hipster), Boulevards offers an alternative guide to cities in the U.S. and abroad.

ing that by buying a ticket *exactly* forty-eight hours before a sched-
uled show time, you may end up with one of the best seats in the
house.

3. PHONING IS BETTER THAN GOING.

Those idiots who are still camping out for three days in front of the
box office are wasting time—ticketing for long lines is now regularly
done by lottery, so being first in line doesn't mean a thing anymore.
Your best bet is at work. Get ten friends in your office to call five
minutes before tickets go on sale, and work it like a radio contest: the
first person to get through orders the maximum number of tickets.
Going to a popular record store is pointless: even if you're third in
line, by the time you get to buy one ticket, thousands may have
already been sold at other stores and by phone. And that doesn't even
take into account scalpers, who put the kids who work at such stores
on payroll; they in turn hog the best tickets before they wait on a single customer.

4. NETWORK.

Knowing someone—anyone—with access to great seats is the easiest
way to get one. Before a single ticket is sold to us poor slobs who
actually pay to see an event, tickets are swiped by promoters, performers, venue executives, press agents, and ticket sellers to hand out
to their friends and family members. Dating a secretary at
TicketMaster or interning at *Rolling Stone* could do more for your
odds of getting tenth-row tickets to Springsteen than spending a
week's pay at the box office.

5. BEWARE OF THE SCALPING GAME.

Remember that scalping isn't just like organized crime—it *is* an
organized crime. Trying to buy or sell a ticket in front of an actual
venue is now considered insane: cops are everywhere, and even if you
do manage to get a ticket, chances are it's counterfeit. Professional
scalpers who can actually deliver the goods work underground and
on a strictly word-of-mouth basis. Ask around to find one, and make
sure that you trust the person who's making the recommendation.

It's all very arduous, to be sure, but if you want to get in, you do
what you have to.

TALL TAILGATING

It's game day. And you've scored tickets. What's the first thing that comes to mind? All right, the second? You can hear it rising up from the depths of your soul like a primal chant, beating in tandem with your heart: tail-gate, tail-gate, tail-gate.

So are you ready to rumble? Unless you're going to one of those fancy-schmancy team-sponsored tent parties, there's some planning to be done, son, options to consider, possibilities to examine.

Tailgating, after all, is the ultimate male rite of expression. It separates the Bud Boys from Single-Malt Men. So while you don't want to get bogged down with a lot of things to pack, you know that a six-pack and a bag of chips just ain't gonna cut it. Consider this basic checklist:

FOOD

The Official Food of the U.S. Tailgate would have to be the burger. It's easy to buy and, unlike our good friend Mr. Chicken, grilling takes minutes. Hot dogs are easy, too, though for some, beer burps are a consequence to consider here. And like virtually everything else, tailgating has definitely edged upscale—it's no longer blasphemy to consider steaks or lobsters to throw on the grill (don't forget the utensils if you go that route.) Essentials include beer pretzels, chips, dips, and salsas; mustard and mayo. Also, remember to set aside some of the goods if you plan to continue after the game.

IBUPROFEN: Goes great with water. Don't leave home without it.

DRINKS

This depends entirely on where you stand on the evolutionary chart. Late teens: Bud and Everclear Pure Grain Punch; early twenties: ice beer and Dewar's; in your *P.O.V.* prime: Guinness and Royal Lochnager with a big fat Cohiba. Whatever your pleasure, keep in mind that you're responsible for taking in or throwing out anything you bring. So a quarter-keg of beer is nifty in the parking lot; flasks usually go undetected later on. A gallon of water is always a good idea, and no matter what, don't forget the bottle opener.

LOCATION

Obviously, near the parking attendants or security hut would be stupid. Consider where the sun is in relation to the stadium, and decide whether you need it or its shadow. Of higher importance of course is, Where's the Porta-John? Pissing on other people's cars is a definite tailgate faux pas.

Things not to forget: radio, matches, plastic cups, paper plates, a blanket, and a thermos if it's cold, ice if it's warm, plus the Number One Most Obvious Thing, a football. It wouldn't be a tailgate without tossin' the old pigskin.

Tailgating around the country takes on amazing regional zeal. Everybody's is the rowdiest, craziest, wildest, best in these here U-nited States. We'll let you be the judge:

NEW YORK

TAILGATE TYPE: The Goombah Gorge

WHAT THEY EAT: "They're eating and drinking just about everything out there," says Bill Smith, assistant director of marketing for the New York Giants. "It's not just hot dogs and Budweiser anymore." Sausage 'n' peppers is numero uno among the cognoscenti, but anything Italianized will do, such as mozzarella burgers or hot dogs with red onion sauce. Whatever it is, bigger is always better.

WHAT THEY DRINK: Veterans drink Gallo Rosso right outta the jug, but anyone who goes to the game via the Jersey Turnpike is usually inspired by the flying neon Budweiser eagle near Exit 14. Bud really is the King of Beers at the Meadowlands.

THE PLACE TO BE: If you're on the waiting list for Giants' season tickets, you'll have to tailgate in the parking lot with the rest of the commoners for at least fifteen years before being admitted to the Touchdown Club tent. According to Rusty Hawley, vice president of marketing for the Giants, season-ticket holders pay an extra seventy-five dollars per game to rub elbows with Dan Reeves and the boys, play virtual-reality games, and eat like kings.

PRE-POST-TAIL STATS: "The Touchdown Club is a cool idea," says fan Diego Chavez, "but there's something queasy about it being so fancy and organized. It doesn't feel like tailgating."

TWO CLEAN JOKES:

Everyone likes to laugh.

BOSTON

TAILGATE TYPE: The Boston Pee Party

WHAT THEY EAT: New England clam bake (throw lobsters, steamer clams, mussels, and corn in a pot, and boil on top of a barbecue).

WHAT THEY DRINK: The pregame feast is usually more of a brunch, says Dan Kraft, vice president of marketing and sales for the Patriots. "I'd say 40 percent of the fans show up three to four hours prior to the game to drink bloody Marys and champagne mimosas before the game." Throughout the day, however, Sam Adams flows like water in Beantown.

THE PLACE TO BE: Within field goal's reach of a Porta-John. "I had to walk a mile to take a piss," says visiting Redskins fan Dion Morreale. "People were pissing everywhere."

PRE-POST-TAIL STATS: "It's an all-day affair" says Morreale. "But it seemed like there were a lot of families there, so it was kind of mellow compared to a Redskins tailgate."

MIAMI

TAILGATE TYPE: Latin Fiesta

WHAT THEY EAT: Rhett Ticconi, promotions coordinator for the Miami Dolphins, says that tailgating at Joe Robbie Stadium is quite a gastronomic scene. "People are out there making black beans and rice over sternos to have with their roasted chickens and grilled steaks."

WHAT THEY DRINK: Bacardi rum is everywhere, although pina coladas and strawberry daiquiris are pretty lame without a blender to plug in. The beers of choice are Heineken and Coors Light.

THE PLACE TO BE: Ticconi says the franchise set up a general-admission tent in the parking lot to offer shelter from the Miami sun. "Sports Town opens three hours before each game, and there we serve just about every kind of food imaginable—we have the most diverse population here."

PRE-POST-TAIL STATS: "The tent's a great deal," says Dolphins fan Jose Perez. "They have everything there for you, because who wants to have to plan things to bring when it's really hot out?"

**FREQUENTING
ONE BAR:**

Create a place
where everybody
knows your name.

NEW ORLEANS

TAILGATE TYPE: Big-Easy Experience

WHAT THEY EAT: Mike Sullivan, general manager of concessions at
the Louisiana Superdome, says "Our food can't be beat—pan-fried
Creole crabcakes, cajun-barbecued pork sandwiches, southern-fried
chicken, and chicken-andouille gumbo."

WHAT THEY DRINK: Locals will tell you the beers of choice are
Bud on tap or the New Orleans microbrew favorites Abita or Dixie.

THE PLACE TO BE: There is no proper parking lot, so the Saints
had to come up with something to offer displaced fans. "We set up
the Saints Experience, which are these tents on a bridge connecting
the Superdome to the city," says Sullivan. "We offer a variety of services for fans, such as head shaving/logo imprinting by Super Cuts
and virtual-reality sports games."

PRE-POST-TAIL STATS: Skinheads love the Super Cuts conve-
nience, and fans consider themselves the best-fed in the country.

CHICAGO

TAILGATE TYPE: Sausage City

WHAT THEY EAT: Bears fan John Sideris says a lot of people grill
sausages, which can be eaten for breakfast, lunch, or dinner. "They're
great for egg sandwiches in the morning and with peppers and onions
for lunch."

WHAT THEY DRINK: Old Milwaukee.

THE PLACE TO BE: On a party bus. "When it gets cold, and that
wind starts up, you run for cover," says Sideris.

PRE-POST-TAIL STATS: Chicagoans party hard. (Remember the
N.B.A. playoffs?) You might not want to stick around if the Bears
win.

SAN FRANCISCO

TAILGATE TYPE: Savvy Savages

WHAT THEY EAT: Lori Albrecht, director of marketing for the
49ers, says it's all about presentation. "You have people setting up

tablecloths on the hoods of their cars—replete with candles and silver platters—on one side of the aisle, and a group of guys grilling burgers with a keg on the other. It's total self-expression. It's all about just having fun."

WHAT THEY DRINK: Anchor Steam, and don't tell native Charlie Miller that San Fran fans are late starters. "That's bull, we start drinking at dawn," he crows.

THE PLACE TO BE: As far away from Charlie Miller as possible.

PRE-POST-TAIL STATS: "We have the absolute wildest, vilest, most rabid fans in the country," cheers Albrecht.

SEATTLE

TAILGATE TYPE: Communist Crapola

WHAT THEY EAT: Sandwiches in their cars. According to a spokesperson in the Seahawks' public-relations department—who asked to remain anonymous—the team and local government do not sanction tailgating. He admitted, however, that although security is high in the parking lot, flickers from renegade hibachis can be seen on premise occasionally. Yikes.

WHAT THEY DRINK: Whatever they can hide on their person.

THE PLACE TO BE: Anywhere but here!

PRE-POST-TAIL STATS: "I don't make the rules," say Mr. Anonymous, "I just tell it like it is."

A GOOD FLASK:
Is that bourbon in your pocket, or are you just glad to see me.

WINNING AT THE TRACK

The British dubbed it the "Sport of Kings," but no matter: there is perhaps nothing as truly American as a day at the racetrack. It has athletic competition. It has lots of wanton money coming and going. There's beer and hot dogs. Majestic animals and cheap smokes. Then there's the little Horatio Alger twist on it all: the idea that the smartest guy who works the hardest will walk away with the most loot.

And that's the beauty of it. Compare it with casino gambling: you basically need the brainpower of a trained chimp to find excitement in sitting on a stool and pulling a slot-machine handle. Craps is better, especially if you know what you're doing, but it still boils down to blind luck. Blackjack has a bit of skill, but while you may fancy yourself quite the player, we all know we should split our eights and double down when we're holding an eleven and the dealer shows six. Learn the basic strategy, and it becomes a slot machine with playing cards.

Now let's ponder the $3.50 marvel that is the *Daily Racing Form*—nothing but an inchoate, incomprehensible mass of numbers to most people. But it's the key to riches for you, smart guy.

Conventional wisdom holds that you'll do OK at the track by grabbing a tip sheet or newspaper and following the advice of the experts. Well, look around you after a day's races have ended. You'll see an empty grandstand littered with thousands and thousands of losing tickets. Five-dollar exacta boxes in the second race. Ten-dollar daily doubles on the eighth and ninth races. Two-dollar win tickets from the fifth race. Twenty-dollar show tickets from the third. Twenty-four-dollar trifecta wheels from the seventh. The bulk of them are bets made by following the picks of the so-called experts.

Here's the skinny: Half of the "experts" in the newspaper know no more about racing than the guy who sits next to you on the train every morning. In fact, some of the most well-respected handicappers in the country do little more than pick favorites in each race. Guess what? Favorites win about, oh, 30 percent of the time. And with heavy favorites returning only three dollars or so on a two-dollar bet, you could bet on the favorite in every race on a nine-race card and be rewarded by taking home half the money you had brought in. Sure, a conservative approach can protect your money, but it does little to grow it. And to be brutally honest, rooting home a 2–1 shot on a two-dollar ticket to show isn't exactly the most thrilling two minutes in sports. ("Whoopee! I just won ten cents.")

On the flip side, the heart-pounding excitement of watching two thoroughbreds slug it out down the stretch, knowing a head bob can mean a thousand dollars in your pocket, can't be found anywhere else—not at the casino and certainly not on the local television news, watching the lottery girl call out those six numbers (unless, of course, you happen to be holding a ticket with the first five).

How do you become part of the horse-racing action? Unless the gambling gods are smiling on you, it doesn't come from fourth-hand

A PEN:

Relieves your mental notepad and allows you to get numbers at any time of night.

hot tips from someone's Uncle Mel or by betting lucky-number combinations, gray geldings, girl jockeys, or horses named Harry. The only good thing about plays like that is a good portion of the other people at the track actually bet like that, and their stupidity translates into a better return for you. (This is the essence of pari-mutuel wagering—outsmarting everyone else in the house—and why, unlike legal casino wagering, it is actually possible to make a living betting racehorses.)

Now this is not intended as a primer for would-be professional gamblers. But if you're dead serious about quitting your day job, there are a few excellent books on handicapping, notably Steven Davidowitz's *Betting Thoroughbreds,* Andrew Beyer's *Picking Winners,* and Dave Litfin's *Expert Handicapping.* These gentlemen all spend considerable time at the racetrack doing magical things with numbers and winning money on horses; however, it should also be pointed out that they all have real jobs that call for them to actually be *at* the racetrack. It is therefore acceptable to refer to Davidowitz, Beyer, Litfin, and people of their ilk as "those lucky bastards."

Although professional horseplayers will tell you you're throwing away your money if you don't spend hours and hours researching the field (or at least buying one of their books), there is a happy medium. You needn't blindly follow the advice of newspaper tipsters with ridiculous names like Lucky Hal or The Speed Buddha, who think they know a lot more than they probably do.

What it all boils down to is information. There are an astonishing number of parallels between successfully playing the horses and successfully playing the stock market, most of them based on money management, performance, and value. Just about everything you need to know is contained in the horse player's daily bible, the *Daily Racing Form,* which lists not only the past performances for every horse but such arcane information as the fractional times of the leader in its past races, whether a horse has raced on medication or with special equipment such as blinkers or mud calks, the "speed figures" for each, the odds at which it went off, and so on. Some of this information is critical, some of it is downright confusing. Almost all of it is very, very important.

Just as in picking a stock, the important thing is to be able to know what a particular horse is capable of doing in a particular race. The fact a horse has won six straight races doesn't mean anything if all those races have been at a mile or less against less-talented claiming horses—horses that, for a price listed in the *Racing Form,* an

LEARNING TO READ
HOW TO DECIPHER THE DAILY RACING FORM

THE HORSE'S NAME. Useful if you don't want to stand at the rail yelling "Come on...six!"

THE JOCKEY'S NAME, RECORD AT THE MEET AND RECORD FOR THE YEAR. Shane Sellers is a very good jockey who's just beginning to crack the upper echelon of riders. Go by the record but also go with your gut: if you've heard of a jockey, that's a good sign. It means he's probably already won at least one prestigious race.

THE DATES OF THE HORSE'S LAST TEN RACES. A line denotes the horse is coming off a layoff. In this case, City by Night had a three-and-a-half-month break from April to August of last year, then came back and raced miserably on August 5, after which he then had a nine-month layoff. In other words, he ran once during a thirteen-month period. Obviously his trainers did excellent work with him during that time, because since coming back, he's been gangbusters.

THE NAME OF THE RACETRACK THE HORSE RACED AT AND THE CONDITION OF THE TRACK SURFACE. In this case, City by Night made his last start at Churchill Downs over a sloppy track, and his previous start there over a fast track. Prior to that he raced at Saratoga on firm turf, and at Keeneland, the Fairgrounds and Gulfstream Park on fast tracks. A guide to these abbreviations can be found in the *Form*.

INDICATES A RACE ON GRASS INSTEAD OF ON DIRT. The vast majority of races in this country are on dirt.

IF A HORSE EXPERIENCED PROBLEMS IN A RACE, THE TRACKMAN WILL NOTE THIS IN A TROUBLE LINE. City by Night had a peck of trouble in his last race and still won by three and a half lengths. Cool.

THE DISTANCE OF THE RACE. Races of a mile or more are denoted as 1 1/8th miles, 1 1/4 miles, etc; sprints are written in furlongs (one-eighth of a mile). A three-quarter-mile race is known as a six-furlong race.

THE WINNING FRACTIONS AND FINAL TIME OF THE RACE. If the horse didn't win, figure his time by adding one-fifth of a second for every length behind the winner. In the Hall of Fame Stakes, City by Night finished seven and a half lengths behind Sir Cat, so figure he clocked in at about 1:41 4/5. Generally speaking, a horse runs a furlong, or an eighth of a mile, in about twelve seconds. Faster is good.

THE HORSE'S BREEDING. This is important only in races featuring two-year-olds, when you're trying to get a line on how an inexperienced colt or a first-time starter is going to run. A good horse can come from anywhere, but some good sires are Forty Niner, Mr. Prospector, Storm Cat, Gone West and A.P. Indy.

THE TRAINER'S NAME, HIS RECORD AT THE MEET AND HIS RECORD FOR THE YEAR. Trainers are considered successful if they win 20 percent of the time. Byrne has won nearly 40 percent of his races this year. Bet anything he starts.

6 City by Night

Own: Kaster Nancy & Richard

SELLERS S J (—) 1997:(867 178 .21)

B. c. 4
Sire: Slew City Slew (Seattle Slew
Dam: Shift Surprise (Night Shift)
Br: El Batey Bloodstock (Fla)
Tr: Byrne Patrick B (—) 97:(71

115 5 5 43 31 13½ 13½

14Jun97– 9CD sly 1⅛	:47	1:12	1:37²	1:50² 3↑ S Foster H-G2				
Broke in air, leaned in, bumped 3/16, driving clear					103	3 1 2¹	1hd 12¼ 12½	
9May97– 9CD fst 1⅟₁₆	:24³	:48³	1:12⁴	1:43⁴ 3↑ Alw 41160N$Y	84	1 5 41½	62¼ 9³⅜ 87½	
5Aug96– 8Sar fm 1⅟₁₆ ①	:23²	:47	1:10⁴	1:40² NMsmHllFame-G2	99	6 4 41½	2½ 2½ 1no	
21Apr96– 8Kee fst 1⅟₁₆	:22³	:45⁴	1:10	1:42¹ Lexington-G2	83	7 2 2¹	2¹ 32½ 611	
17Mar96– 9FG fst 1⅟₁₆	:23¹	:46²	1:11²	1:42³ La Derby-G3	92	5 3 31	3½ 2hd 11	
26Feb96– 9GP fst 1⅟₁₆	:23⁴	:47⁴	1:12¹	1:44 Alw 28000N1X				
Six wide top stretch, driving								
25Nov95–10CD fst 1⅟₁₆	:24²	:48²	1:12⁴	1:44¹ KyJockeyClub-G3	69	3 5 5³½	51½ 59 514	
Drifted out 2nd turn, no factor								
5Nov95– 8CD fst 1	:23	:46²	1:11²	1:36⁴ Iroquois-G3	81	2 4 41½	32½ 23½ 34	
8Oct95– 4Kee fst 1⅟₁₆	:22²	:46¹	1:11	1:43¹ BreedersFty-G2	97	2 4 44	33 33½ 22	
4-wide stretch, no late gain					76	5 4 42½	2½ 25 2	
4Sep95–13RD fst 1⅟₁₆	:24	:48	1:11⁴	1:45 MillerHghCrd200k				

WORKOUTS: Jun29 CD 4f fst :49 B 6/34   Jun13 CD 3f fst :36³ B 2/16   ●Jun7 CD 5f sly :59⁴ H 1/20   Jun

THE KIND OF RACE. Stakes races—with grade three being the lowest, grade one being the highest—are referred to by name, with allowance races containing the purse and the conditions of a race. For example, Alw 28000n1x means a $28,000 purse for nonwinners of one race other than maiden or claiming. There are high-priced claiming races, but most are for the least-talented horses. Any licensed owner can "claim," or buy, any horse in a claiming race for his claiming price.

THE ALL-IMPORTANT BEYER SPEED FIGURE. Based on a complicated mathematical formula, this figure determines how fast a horse ran relative to the other horses in the race on a particular racetrack. Anything over 100 is pretty good, anything approaching 120 is awesome. Look for figures that are rising instead of falling over a set period of time. Most handicappers make their own speed figures; Beyer's are very reliable.

THE CALL OF THE RACE, OR WHERE THE HORSE WAS AT CERTAIN POINTS IN THE RACE. In this instance, City by Night was fifth after a quarter-mile, fourth by three lengths after a half-mile, third by a length after three-quarters of a mile, first by three and a half lengths at the head of the stretch and three and a half lengths in front at the finish line. City by Night has come from behind in all of his races, which means that he has to have a quick pace up front to run at. If there's no speed in the race, he'll have a more difficult time catching the front-runners.

THE WEIGHT THE HORSE CARRIES IN THIS RACE AND HAS CARRIED IN PREVIOUS RACES. Not crucial, unless there is a ten-pound swing in either direction or the horse is getting or giving that much weight to his rivals.

DENOTES EQUIPMENT USED. City by Night raced in front bandages (which is not considered a good thing, but there you have it) and with blinkers his last two races, and won both times.

THE FIRST THREE FINISHERS IN THE RACE, THE WEIGHT THEY CARRIED AND THE DISTANCE SEPARATING THEM FROM EACH OTHER.

THE TRACKMAN'S BRIEF COMMENT ABOUT HOW THE HORSE RAN.

HOW MANY HORSES ARE IN EACH RACE.

Lifetime Record :	14	5	4	2	$384,959					
						Turf	2	1	0	0	$6,40'
1997	2	2	0	0	$124,217	Wet	2	1	0	1	$103,95
1996	4	2	0	0	$140,273	Dist	1	1	0	0	$101,64
AP	1	0	1	0	$8,664						6

L 116

L 113 fb   4.00   92 – 19   City By Night$113^{3}\frac{1}{2}$ Victor Cooley$115^{3}\frac{1}{2}$ Semoran$113^{2}1\frac{1}{2}$ Well rated, ridden out   6

L 118 fb   *.70   92 – 16   CityByNight$118^{2}\frac{1}{2}$ Dynpopper$120^{5}\frac{1}{2}$ PerryJmes120^{3} Saved ground, tired   9

L 113 b   8.40   89 – 05   Sir Cat113^{1} Fortitude113^{nk} Optic Nerve120^{1} Driving, lasted   11

L 113 b   17.30   98 – 02   City By Night113^{no} Prince Of Thieves$118^{1}\frac{1}{2}$ Roar$118^{2}\frac{1}{2}$ Faltered midstretch   8

L 118 b   3.60   86 – 13   Grindstone$118^{3}\frac{1}{2}$ Zrb'sMgic122^{4} CommndersPlc118^{2} 7

L 117 b   *1.50   88 – 13   City By Night117^{1} Rebecca's Storm117^{4} Murray Novack$120^{2}\frac{3}{4}$ 5

L 111   9.50   76 – 08   Ide$122^{3}\frac{1}{2}$ Editor's Note$119^{2}\frac{1}{2}$ El Amante113^{5} Inside, no gain   8

L 114   3.70   88 – 14   Ide121^{4} El Amante$116^{1}\frac{1}{2}$ City By Night114^{4} 10

L 121   21.50   90 – 16   Honour And Glory$121^{2}\frac{1}{2}$ City By Night$121^{2}\frac{1}{2}$ Blushing Jim121^{2} Strong bid, 2nd best

LB 120   3.70   94 – 01   Devil's Honor120^{5} City By Night$120^{3}\frac{1}{2}$ JPHamer120^{nk}

May28 CD 4f fst :50 B 30/50   May7 CD 4f fst :51 B 53/76

THE ODDS TO THE DOLLAR. Signifies only the public's opinion of the horse at that time, with that class, and is generally useless unless you like to bet beaten favorites (favorites have a star next to the odds).

THE FORM'S SPEED RATING AND TRACK VARIANT. No one I know pays any attention to this.

DENOTES THE USE OF LASIX, a common diuretic used to prevent nosebleeds, which can interfere with a horse's breathing. First-time users of Lasix often improve dramatically.

THE DATE, PLACE, DISTANCE AND TIME OF A HORSE'S WORKOUTS. If accurate, these can give vital clues as to a horse's condition. Nice, steady "works" are a good sign; spotty, irregular works are not. A bold dot next to the work means the horse turned in the fastest work of the morning at that distance.

DENOTES THE USE OF BUTAZOLIDIN, AN ANALGESIC. You either love horses on bute or hate 'em. Good sense dictates the latter: A horse on bute is a horse with sore legs, and why would you want to bet money on a horse with sore legs?

THE JOCKEY'S NAME. Handy for vocalizing your feelings about a particular ride, as in "Way to go, Sellers!" or, maybe, "Sellers, you suck!"

(e Slew)
hift)
'la)
7:(71 26 .37)

13$\frac{1}{2}$ Sellers S J

12$\frac{1}{2}$ Sellers S J
87$\frac{1}{2}$ Sellers S J
1no Sellers S J
611   Sellers S J
11   Sellers S J

5 14$\frac{1}{4}$ Martinez W

34$\frac{1}{2}$ Martinez W
22$\frac{1}{2}$ Martinez W

25   25   Martinez W

Jun1 CD 5f sly 1:01^{3} B 4/24

PLACE YOUR BETS

It's hard enough getting to the betting window just before post time—don't disgrace the sport and yourself by making your bet in the foreign tongue of the track neophyte. Learn the terms. Impress your girlfriend. Make some money. And have more fun: Why bet a horse to place when you can step up to the window and say, "Dollar triple key 1 with the 2-3-5."

Here's how it's done: State the amount of the bet, then the type of bet, then the number of the horse or horses. For example: "Two dollars win 4," "Dollar exacta box 1-2," or "Dollar part wheel 1 with the 5-7-8."

Alas, the more exotic the bet, the less that returns to the bettor. The "vig"—which is gamblingspeak for the house's take (the house in this case includes the track, the state, the breeders, and the purses)—ranges from approximately 15 percent on simple win, place, and show bets to 20 percent on more complicated exactas and doubles, and 25 percent on trifectas and pick threes and sixes. Then again, the payoffs are much bigger. *Caveat emptor.*

Bet: win
What it means: horse must finish first.
The skinny: the three simplest bets, for when you don't want to think. Only long shots will earn you any real dough.

Bet: place
What it means: horse must finish first or second.

Bet: show
What it means: horse must finish first, second, or third.

Bet: across the board
What it means: horse must finish first, second or third. Basically, you're betting win, place *and* show.
The skinny: still simple, but more bets mean more chances to win.

Bet: daily double
What it means: horses must finish first in respective races. The daily double is generally available for races one and two; also races eight and nine. You win all or nothing.
The skinny: when you want your fun to last more than just one race.

Bet: exacta
What it means: horses must finish first and second in exact order.
The skinny: expertise and luck required, but the payoff is worth it.

Bet: quinella
What it means: horses bet must finish first or second in any order. Generally only offered on races two and four.
The skinny: like an exacta box (which covers either order of finish), but allows you to bet as little as a dollar.

Bet: trifecta
What it means: horses bet must finish first, second, and third in exact order.
The skinny: you've got to be more than good to pull this off, but even coming close is a thrill; huge potential payoff, and the right to brag, "I hit the trifecta!"

Bet: pick three
What it means: horses bet must finish first in three designated races. If no one selects all three winners, the pool gets distributed to the person(s) picking the next highest number of winners.
The skinny: a simple way to add some spice to your night by betting on multiple races.

Bet: pick six
What it means: if you pick the winners of races three through eight, you win or share in 75 percent of the day's pool, which can swell due to carryovers. (The other 25 percent is returned to people who pick the next highest number of winners.)
The skinny: lotto with horses.

Parlay: combine at least two races to a maximum of six races; like the daily double, you win all or nothing.
The skinny: if you don't like the races in the daily double, make your own.

Bet: wheel
What it means: you bet on one horse with all the others. For example, in an exacta wheel, you'd bet one horse to win with each of the others to place. Naturally, this costs more, since you're actually placing as many bets as there are horses running.
The skinny: bet this if there is a clear winner, but several horses have a chance to run second.

Bet: key or part wheel
What it means: you bet on one horse with some of the others.
The skinny: when you want multiple chances to hit the exacta or trifecta, and have one horse you feel extremely sure about; here, you're eliminating the horses you feel don't have a prayer to place or show.

owner can "claim" by offering to buy before the race begins—and the horse is now entered in a one-and-a-quarter-mile allowance race against a couple of stakes-class horses. (Horses generally race in three classes: stakes, allowance, and claiming [stakes is the highest].) On the other hand, a horse that has lost six straight races at one and an eighth miles or more against stakes horses, and who is dropping down into a one-mile race against claimers—such a horse has an obvious class edge (and will no doubt wind up the 1–5 favorite).

But your eye might be caught by a horse who has finished third, fourth, and fifth in similar races but who has a new rider, or a horse who's now being trained by one of the more successful trainers in the area (the records of both jockeys and trainers are listed next to their names in the *Form*). Or perhaps you like the way the horse's Beyer Speed Figures have been improving over his last few races, or you notice that the horse has raced well when given at least three weeks between races and is now coming off a four-week layoff.

The key is to make your own decisions. Trust yourself. You'll win some, you'll lose some, but you will be in charge. And chances are that if you educate yourself by turning the page and using our guide on how to actually read—and analyze—the *Racing Form,* you'll be making a pretty darn good selection. There's no better way to be part of the action.

A SMALL TRIAL-SIZE BOTTLE OF COLOGNE:

Handy in the glove compartment, just in case.

BE A VEGAS BIG SHOT

Ever been in a casino and seen management delivering a box of cigars to a special player? Wonder who pays those ridiculous prices for entrées in a casino's fancy dining rooms? Think you have to have a cousin named Joey to get a free room in Vegas or Atlantic City?

Well, if you're even a smidgen more than a casual gambler, you can tap into those cigars, free dinners, and comped rooms if you play it right. Here's the deal: Casinos want your business and will reward you if you're willing to play several hours a day. Entire marketing teams cater to such players, and you don't have to be pushing out hundred-dollar chips at the baccarat table to catch a casino's interest; even twenty-five-cent slot players can earn freebies if they play long enough.

The goal can be summed up in three letters: "RFB." That's casino shorthand for "room, food, and beverage," which means where you sleep and anything you eat or drink is on the house. The real big players get "RFBI," the last letter standing for "incidentals," such as phone calls, dry cleaning, and spa treatments. Here's how to enter the world of comps.

1. GET RATED.

If a casino employee approaches to ask your name, don't recoil in horror. You're about to be "rated," which means, if you're willing to give your name, the casino will begin tracking your play, noting the average size of your bets, and the length of time per day you gamble. You'll probably be given a plastic casino card that you can present every time you play or use the slots. This is the first step toward collecting the free stuff.

2. BE AWARE OF HOW LONG YOU PLAY.

In order to be comped, a player must bet about four hours a day. So as soon as you sit down to wager, ask to be rated. If you switch tables or games or leave for a few hours and return, always give your name to a pit boss immediately so the clock can resume running. Your history of play will be entered into a computer each day.

3. MAKE A CONTACT.

Get known at one casino, instead of hopping from one to another, and keep the card of any casino exec who proffers one. Remember, these are the guys who, with the "power of the pen," can decree you RFB for almost any reason. If your play is sufficient to earn comps, you'll want to call him before your next visit for a free room or meals.

4. KNOW WHERE YOU RANK.

Casinos generally use an alphabetical or numerical rating. An "A" or "1" player would be someone like Kerry Packer, the überwealthy Australian who gambles millions when he visits Vegas. For Packer the sky is the limit in terms of comps—a player in his category can even negotiate a deal that provides a 15 or 20 percent *rebate* on all losses.

A "D" or "4" player (that's you) might be a fifteen-dollar-a-bet blackjack player or steady slot player. You won't get a suite, but a buffet lunch should be within your reach.

BEEDIE CIGARETTES: Ebony-leaf wrapped Indian pleasure.

5. ASK.

Let's say you've been playing a few hours at a blackjack table, maybe pushing out twenty-five dollars a bet. Chances are, no one is going to approach you to buy you dinner. Ask the pit employee who has been watching your play. (The dealer is of no use in these situations, by the way.) A request for a dinner at one of the house's midrange restaurants is entirely reasonable, and chances are quite good they'll say, "Yes."

Remember, it doesn't matter if you're winning or losing. All the casinos want is a crack at your money. You give 'em the time and the action, and they'll give you the comps.

BEAT THE CASINO

Whether you're gambling in Vegas or at your favorite Indian reservation, one thing remains consistent: those casinos structure every game to give them the edge. In English, "the edge" means they get the money, not you. In math, "the edge" is expressed as a percentage. A 5-percent edge means that, in the long run, the casino wins five dollars for every hundred-dollar bet at that game. Roulette, the big wheel, Sic Bo, Caribbean Stud, many bets at craps, and most slot and video-poker machines have edges of 5 percent or more. Tough odds.

But there is a way for the smart and the patient to beat the house. Thankfully, the casinos haven't quite succeeded in making all games and all bets favor them. For example, card counters in blackjack and expert video-poker players can get slight edges over the casinos. But beating the system this way is like getting to Carnegie Hall: it takes practice, practice, practice. And most casino players have no interest in putting the kind of effort usually associated with the LSATs into an evening's entertainment.

Still, there are good ways and bad ways to play the casinos. Every one of the following bets comes in with an edge of around 1.5 percent or lower—your best chance of bringing home the bacon from the casinos' hide.

BACCARAT/MINI-BACCARAT

Bet bank bets or player bets only. Both of these have house edges of less than 1.4 percent.

BLACKJACK

Basic strategy, which can be found in any decent blackjack book [See our handy cheat sheet for a quick primer], reduces the house edge to .5 percent or less, certainly the best bet going. Play blackjack at casinos that deal single-deck games, keep count of how many aces have been played, and the odds might even swing slightly in your favor.

CRAPS

Make pass line or don't pass, come or don't come, along with full odds (full odds are the "behind-the-line" bets that up your total outlay but do not give the casino *any* advantage); once the full odds are accounted for, these bets reduce the house edge to .6 percent or lower, depending upon how much you're allowed to put in odds. (Ten times your initial bet is good; some Vegas casinos now allow you to put a hundred times your first bet behind the line, but that's a pretty hefty bet on each roll of the dice). Alternatively, try placing the six and eight, which reduces the house's edge to 1.52 percent. If none of this means anything to you, make sure to get a lesson from a friend before going near a craps table.

ONE DARK, CLASSY BLAZER: Dresses up any outfit.

SLOTS

If you simply must play the slots (despite the lack of reward for either skill or strategy), play the five-dollar machines. They are the "loosest" machines in the casino, meaning they routinely give the best return, even if you only play a single coin.

PLAYING PERFECT BLACKJACK

Dealer's Up Card

Your Hand	2	3	4	5	6	7	8	9	10	A
17–21	S	S	S	S	S	S	S	S	S	S
16	S	S	S	S	S	H	H	H*	H*	H*
15	S	S	S	S	S	H	H	H	H	H
14	S	S	S	S	S	H	H	H	H	H
13	S	S	S	S	S	H	H	H	H	H
12	H	H	S	S	S	H	H	H	H	H
11	D	D	D	D	D	D	D	D	D	H
10	D	D	D	D	D	D	D	D	H	H
9	H	D	D	D	D	H	H	H	H	H
8 or less	H	H	H	H	H	H	H	H	H	H

Combinations with Ace

	2	3	4	5	6	7	8	9	10	A
A:9	S	S	S	S	S	S	S	S	S	S
A:8	S	S	S	S	S	S	S	S	S	S
A:7	S	D	D	D	D	S	S	H	H	H
A:6	H	D	D	D	D	H	H	H	H	H
A:5	H	H	D	D	D	H	H	H	H	H
A:4	H	H	D	D	D	H	H	H	H	H
A:3	H	H	H	D	D	H	H	H	H	H
A:2	H	H	H	D	D	H	H	H	H	H

Double Cards

	2	3	4	5	6	7	8	9	10	A
A:A	SP	SP	SP	SP	SP	SP	SP	SP	SP	SP
10:10	S	S	S	S	S	S	S	S	S	S
9:9	SP	SP	SP	SP	SP	S	SP	SP	S	S
8:8	SP	SP	SP	SP	SP	SP	SP	SP	SP*	SP
7:7	SP	SP	SP	SP	SP	SP	H	H	H	H
6:6	SP	SP	SP	SP	SP	H	H	H	H	H
5:5	D	D	D	D	D	D	D	D	H	H
4:4	H	H	H	SP	SP	H	H	H	H	H
3:3	SP	SP	SP	SP	SP	SP	H	H	H	H
2:2	SP	SP	SP	SP	SP	SP	H	H	H	H

H = hit; S = stand; D = double down; SP = split

*In casinos where surrender is offered, surrender this hand.

TEN RULES ON WHERE NOT TO GO DRINKING

1. Never go to a bar that serves umbrellas in your drink or colors your drink. Especially pink.

2. Never go to a bar that has a "Happy Hour." Nobody there ever is.

3. Never go to a bar where the bartender has more problems than you do.

4. Never go to a bar where you raise the average age of those inside by more than five years just by walking in.

5. Although the best pubs are Irish pubs, never go to one on St. Patty's Day. It's amateur night and a good time to get a reservation at a Chinese restaurant.

6. Never go to a bar where there is more than one bouncer unless you're expecting the trouble they are.

7. Never go to a bar where they allow cell phones. A bar is a place of sanctity—check your self-importance at the door.

8. Never go to a bar that doesn't ask you what brand you prefer but instead pours something called "Old Panther Piss" aged in the woods from the well underneath the counter.

9. Never go to a bar that doesn't allow cigar smoking. Tell anyone who complains, "If it wasn't for twenty cigars a day smoked by Winston Churchill, you'd be speaking German."

10. Never drive and drink. The world needs designated drivers— and where would they be without designated drunks sitting in the backseat getting sick all over themselves? They'd be out of work, that's where.

POLISHED SHOES:

Class starts from the ground up.

CHAPTER 12

TRAVELING

Q: WHAT ARE SOME TIPS FOR SUCCESSFUL ROAD-TRIPPING?

DO YOUR HOMEWORK:
Read up on where you're going. It's your trip, make the most of it.

DRIVE SLOW

If you can't arrange the trip so that it's 150 miles a day or less, then you might as well fly, because you're mostly going to see the inside of your car.

DRIVE FAR

It takes at least a week for the average person to wind down from work and the daily routine. After that, you'll be more open to people and better adjusted to the rhythm of the journey.

LEARN

Any town has more history and texture than you'll ever get from a guidebook. Being a tourist gives you license to ask; use it. Every local can tell you something that you didn't know, and a simple question might eventually lead to a new friend.

Books on tape are another great avenue for learning on the road, plus they keep you from having to hear the Eagles sing "Hotel California" another thousand times. You can learn foreign languages at a survival level with Pimsleur tapes from Sybervision (800-888-9980). The most directly educational tapes available are from The Teaching Company (800-TEACH-12). They bring the nation's best university lecturers into your car at a $29,950 savings off the cost of one year at an Ivy League college.

CHEW GUM

It'll keep you awake.

TRAVEL RESOURCES FOR THE CYBERSAVVY

Planning a honeymoon? Or maybe a tropical, babewatching adventure for you and your five-man crew? Tired of dealing with travel agents and guidebooks from Rand McNally? There's good news: The number of travel-related Web sites is soaring, allowing computer-savvy globe-trotters a faster, cheaper way to plan their next trip.

The best way to begin your search for destination information is through an index such as *The Virtual Tourist* II, which lists thousands of local and regional sites worldwide. From there, surf the official tourism sites; they won't tell you which restaurants to avoid, but they will provide basic info on attractions, dining, lodging, entertainment, and events. Then get a little adventurous. Try a cool e-zine, such as *Split* (http://www.lainet.com/nomad) or *The Connected Traveler* (http://www.well.com/user/wldtrvlr), which feature reports from road warriors, foreign and domestic. Or dive into a travelogue posted by fellow footloose Netizens such as Walter and Cherie Glaser's "Images of Istanbul" (http://www.bpe.com/travel/asia/istanbul), a photo-packed exploration of the city.

WASHABLE SUEDE PANTS: For the guy who wants to make sure hands will be all over him.

Guidebooks can provide a sense of security in a strange place, but they can be a burden—first on your wallet and then in your backpack. To pare down the overhead and overload, check out the free offerings from major publishers on the Web. Fodor's (http://www.fodors.com), for instance, includes a Destinations database of info on restaurants, attractions, and hotels for major international cities. The site also offers links to a currency converter and travel and health alerts. The Rough Guide's (http://www.roughguides.com) site includes full-text introductions to its books and links to the HotWired site that contains the entire U.S. and Mexico Rough Guides. Moon Travel Handbooks (http://www.moon.com) and Lonely Planet (http://www.lonely-planet.com) also have sites with samplings of their publications.

Slick travel magazines also are available on the commercial services as well as on the Web—*Condé Nast Traveler* (http://www.cntraveler.com), *Travel & Leisure* (http://pathfinder.com), and *Travel Holiday* (http: //enews.com/magazines/travel_h) among them.

Once you've unearthed the information, you can cut and paste the excerpts, articles, and tidbits from your on-line screen into your word processor or text program and then print out the material and stuff it in a pocket (way lighter than *Let's Go*). And while you're at it, check out the Web's array of mapping programs. One of the best is the graphics-rich MapQuest! (http://www.mapquest.com), which generates free scalable maps. Just type in an address and MapQuest! does the rest.

Booking flights and making hotel reservations also can be time-consuming, especially if you're waiting for airfare sales or studying glossy brochures. Travel-reservations sites let you search for flights and fares and even book seats with your computer— although always remember that, for security, it's best to avoid sending your credit-card information out over the Internet. Sites that allow you to make your reservations or purchase by E-mail, phone, or fax are the safest; the commercial services are more secure as well.

Individual airlines have Web sites, and some offer cybertravelers special discounts and incentives to help build loyalty among surfing flyers. For multiple airline bookings, the slickest site is Travelocity (http://www.travelocity.com), which also features tourist information, maps, and photos on fifteen thousand destinations.

For those who prefer to stay grounded, reservations sites and transportation companies also offer on-line booking for rail, bus, cruise, and rental-car travel. Although the commercial sites are often more about advertising than entertainment, some can leave you feeling relaxed and tanned just by clicking in. The Royal Caribbean Cruise Lines site (http://www.royalcaribbean.com), for instance, features breezy destination guides and a cybercruise virtual voyage.

For on-line hotel booking, one of the best sites is TravelWeb (http://www.travelweb.com), which uses a secure server (safer for credit-card transactions) to provide real-time reservations for thousands of properties worldwide—all searchable by destination, chain, type of lodging, and amenities. The Web is also awash in bed-and-breakfast finders, hostel guides, and other alternative lodging directories.

If you belong to a hotel guest program or prefer a particular chain, corporate Web sites can be time savers. Some, such as HiltonNet (http://www.hilton.com), with its destination guides to major cities, are sophisticated and dense with information, while others offer little more than property addresses. But at least you can find out what's where with a few clicks.

If the Web is like an infinite shopping mall with millions of stores, the commercial services are more like department stores: they have a little bit of everything, but in limited quantities. Nevertheless, AOL, Prodigy, and CompuServe still feature useful travel resources, including the EAASY SABRE reservations service. And for "newbies," they offer a chance to window-shop before getting lost in the endless corridors of the Web.

LOW-FARE E-MAIL

Every Wednesday, a couple hundred thousand cybersavvy shoppers know that they're going to get spamlike E-mail that they'll actually want to read. The senders: American Airlines, US Airways, TWA, and Continental, each offering leftover (read: amazingly cheap) airfares to Vegas, New Orleans, Barcelona, and just about every other major destination. There's a catch, of course: you have to leave almost immediately and stay over a Saturday night. So would you drop everything and just go? The airlines are betting you just might.

Look at it from the airlines' point of view. Once a plane takes off, every empty seat is wasted money; unlike tires or beer, there's no

Roadside America
www.roadsideamerica.
com
A hilarious and enlightening travel site, Roadside America takes you to the far reaches of the nation—attractions like Lambertville, New Jersey's Penis Bone Collection, and the World's Largest Thermometer in Baker, California—with the guidance of three "roadside geneticists." Fun for a virtual voyage, useful for a genuine getaway.

GoSki!
www.goski.com
Looking to abandon Aspen for someplace more adventurous? The Tein Shan mountains of Kazakhstan, perhaps? Wherever you want to go, here's where to learn the latest. Down-home reviews by people who've been there.

hope of selling it tomorrow. So the major airlines have begun offering last-minute discounts on airfares to people who subscribe to E-mail distribution lists. We're talking round-trip tickets coast-to-coast for $179, Mexico for $99, even Europe for $198.

Here's how it works. Would-be jet-setters enter their E-mail addresses at the Web site of one of several airlines. Some of the higher-maintenance sites ask for a list of likely departure cities or routes. Then, typically on Wednesday morning, the airlines send a list of available flights they predict will be undersold by the weekend. Obviously, these flights are not for the planner. They're for the desperate wage-slave flyer who decides at the last minute to jump a plane bound for Anywhere.

To keep the discounts unpredictable, the flights are offered on a rotating basis. That way last-minute fares don't compete with their bread-and-butter fourteen-day advanced purchase fares.

These kinds of alerts began 1995, when Fort Worth–based American Airlines began airing last-minute fares called "cable savers" on a local cable television station, along with an 800 number for booking. Cable viewers got dirt-cheap fares, as much as 40 to 70 percent less than booking the flight normally; and that the airline got to increase its "incremental revenue"—earnings, until then, it had written off as a cost of doing business. When American Airlines came on line with a Web site last year, it became clear that the Internet was the cheapest, most efficient way to deliver the service. Continental, TWA, and US Airways have since followed suit.

And while just about every major airline offers booking and purchase of tickets over the Web, only a blessed few have caught on to the genius of E-mail. The premise makes sense: ask me to drop everything and jump on a plane to Puerto Vallarta, but don't make me slog through a dozen Web sites to find the deal. (But if you'd prefer to slog, a tidy list of airlines with links appears at the Web site of University of Texas at Austin assistant professor of management Marc-David Seidel (http://itn.net/airlines/). So far, American Airlines has 630,000 subscribers getting the weekly E-mails. Only nine months up and running, TWA sends out 33,000 E-mail messages a week.

American Airlines either created a monster or a market. Either way, it adds a whole new dimension to weekend wanderlust.

FLY FIRST CLASS—
WITHOUT PAYING

Champagne tastes, beer drinker's budget. It's a problem we know well. After all, how can you enjoy rubbery chicken in coach, when you know full-well those seated in first class are sipping bubbly and getting their pillows fluffed? It's a serious problem—but it's far from insurmountable.

Two words for those who've ever wondered what it's like to travel on the other side of the curtain: it's terrific. First-class passengers board before coach passengers. They don't jostle for overhead space. The flight attendants check their coats and call them by name. First-class seats are roomier and plusher, with big armrests and tons of legroom. And those are just the obvious perks.

Less well-known advantages: First-class baggage is loaded last and comes off first, allowing for quick airport getaways. If there is a delay or cancelation, first-class passengers will be rerouted first, getting the best selection of alternative flights. Nothing costs extra, not drinks nor headphones. The food is much better, and on long-haul flights you enjoy better entertainment, hot towels, and multiple entrée choices. First class even has its own bathroom, adorned with fresh flowers, so there's no waiting to get past the cart in the aisle.

So how do you get to the other side of the curtain while traveling on a budget? The two aren't mutually exclusive. And you don't even have to resort to bald-faced lying, such as pretending it is your honeymoon or feigning a leg injury. It won't work, folks. You'll be about the twentieth person that day, and the counter person will have heard the story hundreds, if not thousands, of times.

Here's the real deal: by far the best way to travel in style is to strategically use frequent-flier miles. Tread carefully, as the airlines all have different rules. If you travel for work, it's pretty easy to reach a tier level, which usually offers automatic upgrades or coupons. If you make it to the highest level, you'll almost always fly first class, and can be put on the upgrade list when you buy your cheap coach ticket, weeks in advance, ahead of people checking in that day. For example, Delta offers unlimited, confirmed upgrades for any price ticket for their highest-tier members.

Of course, most of us won't hit those levels. A viable alternative is to hoard frequent-flier miles—especially through affiliated credit-

travlang
www.travlang.com
Wanna learn a few phrases for your trip to Tokyo, Jerusalem, or Lisbon? At travlang, you select the language you speak (English, we presume) and the one you want to learn (the usual choices, plus Zulu, Hindi and lots of others). Voilà, you've got a lesson, plus a selection of ten translating dictionaries.

Rec.Travel Library
**www.solutions.net/rec
-travel/**
The site doesn't have the slick look of its commercial brethren, but it does offer lots of tips, advice, and stories from fellow travelers.

card and long-distance plans—and use them solely for upgrades. Frequent-flier miles should almost always be redeemed for upgrades, not free tickets.

This may fly against your instinct, but it's simple math, really. As long as you have a little advance notice, the most expensive domestic coach ticket you will ever buy (assuming you're going to stay over a Saturday night) might run around four hundred dollars, and tickets on popular or competitive routes are generally far cheaper. When you use twenty-five thousand hard-earned frequent-flier miles for one of those seats, you are receiving maybe one and a half cents per mile, probably less—and you don't earn new miles for the flight. This assumes you can get a seat at all—the airlines are notoriously stingy about allotting free seats and will almost never fork over one that they think they could have sold. Which means forget about trading in for a midwinter ticket to Miami or Denver. Tulsa in July is more like it.

Upgrades are a much better value. Crunch the numbers: On US Airways, you can get one-way upgrade certificates for 2,500 miles, and these can be used on all but the most bargain basement of tickets. Say you fly to Chicago from your home in Vermont. You can buy a round-trip for about two hundred dollars—less than a penny a mile of value if you're trading in for a free ticket. A first-class round-trip, however, would cost more than a thousand dollars. Considering that it's only five thousand miles to bump you into first class in both directions, the extra eight hundred dollars or so in benefits comes out to a whopping sixteen cents of value per mile. Plus, you earn enough miles on that very flight for yet another one-way upgrade.

AIRLINE UPGRADES:

There's a reason they call it first class.

AIRLINE	URL	PROGRAM NAME	SAMPLE DEAL— DOMESTIC (All Fares Round Trip)
American	www.americanair.com	Net SAAvers	Oakland to Dallas, $159
Continental	www.flycontinental.com	CO.O.L. Travel Specials	Newark to San Francisco, $229
TWA	www.twa.com	Trans World Specials	San Jose to Washington, D.C., $179
US Airways	www.usairways.com	E-Savers	New York to Charlotte, $99

For the cost of one free ticket, you can upgrade as many as five round-trip flights. Also, while those free tickets are tough to procure, upgrades are almost always available, since so few people pay first-class fares. And here's a no-brainer: when you have miles that are going to expire and don't have enough for a freebie, take the upgrade and run.

If you are a tier member of most programs, which can be reached at as little as twenty thousand miles over a certain period of time, there is another little-known option for securing upgrades. Most airlines sell books of upgrade coupons for a nominal fee relative to their value. While anyone can buy these, only tier members can use them with restricted discount tickets. For three hundred dollars US Airways sells a book of eleven tickets, each good for an upgrade of up to eight hundred miles. Any tier member can use these on a ticket of any price. New York to Chicago would require two coupons each way, a cost of just over a hundred dollars. This turns your two-hundred-dollar back-of-the-bus ticket into a three-hundred-dollars styling ride.

An even better scam for business travelers: If your company springs for full-fare coach, it's almost free to upgrade these tickets, since many airlines are actually selling first- or business-class seats for full-coach fare. If not, you can usually upgrade for a minimal number of miles, or even just by asking. Northwest charges nontier members a flat twenty-five-dollar fee for every five hundred miles of travel to upgrade full coach to first class.

Another way to get upgraded is by becoming demanding when there is a delay. If your flight is late for any reason outside of the

PACKING A LUNCH: Let's face it, airline food sucks.

LEARNING KEY PHRASES: Hand gestures and facial expressions can only do so much.

SAMPLE DEAL— INTERNATIONAL	FREEBIE
Miami to Bogotà, $257	500 bonus miles with Internet purchase
Newark to London, $249	500 bonus miles with Internet purchase
Boston to Madrid, $198	1,000 bonus miles with purchase
Baltimore to Bermuda, $139	Heartfelt appreciation, see TWA

I CAN SEE FOR MILES AND MiLES

Major Frequent-Flier Programs and Their "Links"
Here's a sampling of airline partners that offer frequent-flier miles. Mileage awards vary dramatically with special promotions and other factors. Banks listed offer "affinity cards" with a given airline.

Airline: American
Hubs: Chicago, Miami, Dallas–Fort Worth
Sample partners: Best Western, Thrifty Auto Rental, MCI, FTD, Citibank, Holiday Inn, Hyatt Hotels, ITT Sheraton, Westin hotels
Best deal: earn one mile for each four dollars of purchase price when you buy or lease a new or used vehicle from one of hundreds of car dealers.
Wacky deal: five thousand miles when you attend a three-day golf clinic at Nicklaus/Flick Golf School (800-642-5528)
Rating: ★ ★ ★ ★

Airline: America West
Hubs: Columbus, Las Vegas, Phoenix
Sample partners: Hilton Hotels, Alamo Rent A Car, Sprint, The Flower Club, Holiday Inn, Avis Auto Rental, Bank of America
Best deal: 2.5 miles awarded for every dollar spent at Holiday Inn and Crowne Plaza hotels.
Wacky deal: five hundred miles for every ten days of parking at Allright or Premier parking garages (for "parking plus" members)
Rating: ★ ★ ★

Airline: Continental
Hubs: Cleveland, Houston, Newark, Guam
Sample partners: Marriott, Avis, MCI, Visa, Radisson, ITT Sheraton, Hertz
Best deal: one mile for every dollar spent on American Express corporate cards.
Wacky deal: one mile for every two dollars spent at Randalls Food Markets
Rating: ★ ★

Airline: Delta
Hubs: Atlanta, Cincinnati, Dallas–Fort Worth, Salt Lake City
Sample partners: Hilton, American Express, MCI, Charles Schwab, Hyatt, Inter-Continental Hotels, National Car Rental
Best deal: five hundred miles from Hilton or Hyatt for each overnight stay.

Wacky deal: one hundred miles for taking the Delta Water Shuttle between LaGuardia Airport and Manhattan
Rating: ★ ★ ★

Airline: Northwest
Hubs: Minneapolis, Memphis, Detroit
Sample partners: Crowne Plaza, First Bank, Hilton, The Flower Club, Holiday Inn, Radisson, Westin
Best deal: five miles for every dollar spent on MCI.
Wacky deal: five hundred miles for a donation of fifty dollars or more to St. Jude Children's Research Hospital in Memphis (800-822-6344)
Rating: ★ ★ ★

Airline: TWA
Hubs: St. Louis, New York–JFK
Sample partners: Sprint, Visa, Marriott, Alamo, European American Bank, Avis
Best deal: if you use a gold MasterCard or Visa, you'll earn 1.5 miles for every dollar spent on TWA services, plus a five-thousand-mile signing bonus.
Wacky deal: none
Rating: ★

Airline: United
Hubs: Denver, San Francisco, Chicago
Sample partners: Hilton, Hertz, Budget Auto Rental, Amtrak, 1-800-FLOWERS, ITT Sheraton, Holiday Inn
Best deal: 2.5 miles for every dollar spent at Holiday Inn or Crowne Plaza hotels, five hundred miles per night at Inter-Continental Hotels.
Wacky deal: none
Rating: ★ ★

Airline: US Airways
Hubs: Pittsburgh, Charlotte, Philadelphia, Baltimore
Sample partners: NationsBank, MCI, Alamo, The Flower Club, Marriott, Hyatt, Radisson
Best deal: earn one mile for every dollar spent on a NationsBank Visa.
Wacky deal: none
Rating: ★

weather, which airlines obviously take no responsibility for, head straight to the special-services counter and complain, firmly but politely. Ask for a free ticket. They'll probably say no, but then make a counteroffer. Ask for an upgrade and some bonus miles. It helps to dress well and act like someone whose business they want to keep.

In fact, "it never hurts to ask" just may be the official upgrade credo. Every time you check in for any flight, ask how much it would cost to upgrade your ticket to first class. It usually costs an arm and a leg, but if you appear sympathetic, especially if you are traveling with your significant other, they may take pity on you. Counter personnel are empowered to give away seats when available. Also, they make mistakes.

Shadier methods include telling the gate person you are an elite member but don't have your card and want to upgrade. Can they check your frequent-flier status for you? Not usually. If there are seats available, you might get the benefit of the doubt. This works especially well if you show up just as the plane is boarding, when they have very little time. Another tactic is to pretend you ordered a special meal, such as kosher or vegetarian, when you check in, and then become irate because they lost the record of it. Make it clear that you can't tolerate the food in back because of dietary restrictions. Remember that when you lie, you are probably stealing someone else's seat, perhaps a legitimate honeymooner or weary frequent flier. If you don't care, fine.

Yes, this is all a lot of hassle. Rest assured, though, it's worth it. Imagine if flying becomes the best part of the trip, rather than a way to get you somewhere. That's what it's always like for those in the front of the plane, the people you can't see, but only hear, laughing and talking as Champagne corks pop and glasses clink five miles up in the sky.

LOCALS:
Go where they go.

EARN MILES ON THE GROUND

So you know your way around an airport. Every week, your job flies you from your home in Washington, D.C., to the Midwest farm belt. You're a member of six frequent flier programs. The last thing you need to do is earn extra miles. Right?

Wrong. Instead of sitting back satisfied with the miles you accrue in the air, it's time to work the system and match them almost mile for mile on the ground. It's called "linkage." Welcome aboard.

Yes. Gone are the days when the only way to build frequent-flier miles was to get on a plane. Today, opening a mutual fund account, renting a car, or just sending your mom some flowers (a good idea anyway) can earn you miles. Cutthroat competition among airlines has produced thousands of new ways to earn miles without ever flying. Hook up with the right programs, and you can watch hundreds of miles pile up every single week.

All of this is possible because today airlines sell their miles to practically anyone who wants a piece of the action, linking with businesses that buy (usually for one to two cents per mile) trillions of "free miles." These businesses then turn around and dangle the miles like money-saving carrots to lure travel-hungry customers.

The most aggressive airline hustling these deals is American, which shouldn't be surprising: it started the first frequent-flier program in 1981 as a way to build customer loyalty. Today, American offers a staggering 3,500 deals through two thousand participants passing out the free miles. To you, that means a mailbox full of promotions—and the chance to earn thousands of those miles.

LAS VEGAS:
Unless you're not interested in free beer, $1.50 steak and eggs or the promise of an unparalleled pay-day.

First step: patronize the right frequent-flier program. Since membership is free, it doesn't hurt to join them all. But it pays to bunch as many miles as possible on one specific airline. Focusing on an airline with a hub at the airport nearest you is usually the logical strategy.

Next, take a look at your credit cards. If you have an American Express card, sign up for its Membership Rewards program. For every dollar you charge on American Express, you will earn points that can be transferred over to one of thirteen major airline frequent-flyer programs and redeemed for miles. If you charge an airline ticket on Amex, you'll get the miles from the airfare as well as the points from using the card. Although the program doesn't offer a bonus for signing up, there's no expiration date on the miles, a major plus. You can link in your corporate Amex for free. The program also will swamp you with promotions: one recent offer pledged 2,500 points for a free consultation with an American Express financial planner. Sure, the free consultation may be accompanied by a hard sell, but what the hell—planning for an early retirement ain't such a bad idea, either. (More time to fly.)

Airlines also team up with credit-card companies to offer "affinity" cards, like the First Bank WorldPerks Visa card from Northwest or the United Airlines Visa card. Many of these cards will give you several thousand points just for signing up. But check the fine print: some cards limit the number of points that can be earned each year.

Of course, some of the most lucrative ways to earn miles involve using travel-related services. Nearly all the airlines are connected to big-name hotels and rental-car companies, where you can earn up to five hundred miles at a clip. Airlines also sponsor "dining-out" programs where you can earn miles by eating at certain restaurants. And again, it's a snap to double points at any time—just charge your purchase on the credit card linked to your frequent-flier account.

Phone companies are another big source of airline miles. You can get miles for signing up, using a cell phone, or buying a calling card. You can switch long-distance companies and your original phone company will offer you free miles *for switching back.* It's a shell game—play it. Sometimes even a little whining or begging can get you a better deal.

In addition to the big programs, there are thousands of smaller promotions that can rack up miles. If you donate fifty dollars to the National Parks Foundation by the end of April, you'll pocket five hundred miles on American. Delta has a partnership with Charles Schwab, the discount brokerage house, in which you can earn three thousand miles when you deposit or transfer thirty thousand dollars into one of their accounts. If you buy or sell a home through Better Homes and Gardens Realtors? That's ten thousand to forty thousand miles on TWA. Need a new computer? Consider going to Best Buy: they'll cough up three thousand miles on Delta, American, Northwest, United, or US Airways when you buy a notebook. With all of this keep in mind that buying something you don't need just for the miles is folly—the idea behind frequent-flier programs is to *save* you money. Take advantage of these programs only if you were going to make that purchase, or a similar one, anyway.

How to find the best deals? Reading your junk mail and tooling around on the Internet are best. But be wary. A recent on-line ad promised five thousand bonus miles for using Continental's dining program. But two calls to Continental's 800 frequent-flier number proved the promotion to be a bust. Both customer-service representatives said no such deal existed. It seems that even with frequent-flier programs, you have to check everything at the gate.

A CURRENT PASSPORT: Whenever opportunity arises, you'll be ready to go.

A GOOD TRAVEL AGENT: The key to your best vacation deals—no cost, hassle-free.

THE FINE ART OF HOTEL HAGGLING

"Ramada reservations. This is Amy. What city and state can I help you with?" Man, from the moment you call to book hotel reservations, you've got to spit out answers—fast.

How many people in the room? How many nights? King bed or two doubles? Smoking or nonsmoking?

It's all quite ironic, given that the key to booking affordable hotel rooms rests largely on you asking a few questions of your own.

Allow us to tip you on the hotel industry's biggest open secret— the fixed price for a room is about as rigid as the used-car prices listed in the newspaper classifieds. Last time you stayed in a hotel, we'd bet that the person next door paid a different price than you did. Next time, let's hope he'll be the one paying more.

The key to saving money on hotels is negotiating with abandon. Only the most clueless consumers pay the full "rack" rate for a room. (That's the price the reservations agent quotes you at the beginning of your call.) Sure, haggling takes time, energy, and patience. Like a good poker player, you may need a bluff a few times and know when to fold. But at least you can turn the rather drab task of planning your trip into a contest of nail-biting business savvy. More important, you can save yourself a nice pile of clams.

Consider the hotel's initial price quote an opening bid. Then start finagling your way down, down, down. Prices change from hour to hour depending on who you call and what questions you ask.

There are a number of places you can call to reserve a room: a hotel chain's 800-number reservations line, the hotel itself, or consolidators, who are essentially hotel-room brokers. No one of these methods will always yield the lowest price, but trying all of them allows you three tries at a cheap rate.

The cheery souls on the 800 lines are often free to cut deals. Good old Amy on the Ramada line quoted a seventy-nine-dollar rate for a Saturday night outside San Francisco, and sixty-nine dollars for each additional night. When asked about her corporate price, the numbers drop to seventy-two and sixty-one, respectively. You get the same price for an AAA membership. If you happen to be an Entertainment Card holder, bingo: a forty-nine-dollar rate.

Dialing directly to the hotel you want to stay at often yields an even better price, since front-desk drones are authorized to respond to local business conditions.

The consolidator route is more direct. Consolidators are wholesalers who buy blocks of hotel rooms and offer discounted rates, especially to last-minute travelers. Two favorites are Central Reservation Service (800–548–3311) and VTS/Value Hotels (800–377–2892). Calls to consolidators take less time because there's no negotiation. You are quoted a rate without a fuss. Take it or leave it. They normally do not dicker, so don't waste your time trying to talk them down. At the very least, consolidators are worth calling to gain a basis for comparison.

No matter whom you're haggling with, negotiation depends on leverage. You lose it if you travel when hotels are full or near full. But you can still cut a good deal with a show of polite persistence.

There's another trick to knocking down your rate. While we know that part of the fun of staying in a hotel is raiding the minibar and planning your day around the complimentary breakfasts and other freebies, you pay for these extras whether you realize it or not. If you're willing to go without some of the add-ons, you can save.

Still itching for savings? There are several other tactics. Most travel agents book hotel rooms for their clients by using consortiums. These groups reserve large numbers of rooms in advance and then sell them to travel agencies. Examples of consortiums are Thors, Giants, and Hickory Travel Systems. As a rule, give a few agents who belong to different consortiums a chance to find you a low rate.

Whenever you check in, ask if there's a cheaper room available. Some front-desk clerks will give you a price break if it's not a busy night. Here's an effective way to broach the topic: "Hi. I've got a reservation tonight here. But my boss wants me to stay at [insert name of competing hotel] so that I can save ___ dollars a night. But I'd rather stay with you. Can you help?"

If you have a flexible itinerary, book a room for the first night of your stay, and then do some first-hand research after you arrive. Pop your head in a few hotels, and see what's available. If you're willing to wait until 7:00 or 8:00 P.M. and you're not in a city overrun by visiting conventioneers, you may just find yourself in a room much nicer than you can afford, with change in your pocket to spare.

GRACELAND:
For ten dollars it will change the way you think of the King.

TEN TRIPS YOU MUST TAKE BEFORE YOU DIE

To travel is to appreciate a big, wide, wonderful world that holds . . . possibilities. But where to go? Ideally, you'll hit everywhere. For now, we've culled down the world for you. Consider these ten epic travel experiences as possible bookmarks that can be the beginning, middle, or end of other adventures. Use them as suggestions to make your own memories. Whatever you do, just go.

1. THE PYRAMIDS AT DAWN

Egyptian legend has it that if you visit the Pyramids of Giza at dawn, they will whisper to you. Which is a heck of a lot better than visiting when everyone else does, because there's no whispering then—just the shouts of hawkers offering postcards, film, soft drinks, and photos of you atop a "genuine camel." Visit in the cool, dark hours of the morning, and you're not likely to forget your rendezvous with five-thousand-year-old history.

If you hire a 5:00 A.M. taxi from Cairo, you'll find yourself at the Pyramids just thirty minutes later, with only the North Star still distinct in the sky. Instruct the driver to go around the Cheops pyramid and drive as far as possible toward the Chephren, the middle pyramid. By the time you draw near the Chephren, the sky will look like one of those multilayered drinks bartenders have to make on prom night: the darkest part of the heavens turn blue, then fade into pink light, then darker pink, and then gray over the horizon toward Cairo. Remember not to pay your cabbie until the round-trip fare is completed. This isn't the Luxor in Vegas—you don't want to be stranded.

Climb part way up the Chephren and press yourselves against the cool, rough stone. As the sun comes up, you'll see spread beneath you the ruins of a temple. The oatmeal-colored façades of the Pyramids will begin to reflect the light, with the sides facing east taking on a pinkish cast. As the stone changes hue almost by the minute, you'll forgot your disappointment in not hearing any whispers.

Back to your hotel by breakfast, you'll have beaten the crowds. We guarantee that no matter how many times you visit the Pyramids during the day, it'll be the dawn tableau that is forever etched on your brain.

MINI MAGLIGHT:

As big as a candle but more power, longer usage, and great versatility.

LUGGAGE WITH WHEELS:

Hauling a garment bag around the terminal is but one thing: overrated.

Use Cairo as a jumping-off point for other Egyptian adventures. There are cruises down the Nile through the Valley of the Kings and Luxor. If you'd rather be in the water than on it, dive the Red Sea from the southern tip of the Sinai Peninsula—it boasts some of the best scuba and snorkel action in the world. There are dozens of hotels at Sharm El Sheikh with rooms as cheap as fifteen dollars a night at the Pigeon House (011–20–62–600–996), and up to ninety-one dollars a night at the Marriott Beach Resort (800–228–9290). The Camel Dive Club offers five-day, ten-dive scuba packages beginning at $235. Check out the club's Web site (http://www.cameldive.com/diving_tours.html). For an additional eight-five dollars, they'll take you to a British freighter, the SS *Thistlegorn,* which was sunk during World War II but is still largely intact.

2. ROMANCE IN A PERCHED VILLAGE.

Some people say the south of France isn't what it used to be. You know what? No place is what it used to be. There are McDonaldses in Beijing and Pizza Huts in Bangkok. The whole world is embracing the United Colors of Benetton, and soon every city with an airport will also have a Hard Rock Café or a Planet Hollywood.

So, sure, there are condo developments along the French Riviera, but it's still a gorgeous stretch of land. The climate is generally lovely, the hills are fragrant, the Mediterranean is azure, and the region's cuisine and accommodations are delightful.

Given the opportunity, make a special detour for one romantic dinner at Chateau de la Chevre d'Or (04–92–10–66–66). It's a small hotel with a Michelin one-star restaurant in the tiny seaside village of Eze. The French coastline is dotted with these perched villages, seemingly carved out of stone, usually built centuries ago on hills easy to defend. Eze is on the Moyenne-Corniche, the middle road, that cuts across the hills between Nice and Monaco, about a ten-minute drive from both places. Arrive at Eze and drive up the only road as high as you can, then park. You'll have to hike up stone passageways the rest of the way—just follow the small signs to the Chevre d'Or.

Arrive around dusk for an incomparable view of the Mediterranean and Cap Ferret, protruding like an emerald finger into the water. As darkness falls, the lights of Cap Ferret come on, and if you're with a date, well, you'll both be drunk with romance.

CONSOLIDATORS 'R' US

Hotel Reservations Network:
800–964–6835

VTS/Value Hotels:
800–377–2892

Central Reservation Service:
800–548–3311

RMC Travel Centre:
800–782–2674

Quikbook:
800–789–9887

Room Exchange:
800–846–7000

Phone way ahead and reserve a table by the big windows. Dinner is a leisurely affair that might include a prawn salad, crunchy potatoes, red mullet with a citrus sauce, and croustillant au chocolate. Figure on about $130 per person for dinner, including a good regional wine such as Domaines Ott. Don't miss the cheese cart, a Rolls-Royce-of-a-table that is as fragrant as it is beautiful.

Take coffee and dessert downstairs, by the small, illuminated pool that serves the hotel's twelve cozy rooms. On a warm night, you'll hear the croaking of frogs from the surrounding countryside, a soft symphony of night sounds that will guarantee you a "Yes," no matter what question you're asking. Now that I think about it, you might want to book one of those rooms ahead of time, too.

In and around the south of France, pleasures abound. Caesar's troops marched up and down the Riviera, and you'll find evidence of that everywhere. One of the most spectacular sights is the coliseum in Arles—you'll think you're in Rome. The beaches around Nice and Monaco are mostly rocky, but Cannes has a sandy beach and, of course, the sunbathing is often topless and sometimes bottomless at infamous St.-Tropez. In the hillside village of St.-Paul, between Nice and Cannes, is La Colombe d'Or (33–93–32–80–02), a hotel and restaurant famous for the paintings that impecunious artists traded for food decades ago. Some of those not-quite-starving artists included Picasso, Miró, Léger, and Braque.

Between Nice and Cannes, take a drive around Cap d'Antibes for a little mansion-ogling. Stop at the Grand Hotel du Cap for a drink on the rear balcony, where a sweep of lawn leads to a pool and the sea. The hotel's house drink is Champagne with raspberry liquor, but at about twenty dollars a glass, you might want to sip slowly. This dreamy resort is where Johnny Carson and Bill Cosby like to hide away, and it's the hotel F. Scott Fitzgerald describes in the opening chapter of *Tender Is the Night*. The general manager has to know you for you to get a room during the summer. No credit cards accepted.

Visit the oceanographic museum in Monaco, and then take in the luxury yachts of the very rich in the principality's harbor. The rooms of the famed casino are spectacular, even if they are filled with Vegas-style slot machines. Want to visit the part of the casino you always see in the James Bond movies? *Hoi polloi* don't know it, but those so-called private rooms are farther in the back and require an admission fee. Most fun restaurant? Rampoldi's (just off the square where the main casino and Hotel de Paris rule).

A PACK OF SPEARMINT GUM:

Nothin' worse than getting off the plane and greeting that long-lost love with a bad case of cottonmouth.

3. A SAFARI RESPITE AT THE MT. KENYA SAFARI CLUB

Someday, if you're very lucky, you'll go on safari in Africa. Probably in Kenya, Tanzania, or South Africa, where every October, millions of God's creatures still migrate across the plains and hills.

And if your safari includes Kenya and you're very lucky, you may find yourself spending at least one night at the Mt. Kenya Safari Club (800–845–3692), situated right smack on the equator about a three-hour drive from the capital city of Nairobi. Made famous when actor William Holden bought it in 1959, the Mt. Kenya Safari Club is a sprawling resort that is a throwback to the colonial years, when most every country in Africa was administered by a European power. Kenya, of course, was a British outpost, which explains why you can order your Pimm's Cup or take tea on a Chesterfield sofa while staying there.

Sure, the tented camps at most Kenyan game reserves are more exotic than a Western-style hotel. You'll do plenty of that on safari. There's just something special and whimsical about checking into this colonial-era resort where Charlie Chaplin, David Niven, Bing Crosby, Clark Gable, and other friends of Holden vacationed. Right outside the main lodge window, a manicured lawn sweeps downward to a swimming pool. The lawn is often patrolled by peacocks or wild birds whose plumage—white breast, red head, storklike feet and black "coats"—makes them look like undertakers. Mount Kenya looms impressively in the distance. There's horseback riding and tennis and other lawn sports. Copies of *USA Today* arrive a day late. In the spacious rooms, a large log is arranged and lit in your fireplace while you're at dinner in the relatively formal dining room—it can get chilly at night, thanks to cool winds off the glaciers on Mt. Kenya. Jacket and tie for the men, please. Rates begin at about $325 per couple, per night, including all meals. Steep? Sure. Worth it? Definitely.

Many safari packages even include a night or two at the Mt. Kenya Safari Club. One particularly well-priced safari that does, a twelve-day adventure called "Kenya Kaleidoscope," can be bought through British Airways (800–359–8722) for about $3,650, including airfare from the East Coast and almost all ground costs in Kenya.

4. MOON OVER THE SOUTH CHINA SEA

At twenty-two cents a trip, it has to be the cheapest, most romantic short ride over water in the world. Especially at night. And not even

NALGENE WATER BOTTLE:
Strap it to your bag, obey your thirst.

A TENT:

Everyone should sleep outdoors at least once a year.

the Chinese takeover of Hong Kong can change that about the Star Ferry, the commuter boat line that links the island of Hong Kong with the bustling mainland of Kowloon.

Steeped in tradition and as regular as a metronome, the Star Ferry is to Hong Kong what the Empire State Building is to New York: a functioning monument to a great metropolis. Each day, more than a hundred thousand people cross the choppy Hong Kong harbor on the green-and-white fleet of ten ferries that offers a panoramic view of Kowloon's neon skyline on one side and the majesty of Victoria Peak on the other. For maximum impact, you want to board on the Kowloon side some night when the moon is full. As you head toward Hong Kong island, the skyscrapers of the city glitter against the darkness of Victoria Peak. Put the moon on top like a cherry on a sundae, and you have one of those dramatic views that thrill.

The ferries, all bearing "star" names (such as *Night Star, Morning Star,* and *Celestial Star*), leave every three minutes during rush hour, and every five or six minutes during off-peak hours until 11:30 P.M. All the 39-ton, 110-foot-long vessels have propellers at each end and engines that can provide equal power in either direction. That means the ferries don't need to turn around when they dock. At each docking, the crew, some of whose families have worked on the line for generations, throw off a thick hemp line that is attached to the dock's creosoted wood pilings. Ramps come down from both the upper and lower levels of the ferries, allowing the discharge and loading of a capacity crowd of five hundred people in only three minutes. The fleet makes 450 crossings per day.

The lower deck is "coach" class. It costs twenty-two cents and is the way most commuters travel. The upper deck is first class (fare: twenty-six cents), and first-time tourists sometimes opt for the high-priced ride because the view is slightly better. Both decks are open to the weather, though plastic siding can be dropped down in the event of a major rain.

From Hong Kong you can take a jetfoil to nearby Macau (which gets turned over to the Chinese in December 1999), where casinos attract Chinese gamblers. You can take a train or bus tour north into China. Or stay on Hong Kong and take lunch at Repulse Bay or at a restaurant in the town of Stanley, both of which are on the other side of Victoria Peak, just a fifteen-minute public bus ride away from central Hong Kong. Don't feel surprised upon reaching the other side of the island if your first impression is "south of France." You'll realize that bustling Hong Kong is also an island with crescent-shaped beaches, palm trees, and lush, hillside greenery hiding homes that would fit comfortably in Bel Air.

5. GRAPEVINE MADNESS

For one of the most sensuous experiences of your life, visit a vine-yard during harvest time (mid-August to mid-October), and ask to taste a bunch of grapes directly from the vine. You're going to have to do some schmoozing, of course. Grapes are like gold. By the time they're ripe, they've been tended with care and protected against predators and adverse weather. That's expensive babysitting, and no vineyard is going to take kindly to your walking uninvited onto their property and helping yourself. Maybe buy a few bottles of their best stuff if they have a retail outlet on the premises. Having established yourself as a customer, ask if you can—just once—have the experi-ence of burying your face in a handful of grapes right off the vine. Tell 'em we sent you. Chardonnay and Cabernet Sauvignon grapes will do nicely, but Pinot Noir are generally the sweetest and juiciest.

There are vineyards all over the United States and the world, but we're partial to California's Sonoma and Napa counties because the weather is so pleasant, and both regions have adequate infrastructures to accommodate visitors. Plus, San Francisco is only an hour's drive away. In Napa, bed-and-breakfasts abound, and the Napa Valley Conference and Visitors Bureau (707–226–7459) can offer assistance and information. There are nearly a dozen companies that offer hot air balloon rides over the valley—a spectacular thrill. For names and numbers of operators, call 707–944–8793.

Neighboring Sonoma is the last stop along the El Camino Real, the Spanish-built chain of missions that stretches up from Mexico. Less glitzy than Napa and its towns of Rutherford, St. Helena, Yountville, and Oakville, Sonoma is more blue jeans and Zinfandel, though, of course, world-class Cabernets and whites are also pro-duced in the region that seems custom-made by God for grape growing. Hike or bicycle, and check out vineyards with such recog-nizable names as Ravenswood, Sebastiani, Kenwood, Carmenet, Glen Ellen, B. R. Cohn, and Gundlach Bundschu.

For a self-guided, taped audio tour and other information, call the Sonoma Valley Visitors Bureau at 707–996–1090. There are numerous lodging options; we like the El Dorado (707–996–3030), simple but elegant, with comforters, great water pressure, and a small

A MONEY BELT:

Carry your cash with confidence.

pool. A good deal at $145 for a Friday or Saturday night, $115 other nights.

If Labor Day works for you, make arrangements to attend the annual Sonoma Valley Harvest Wine Auction. It's a fun, informal event that includes winery visits, dinners at wineries, and the final night's blow-out dinner and auction at the Sonoma Mission Inn & Spa. Details: 707–935–0803. There's an early June wine auction in Napa, too, but it's always sold out months ahead of time. Details for next year: 707–942–9775.

6. A WALK THROUGH BUENOS AIRES'S RECOLETA

The most expensive real estate and best address in the Argentine capital of Buenos Aires is a cemetery. In one of the city's most fashionable shopping, living, and dining districts, Barrio Norte, the Cementerio de la Recoleta is where the rich and famous of Argentina hope to someday end up—if they can afford it. It's said it's less expensive to live an extravagant life than to be buried in Recoleta cemetery, and when there was still space available (it filled up about twenty years ago), a plot of land cost about three hundred thousand dollars.

This is no ordinary cemetery with ordinary tombstones, though. Entering it is like entering a small town, with broad, tree-lined walkways and more than seven thousand mausoleums, including seven belonging to past presidents of the country. Ornate sculptures and life-sized statues adorn stone and marble edifices. The history of Argentina is in this cemetery.

In the past, tourism officials have sometimes denied that Eva Perón is buried there because she was not from the upper class. But her tomb is one of the most visited, and she's buried in the Duarte family mausoleum to prevent a repeat of the 1955 scandal when her remains were stolen. Her inscription reads, "I will return to the millions"—though she probably didn't mean via the person of Madonna.

Take a walk on a warm day through Recoleta cemetery, and then take lunch in the gardens of one of the sleek restaurants nearby. You could be in Paris or Rome, given the European architecture, but the energy of the city is definitely South American.

Visit the San Telmo and Monserrat barrios to find couples doing

THE ALL-NEW ROADFOOD:
The ultimate guide to the finest eats in the not-so-finest towns of America.

the tango in the streets and, on Sundays, the best antique market in town in Plaza Dorrego. Dinner begins late in Buenos Aires—sometime after nine. So it makes sense that the clubs don't begin filling up until after midnight. Ask around for the names of the hottest places, but don't expect to get a lot of sleep—the nightlife doesn't wind down until breakfast. In fact, it's not clear when the residents of Buenos Aires sleep.

7. LUNCH IN A BALI RAIN FOREST

A four-wheel-drive Land Rover lumbers up a narrow, muddy, deeply rutted mountain road until it can go no farther. From the Bali rain forest, a barefoot woman appears balancing a fifty-foot-long bamboo log on her head. She smiles shyly and disappears down the road you've just climbed. Your guide shows you a narrow path, and you walk roughly seventy-five yards through thick vegetation until, suddenly, you come upon an open-air dining room perched on bamboo stilts.

"You would like a beer?" a smiling hostess in a crisp, yellow Indonesian tunic asks.

Behind her, long tables hold a feast of satay, fresh fruit, bamboo soup, meats, rice, vegetables, and desserts. Don't ask how they got either the equipment or provisions up there. If Neil Armstrong had encountered a Wendy's on the moon, he wouldn't have been much more surprised.

Lunch in the rain forest comes at the culmination of a day of exploring the heart of Bali away from the tourist towns and resorts. From the sun-baked aerie atop a Land Rover, you'll photograph coffee fields and watch the delivery of offerings of fruits and flowers to rural temples. You'll watch children snare dragonflies on sticks—the insects will be fried later and become munchies. You'll see men chisel building bricks by hand out of the side of rocky cliffs; women balance stacks of the bricks on their heads, carry them up treacherous paths, and stack them neatly by a dirt road. You'll admire the elaborate, handmade dam work that irrigates acres and acres of luminescent, green rice fields.

You'll reflect upon these visions as you indulge in a gourmet buffet offered to you and others who signed up for the WakaLouka Land Cruise, which can be arranged through any hotel in Bali. Cost: eighty-three dollars per person.

PERSPECTIVE AND PATIENCE: Because getting there is not only half the fun—it's often half the vacation.

8. TEA AT THE LONDON RITZ

Afternoon tea in England began in the early nineteenth century, when the Duchess of Bedfordshire decided dinner wouldn't be served until she was good and hungry. To tide everyone over, teatime became a leisurely, afternoon punctuation point, a pick-me-up for the aristocracy. (The working class eventually adopted what became known as "high tea," a six o'clock affair that often included meats, greens, leftovers, and beans on toast with a poached egg; the event often doubled as dinner.)

There's no beans on toast at the London Ritz, the place to take tea. London's prince of teatime is Michael Twomey, a fifty-year veteran of the Ritz, who orchestrates each day's tea in the hotel's Palm Court with the gracious authority of a Philharmonic conductor. He's tended to everyone from Evelyn Waugh to Frank Sinatra, and if only everyone knew that, his job would be a lot easier. You have to reserve weeks ahead—except for hotel guests. (Call 44–171–493–8181.)

Go for the tradition and experience of it. At about thirty dollars per person, it's expensive, but it's all-you-can-eat. Besides a classic selection of tea, you'll receive three-story silver platters piled with smoked salmon, cucumber and watercress sandwiches; scones with strawberry jam and clotted cream; and pastries that include miniature lemon tarts, mini-Napoleons, tiny éclairs, and small pyramids of solid chocolate. A slice of fruit or carrot cake is also offered by roving waiters in the formal room with marble columns.

Dress up. "The Ritz should always be special," Twomey says in explaining why men are expected to wear jacket and tie. Slacks are tolerated on women, but not encouraged; hats are. "The sense of occasion must always prevail."

GOOD BEHAVIOR:
Everyone hates boorish Americans.

9. MOTORBIKING NORTHERN THAILAND

You've heard about the traffic and pollution in Thailand's capital, Bangkok. Chiang Mai is an hour's flight away but a world apart. Bordered to the north by Laos and what most of the world still calls Burma (though the military thugs who run it call it Myanmar), Chiang Mai is cooler, greener, and less crowded, though that last point is in jeopardy as more people flee Bangkok. Surrounded on three sides by lush, green hills, Chiang Mai is where you rent a motorbike for exploring or where you secure a guide for trekking among the hill tribes in the outlying areas.

You can go back to Thailand again and again. Perhaps because it's the only Southeast Asian country that's never been under foreign domination, its people are among the friendliest and most gentle in the world. Even in whacked-out Bangkok, you find beauty and tranquillity behind closed doors; somehow, with flowers, music, and decor, Thailanders manage to create a peaceful oasis in a frenzied setting.

Chiang Mai is home to the nation's woodcrafters and other artisans, some of its best food (don't miss kao soi, a curry noodle soup with coconut milk, lime, and other spices), and certainly some of its most dramatic scenery. And it's cheap. If you walk the streets of Chiang Mai, you'll find plenty of open-air shops offering motorbike rentals for seven dollars a day and guided treks into the hills for eighty dollars for a four-day, three-night trek. It seems everyone in Chiang Mai will take you trekking, and that's a problem. Look for a company that's a member of the Professional Guide Association of Chiang Mai or the Jungle Tour Club of northern Thailand. Don't go in a group larger than ten, and make sure your guide speaks the language of the villages you'll be visiting and that other trekkers won't be there. Ask around for recommendations, and take no valuables.

You can buy food on the street from vendors in Chiang Mai for under a dollar; at night, the downtown market serves up entire meals for three dollars. The gathering spot for local hipsters and foreigners (called farangs) is the Riverside Rim Ping, a restaurant and bar along the Ping River with good food, fruit shakes, and cold beers.

The beauty is in the hills that stretch north to Chiang Rai, the last major town before you enter the opium poppy growing region known as the Golden Triangle, about a three-hour drive from Chiang Mai. But you don't need to go that far to immerse yourself in northern Thailand's hills. Just head northwest out of Chiang Mai toward the Doi Suthep mountain, where the road is good and the scenery stunning. You'll find a hundred shades of green in the rice fields that shimmer in the sun. Pull off the road at a sign offering elephant rides, and revamp your definition of "bumpy ride." Take side roads and admire the teak houses and the saffron-colored robes of the occasional monk. The area's best temple, or wat, is on Doi Suthep, too.

If you go deep enough into the mountains, you'll find villages where opium is still smoked. Just remember that it's a good idea to be very sober and straight when driving in Thailand, because it often appears no one else is on the road is.

LONELY PLANET GUIDEBOOKS:
Let's Go is for college students and losers.

GIGANTIC CARRY-ON BAG:
Skip baggage check.

10. SINGING GONDOLIERS IN VENICE.

It may sound hokey, but find yourself a Venetian gondolier who knows a little opera, open a bottle of Champagne with your date, and . . . it works.

Venice has been written off time and again, and yes, it's all about tourism these days. But it's still a theatrical city, with heart-stopping architecture and atmospheric churches. The trick is not to stay in Venice, which can get hot and claustrophobic. Instead, stay on the nearby island of Lido, where there's beach, greenery, and luxurious hotels. Then take a few-minute ride into Venice for sightseeing.

There are no cars in Venice, so the water is your highway. Vaporetto is the water bus, the cheapest way to get around; the most expensive is by water taxi, or taxi acqueo. Gondolas, too, aren't cheap—use them for the show, not as a way of getting from place to place. A fifty-minute spin along the canals will cost you about fifty dollars— more if you have a gondolier with a good voice.

In Venice, don't miss the Peggy Guggenheim Collection (Calle San Cristoforo 701), the palazzo of the late art benefactress. It's quirky but fascinating, with works by Henry Moore, Jean Arp, Max Ernst, and Alberto Giacometti. Take a drink at Harry's Bar, where the Bollini is said to have been invented, but don't eat there—too expensive. There are plenty of moderately priced options. Along with Lido, visit the nearby island of Murano, the glass capital of the region. Go there for lunch—dozens of pleasant restaurants line the main shopping street of Murano.

But mostly, Venice is about walking. You'll get lost, which is fine during the day, but it can be very confusing at night and—if you ever saw the film of the Daphne DuMaurier classic *Don't Look Now*— very scary. Despite the fact that it relies on tourism for its existence, Venice still means romance with a capital "R." Take a date, grab a gondola, make a memory.

SELF-GUIDED TRIPS:

Leave the package tours to the blue-hairs.

CHAPTER 13

WOMEN

Q: WHAT DO I SAY WHEN MY GIRLFRIEND ASKS, "DO I LOOK FAT?"

This is the question men dread the most—and for good reason. When a woman is standing in front of the mirror, absorbed with assessing the exact circumference of her derrière, she isn't likely to be happy with *any* response. If you answer yes, she'll get upset, saying she feels like a fat cow, and tell you that if you don't like her body then you obviously don't want to sleep with her anymore, and finally mention how cruel you were to bring up her weight in the first place. Say no, and she'll think you're not paying enough attention, or are just humoring her. Danger, Will Robinson! Proceed with extreme caution.

The following answers are not advised: "Not really. Well, maybe in the thighs"; "You know, in some cultures a big butt is considered attractive"; "If you just worked out a little more, like I do. . . ."; and the ever popular, "It's just more of you to love, baby."

The best way to wriggle out of this uncomfortable question is to refuse to allow yourself to get trapped into answering it at all. Don't

FLOWERS:

They may seem trite, but females love 'em. Just watch other women around when someone gets a delivery.

even begin to ask yourself whether she's really any fatter than she was a few weeks or hours ago, because that only gets you involved in her weight obsession—bad idea.

Instead, think about what's really bothering her. It's probably not her fat body. She'll never admit that though, because weight anxieties play such a paramount role in women's psyches. Most women in this culture have a neurotic hatred for their own bodies. Lots and lots of otherwise sane ladies honestly believe that no man is going to want to sleep with them if their hip bones don't inflict bruises.

So the weight thing becomes a shorthand for all kinds of anxieties. Work sucks: I feel fat. Relationship sucks: I feel fat. Weather sucks: I feel fat.

Answering the literal question, in fact, will not only be perilous to your relationship but will also encourage her to sink further into her mire of physical insecurities and not confront the real issues at hand. The trick, then, is to avoid the question without letting her realize that you never answered her.

So are you going to divert her anxieties? Start by giving her bod some nice, positive nonverbal attention. When she pops the weight question, disarm the surface neurosis with a friendly, sexy, unquestionably admiring squeeze or caress. When you feel her body relax and respond, then you're on safer ground and can ask her about what's really bothering her. And if you feel you've got to say something, try, "Listen, I can't tell any difference. You look good to me."

Eventually, she'll start to realize that you aren't going to buy into her weight obsession, which should come as a relief to her—and to you.

After all, if she really wanted a diet cop, she'd date Richard Simmons.

Q: HOW DO I SURVIVE MY GIRLFRIEND'S PMS?

You can see the transformation taking place every month—the edge in the voice, the glint in the eye. She cries at McDonald's commercials and bites your head off for bringing her flowers. And while you get to rule the world and pee standing up, each and every month you also have to face your significant other during that *special* time. Face it, you need help. Here are some tips for PMS survival:

BE UNDERSTANDING

According to the friendly informative recording at PMS Access, "Over 150 symptoms are associated with PMS. Among the most common are irritability, mood swings, weight gain, food cravings, fatigue, backaches, and breast tenderness." Gentleman, if you had to experience this every month for a good portion of your adult life, you'd be pretty cranky, too.

ENCOURAGE HEALTHY EATING HABITS AND EXERCISE

Read this one carefully. "Encourage healthy eating habits" does *not* mean you are supposed to rip the pound of chocolate she is currently gnawing on out of her mouth. This can be very dangerous and, in some reported cases, fatal. A nice dinner somewhere healthy should do the trick. And while she may not feel like moving from the couch, exercise can lessen symptoms and get endorphins going. Suggest going on a walk together. But remember, don't push it.

LIE

Maybe the sight of your sweetie bloated with a Dorito hanging out of her mouth doesn't turn you on. Lie. Listen to me—lie shamelessly and repeatedly. Lie. And don't stop lying.

DON'T EVEN *TRY* TO BE RATIONAL

Think you're confused? Even many women don't know what's going on in their own bodies during this time. Hormonal and serotonin levels are fluctuating, and women are very often confused by their own responses and moodiness. Most women feel terrible when they inflict their moodiness and irritability on a loved one. Don't make them feel worse.

Ask Dr. Tracy
www.loveadvice.com
Whether you're single, on the prowl, or part of a couple, Dr. Tracy's library of love advice has something for you. Read celebrity interviews. Post a question of your own.

Mars and Venus Home
www.marsvenus.com
Dr. Gray's official home page. Join live relationship chats. Read answers to past questions, and find out when the doctor will be visiting your hometown.

goodfella's
"Ballbreakers" page
www.baynet.net/~scru b/Ballbreakers.htm
If things get ugly, come here to get even. School your ex by posting a picture of her at her worst.

RUN A BATH OR GIVE A MASSAGE

Aside from the sensual element of these activities, they will relax your partner and reduce some symptoms, such as headaches and backaches. Plus, you'll get sensitivity points to cash in on when Dr. Jekyll returns.

BE INFORMED

Try to learn as much about PMS, why it occurs, when it occurs, and to understand that it does occur. "This is no longer in a woman's head." So make like Alan Alda, and get sensitive. For a free information package, call PMS Access at 800–222–4PMS.

And if you should fail, don't worry, there's always next month.

VALENTINE'S DAY:

Make a big deal out of it. You may not care, but she actually does.

ASK:

If you want something in bed, ya gotta speak up. Most women aren't mind readers.

Q: HOW DO I BUY MY GIRLFRIEND A BIRTHDAY PRESENT?

The discerning birthday gifter must understand the offering's central purpose: to keep you around long enough to have the problem of what to buy her again next year. Ask yourself these two basic questions before you start shopping: (1) Is it appropriate for the amount of time the two of you have been romantically involved? (2) Is it something that will reflect back positively on you both when she uses it and when she explains it to others? With that in mind and some advance planning, giving the perfect gift can be as easy as selling a million records when you have Puff Daddy as your producer.

As different as every relationship is, so, too, every present should be. If you met over tequila poppers, then think a bottle of Patron, lemon, salt, and two classy glasses. It's thoughtful, appropriate, and involves you. If you don't know where to begin, become a cross between Casanova and Columbo. In other words, before you open your mouth or your wallet, you need to open your eyes.

Always, always give pleasure. Let her dad buy her that laptop, her sister give her a membership to the gym. Your job as the boyfriend is to give the gift of decadence. A certificate to a health spa for a pedicure, manicure, and facial. A satin nightgown. A cashmere blanket. Give her a gift that will remind her of you when you are not around. Apply Pavlov's Law: Make pleasure an involuntary response to her thinking about you.

If you are involved in a serious relationship, there eventually come certain obligations that one must fulfill or suffer the consequences. Unfortunately, no matter how well you boil that rigatoni or write that sonnet, nothing makes the impact of tasteful jewelry. If after a few years your gift isn't round, skinny and gold you'll be out like Grandmother's teeth at bedtime.

One final caveat: Be careful not to choose too wisely—the birthday gift sets the standard that the anniversary has to surpass.

TO MOVE IN, OR NOT TO MOVE IN

REMEMBER YOUR ANNIVERSARY: Married or not, learn the date. Not sure? Ask her way, way in advance.

On the surface, living together with your girlfriend is a good idea—hell, on the surface, it's a *great* idea. Someone to keep the place clean! Someone to use the stove for something other than a storage box! Someone who will change the sheets, and not just in months with an R! Sex anytime you want it! Oh, man . . . .

Down, boy. If your motivation is simply to make your life easier and cleaner, then you've got a problem already. As with everything else in this world, there is a right way and a wrong way to go about this.

What makes living together tricky is that the Laws of Commingling are not written down, at least not in any place *men* have access to. But if you've made up your mind to do this, then we're not going to stop you. Just remember a few things:

MEN AND WOMEN ARE FROM DIFFERENT CULTURES

An Australian aborigine will spend hours digging grubs and honey ants out of the ground with a stick. He'll then eat the squirmy bugs raw, popping them into his mouth like so many bits of wild cherry Pez from a Tweety Bird dispenser.

While aborigines are also very intelligent, highly philosophical, artistically inclined, and musically proficient, surely you can see the difficulties of rooming with one. You come from two different cultures, two different backgrounds that might often conflict.

Then why are you considering *even for a minute* living with a woman to whom you are not married? Why? Did we lose you there? Aborigines . . . women. Women . . . aborigines. The point is, you are a man, and she is a woman and, like the aborigine, she comes from a different culture. *Culture,* dude. Think about it.

Just because you grew up in the same country, maybe even the same state and city as your loved one, does not mean you share the same culture. In fact, you never will. Look at the evidence: Growing up, she wore pink and you wore blue. She played with Barbie's Happening Hair Parlor, and you melted little green army soldiers with flame throwers made out of lighter fluid cans. She learned how to prepare an entire Thanksgiving dinner for ten while you struggled to learn not to put metal TV dinner trays in the microwave.

And now you think you can *live* together. The good news is, you are not alone. There are 3,668,000 "unmarried-couple" households, according to the U.S. Bureau of the Census: twice as many as in 1980. That's 1,834,000 men living in conflicting cultures with 1,834,000 women—and those are the ones who admitted it to the government. But before you double your kitchen utensils, keep this in mind:

COOKING IN:

Invite her over for a home-cooked meal, and we promise she'll be calling you Chef Tell Me More.

COHABITATION MEANS FIDELITY—OR DIDN'T YOU KNOW?

As much as it's going to hurt, Casanova, get rid of your "little black book" of girlfriend phone numbers, *especially* if you have a star rating next to their names. Just pitch it. And don't make the mistake of one clever guy we know who created a secret database of exes in his computer; one day his live-in lover accidentally pushed Shift/9 and read all about Debbie S.'s four-star bedroom gymnastics.

Then there's the case of "Horny Dog" (not his real name), who kept what he called "The List" in a drawer under his boxer shorts in the bedroom. The List contained the names of every woman he'd ever slept with, including the dates of each conquest *and* hatch marks indicating the number of times they did it *per session.*

He never told his live-in about The List. She found it. She read it. She was shocked. Shocked, not just by the sheer numbers of different women, or by the numbers of single-session trysts—including one that had /////// (eight) marks next to her name *for one day*— but by the several names that came *after her own entry.*

Don't try to hide the evidence—get it out in the open. If your cohabitant is on the pill, put your condoms where she can see them, and tell her you're keeping them for those times you both need them (yes, Junior, there are times of the month they will come in handy). Count them out for her, and leave them there. Do not keep any in your wallet, glove box, or Filofax. These will only lead to suspicious minds.

Remember, even the things that in *your* mind are utterly harmless may be potential points of contention for *her.* Box up any old love letters and souvenirs from childhood romances and past conquests, and give them to your mother. If you toss these mementos away, you may regret it twenty years down the line when you want to see a photo of your first love. But to have these things around the house, before you are entangled in the safety net of matrimony, poses a threat to your shackee.

THE FINE PRINT AND THE DOTTED LINE

DO NOT move in together just to save money.

There is a whole subsection of the legal industry that is flourishing quite nicely, and that's the practice of cohabitation counsel. You've heard of prenuptial agreements? Well, there are plenty of family attorneys who are prepared to whip up a cohabitation agreement along the same lines. It's the "pre" without the "nup."

Because you're not just sharing the rent, friend. Did you ever stop to wonder about all those new clothes she's always wearing that make her look so delish? Have you never asked her about her credit rating because you think it's "too personal"? Listen, if you're going to live together, there are *lots* more personal things you're going to be sharing—like toilet paper and rectal thermometers, so get over it.

Legal protection is worth considering—if not just for peace of mind. Because if all goes well, you and yours might wind up with a

CANDLES:

Romantic, moody, cheap. Good for taking a bath or impressing her with dinner.

joint bank account full of mutual money. You might buy the condo you share, you may help her pay off her student loans because you make more money, or you might stay together until you die and leave her with a huge estate tax to pay.

And what happens if, God forbid, Houdini the Slippery Sperm gets past the rubber barrier? What's that? What was that word you just uttered? Did it start with "M"?

Which brings us to the most important thing:

SHE WANTS TO GET MARRIED, NO MATTER WHAT SHE SAYS

Don't make the mistake of moving in without clarifying expectations. You may be thinking you'll live together for a while, so you can save enough to put a down payment on a house to live in—maybe even with her. She may very well be thinking that you're going to get married.

Now how did that happen?

Most people shack up thinking it will determine whether or not it makes sense to take the next step. That being the case, a little pre-cohabitation counseling may help iron out any problems and ensure success. After all, professional help isn't just for people with problems.

No one knows how many cohabitants "take the next step" and get hitched. Some therapists say the cohabitant "divorce" rate is similar to the married couple divorce rate, approximately 50 percent. In fact, there are some who blame society's leniency toward "living in sin" as contributing to the divorce rate, which, according to the National Center for Health Statistics, is double what it was in 1960, when living together just wasn't done. But why blame yourself for everyone else's divorce?

IF YOU'RE STILL GOING TO TAKE THE PLUNGE

OK, you've still made up your mind to mix your linens with hers. (And don't be offended when she throws out all of your linens, towels, and probably underwear because they're *gray*. When was the last time you separated your colors in the laundry?) Here are some other things to sort out, arranged by degree of difficulty:

LOW-MAINTENANCE: The other kind will kill you.

EASY.

Is there enough parking for both of your cars?

DIFFICULT.

How will you decide who does which household chores? The best answer: take the jobs that bug you the most. If having a grungy toilet racks her nerves, let *her* clean it—she'll probably do it more often and more thoroughly than you will. If having a dishwasher always filled with clean dishes irritates you, then *you* take the duty of emptying it.

MOST DIFFICULT.

How do your folks—and hers—feel about your shacking up?

Why is this touchy? While you don't see them a great deal right now while you're just dating, all of that will change when you become a "couple" and begin attending family reunions, holiday gatherings, weddings, christenings, and other functions that she can't miss. And neither can you, bunkie. It's best to have a good relationship with the 'rents, especially for those times you need someone to cosign on a car loan. Don't neglect this issue, or you'll be a swinging single again in no time.

WOMEN: CAN'T LIVE WITH 'EM, CAN'T SHOOT 'EM

This is so true. You can't live *with* them the way you live with your dog. You have to live *for* them. You have to accept the woman you live with as your hero, your best friend, your lifelong compatriot, because if you don't, if you plunge headlong into cohabitation with just a shred of doubt in your little pea brain, then, my friend, you may as well save yourself a bunch of time and throw your beloved couch, bed, coffee table, and framed prints of Vargas nudes into the nearest body of water.

There really is no reason for two people who live together and—here comes the "L" word—*love* together ever to fall apart, not if it's done with genuine mutual respect for the other's *culture*.

Hey, look at it this way. What if you really *did* get an Australian aborigine for a roommate? If you were smart, and you had him share *his* culture with you, he could show you how to shoot a spike dart 150 feet from a really cool .40 caliber blowgun.

That wouldn't be so bad now, would it?

A MUSICAL INSTRUMENT: Billy Joel got Christie Brinkley. Perhaps you'll manage your own little scene in an Italian Restaurant.

TYRA AND FRIENDS TELL ALL

When it comes down to figuring out what women want, you don't want advice from a bunch of guys. What the hell do we know? So to get you the scoop, we decided to convene a council of women. Not just any women, mind you. Try supermodels Tyra Banks, Rebecca Romijn and a bunch of their twentysomething friends—Cassandra, a marketing consultant; Gayle, a waitress; Kara, a teacher; Robyn Roth, a singer; Cen, an aspiring broadcaster; Liba, an art director; Remi Watson, a publicist. Sheri, *P.O.V.*'s sex columnist, joined in to keep things moving. The wine started flowing, the tape recorder started rolling, and the unfiltered truth started emerging.

TYRA: OK, girls. Let's hear it straight. What is the best place for a man to meet you?

CEN: Health food store.

REMI: Coffee shop, supermarkets.

TYRA: How about clubs?

CHORUS: No. Never clubs.

ROBYN: It's the frame of mind guys are in at clubs. They're out for one thing. Sex is really on their mind.

SHERI: How about the gym?

LIBA: I don't like the gym.

TYRA: Oh, I do. Being sweaty and working out is very sexual. . . .

SHERI: Should a guy approach you? With what line?

CHORUS: No lines.

REBECCA: I don't even like being approached. I feel like guys should not just come up and say something to you. I don't like men who approach. I like mutual meetings. You know, just referrals, basically.

ROBYN: Somebody who is really good, you start to wonder how many times they've done it. I like the more loose guy who just looks like he's there.

KARA: I like a nervous guy. I put myself in the position to talk to a nervous guy to make him feel a little less nervous. This happened a couple of months ago with a guy I'm dating now. We had eye contact. Later he told me, "Do you know why I went into that bar? I saw you from the outside, and I told my friend that we have to go in there, I have to meet that woman."

REBECCA: I love a man with a mission.

SHERI: How do you like a man to approach you?

SWING DANCE LESSONS:

A good way to break the ice if you're afraid of a dance floor. Your girl will love you for it.

PABLO NERUDA'S *THE CAPTAIN'S VERSES:*

No one knows how to romance a woman like Neruda.

ROBYN: Oh. Just really, really honest. You can tell when a guy is being honest. If they are putting you on or not. As you get older, you become a really good judge of character.

TYRA: What type of guys do you like?

LIBA: I really like funny. Funny is important for me. I like to laugh.

SHERI: I think most guys would really like to know if you take funny over handsome. And would you take smart over handsome?

CHORUS: Smart. Definitely smart. And, yes, funny.

SHERI: Powerful and sexual over handsome and sexual?

CEN: I like men who are fun but can be serious about life. Goal-oriented, but spiritually well rounded.

CASSANDRA: And very decisive. Decisiveness is one of the most important things to me, you know, because of the fact that we are working all the time. Someone who can plan. Someone who has somewhat of a plan, who can come up with creative and different ideas of what to do as opposed to just the movies or just eating. And a guy being funny totally affects the way they look to me. . . .

KARA: And that makes them attractive—their just being peaceful, having some kind of inner peace about them.

ROBYN: Yeah, I've never gone out with a really gorgeous guy; I've had some ugly boyfriends. Ugly at first, and then they turn into something else.

TYRA: They say that women fall in love or become attracted to men who love them, and men fall in love with the women who are attracted to them.

CASSANDRA: I think that with women it is much more mental. I have definitely seen men who I think are attractive, yet mentally they are not there in any way, so they are the ugliest people in the world.

TYRA: I like men who give me a mental orgasm more than anything else.

SHERI: Would you date a guy who was really nice, sweet, funny, and great, but to whom you were just not sexually attracted?

CHORUS: That's hard.

ROBYN: I think that comes after. Yes, after a while you could be sexually attracted to him. I don't think that needs to come first.

TYRA: I like happy guys with a sense of humor. But I am not necessarily sexually attracted to him first.

SHERI: But if there is really no spark, would you go ahead with the relationship?

CASSANDRA: I would be friends at least, because my boyfriend or whoever I'm dealing with has to be my best friend first of all. I've

PICKING UP THE TAB:

A true gentleman would.

dated a lot of enemies. Because you end up feeling that the man you are dealing with is resentful of you. Jealous of you. Then the sex is nothing anyway after a while.

SHERI: Are the best relationships the ones that started as friend-ships?

CEN: I have a rule that if we were friends and then lovers, when it ends, we should be able to be friends afterward. I can't respect you if you cannot be my friend once it's over.

TYRA: There is another thing they say—that your boyfriend should be the kind of man who would still be your friend if you took away all the sex.

GAYLE: It's true—friendship is so important because sex is only gonna be so frequent when you are first dating. You know the gum-ball theory? If you put away a gumball every time you have sex when you are dating, and then, after you get married, you take one out every time you have sex, you'll have gumballs forever.

SHERI: What about guys when it comes to the whole money thing?

CASSANDRA: For a very long time I wanted to date someone who I thought was up and coming, with no money. The starving artist. Because I am a career-oriented person, I think it was all about putting me in a powerful position.

SHERI: Does anyone like younger guys?

CHORUS: We love them.

TYRA: I met an eighteen-year-old guy at this dinner yesterday. He is adorable. I was just like, "Only eighteen, but is he legal?"

KARA: I think that what women want is not the money, it's not the prestige—they want somebody who is ambitious in whatever they're doing.

ROBYN: But then you have to distinguish between falling in love with their potential or falling in love with their ambition.

REMI: I think you could be supportive, but not the support.

TYRA: Society is just set up for men to have more and for women to have less, and for the woman to look for the man with money and all that. So I think it is weird for a man to date somebody who is more affluent than he is. It's a constant struggle.

CASSANDRA: I dated this one guy who didn't have a car, a house, a job. He didn't have a phone. He didn't have anything, and it was hor-rible.

REBECCA: I think what you are saying is a little outdated. I don't think that there are a lot of men who have a problem with that any-more. I have had men live off me, and they had no problems.

LISTEN:

There's nothing uglier then a guy who's in love with the sound of his own voice.

LIBA: Those are called freeloaders.

REBECCA: I like to date men who are successful as well. They're secure, and you can learn from them.

REMI: Have you found that you have met guys who have total pipe dreams? That's a real turnoff.

TYRA: There is another side of it, too. I've dated very successful, very wealthy men who still can't handle the fact that I've made even one-eighth of what they make. You know, they want me to be a house-wife. I can't tell you names, but . . . [everyone laughs] You know what I mean? They still can't deal with it. So it is weird that men still want us to be there only for them.

CASSANDRA: Men fall in love with the idea of you being independent and working and doing all these things, but that's not what they really want.

SHERI: Before we leave the money question, we have to ask this question: Who pays the first date, and who continues to pay?

TYRA: I think the man should pay for the first three dates, and after that it should be dutch or back and forth.

REBECCA: Modern women don't play games. Whatever happens, happens.

SHERI: Even the first date?

KARA: The first date he should definitely pay. I appreciate it when a man pays, but then I'll offer to buy drinks later on.

ROBYN: I think that it should be just like you're going out with your girlfriend. Sometimes your friend says, "Oh, it's my treat tonight," or it should be dutch.

TYRA: Whoever comes up with the plan should pay.

KARA: I'd prefer their making an emotional investment.

ROBYN: Can we go back to that orgasm thing we were talking about? It's mental for the women, and it's physical for the men. It's innate for a woman to be romantic and want romance, and the guys really have to think about it.

TYRA: If there were guys sitting here having this same discussion, they'd see how our body language is, they'd be . . . [leans back in posed disinterest; laughter]

REBECCA: I heard a theory that a man is able to, like, get over a one-night stand without a second thought. But forget about a woman—the very next day she's asking, "Where is he?" A woman will, like, hang on to him, fret over it, for a long time. On the other side of the coin, a woman can fall out of love after a year or so in the relationship—overnight, almost—whereas a man can't let get go.

DESSERT:
A quick way to her heart.

"YOU LOOK BEAUTIFUL":
No, as a matter of fact, you *can't* say it too much.

GAYLE: Guys are big kids.

SHERI: The moment you sleep with somebody, do you think that's the start of a relationship?

CHORUS: No!

SHERI: At what point do we expect commitment?

CASSANDRA: If we're spending every day or every other day together, then that's fine. A label doesn't have to be put on it.

TYRA: I haven't had a boyfriend since I was sixteen. And that was the last time I really wanted somebody to be my boyfriend.

SHERI: What about the age thing?

CASSANDRA: I'm twenty-nine years old. I've dated as young as twenty-two, and had a great time, and my boyfriend right now is twenty-three and is going to be twenty-four in a month. For some reason, I like younger men. I like the energy.

LIBA: My boyfriend of the last four years is the the same age as me, which is twenty-eight. He's the youngest person I've ever dated; everyone else has always been five to six years older than me. Now, we broke up four months ago, and of all the dates that I've gone on, the most appealing guy who I went out with was twenty-four. The energy is just there.

TYRA: I'm twenty-four years old, and one of the most appealing guys I've dated was twenty-two.

REBECCA: I don't want to date someone younger than me. My boyfriend is ten years older than me.

SHERI: Doesn't that feel like an age gap?

REBECCA: I don't feel an age gap at all. I feel just as mature and ready for life situations as he is. Like I was saying earlier, women feel maternal at a younger age. Women are ready to have babies at a younger age than men are. They think about the wedding day, just that one day. That's why women make the mistake of jumping in marriages early.

REMI: I love the idea of love, and I'm not against long-term relationships, but I don't necessarily have wonderful feelings about marriage. I don't think it is an awful thing, but I don't think that marriage is or should be the end point. Frankly, I think marriage is overrated. People think that once they walk down the aisle and they have a dress on and the confetti is thrown and presents are everywhere, all of a sudden it's all roses. Really, it is just an extension of a boyfriend/girlfriend relationship, glamorized and romanticized.

SHERI: Do we really like bad guys?

REBECCA: It's the whole fantasy—the bad boy edge. It's a real turn-on. It's tricky though. Like in *Gone With the Wind,* he whisks her off

PEACH ROSES:

Red? Predictable. Yellow? Boring. White? Strictly for funerals. Try a horse of a different color— she'll appreciate the ride.

her feet and sweeps her away. It's a fantasy. In fact, he's going to rape her.

ROBYN: I hate to admit it, but when it comes to a bad guy really sweeping us off our feet, we really want that.

SHERI: What's the best lie a man ever told you to get you into bed?

ROBYN: That women have to please a man, because once they start, we are responsible for that thing, that erection. We must rescue him from pain.

CASSANDRA: I have to say, I've been in enough relationships with lazy lovers, and I would rather just not have sex than to deal with a lazy lover.

KARA: I think men also need to understand women's bodies more and think about what they are doing.

SHERI: Has anyone ever used a guy just for sex?

KARA: I was really interested in this guy. He was so sexy, so dynamic, so much fun. He was moving to be with his girlfriend in Chicago. While he was in L.A., we were together and having a great time. We hadn't had sex yet because he was leaving soon. We were together for his last night at this bar with all my friends, partying and having a good time. He's jumping up and down, going, "Please have sex with me; please sleep with me." He was kidding around, but I knew he was serious. I'm just thinking, "Why would I have sex with you tonight and you're leaving tomorrow? Like, I'm going to give you a good-bye present?" Well that's what I did!

SHERI: Besides a one-night stand, any of you date a guy just for sex?

CHORUS: It's great.

CEN: I think that's fine.

ROBYN: If that's what you want at that point in time.

LIBA: Has to be mutual.

KARA: If the person is very cool and they're cute, too.

CASSANDRA: As long as we both know that we both go into it in the same frame of mind.

ROBYN: I could never do that because I always romanticize it. Even if I don't like the guy that much, I want the guy to like me.

REBECCA: Yeah. I hate to admit it, but I agree with you.

ROBYN: You want all these guys to admire you and want you, but you don't want them. You just want them to like you, so you get them to like you. Then, when they really, really like you, you say, "Later." You blow them off.

SHERI: How much should you tell a guy about your sexual history? This is about diseases, prescreening for everything possible...

CANDLES:
The perfect amount of light and sultry smells.

CEN: You never tell him everything.

GAYLE: I agree with that.

CASSANDRA: That's your history. He has no right to know everything,

LIBA: All they need to know is for safety. Because ultimately you could get AIDS. So you better know who you are with!

ROBYN: Let's say you go and have HIV testing together and you're negative. Why does it matter, your sexual past?

REMI: Well, you're not going to get an AIDS test before a one-night stand.

CASSANDRA: In the nineties we've become more mature. When I had an AIDS test a couple of years ago and I was OK, I decided that I would never have sex without a condom; never, ever. If I start a new relationship, we will take an AIDS test together but afterward still use condoms. Remember, there's that six-month time period when the disease can be incubating. Also, I'm here with you guys right now. He could be somewhere doing something else.

KARA: You can't assume that every time you have sex with someone it's going to be a serious involvement or relationship that is long-term. Not everybody has relationships that are long-term. Then you can certainly say, "Since we've been together for five months, lets go get an HIV test." But how can we insist on a test at the start? It's like saying you want to get serious. It's really tricky.

CASSANDRA: I don't think you should tell about the past history, because, ultimately people will always lie. So why tell anything? It doesn't help you to calculate how safe each of you is. Men just are curious to hear about your lovers.

SHERI: Let's say the guy asks what you've been up to, and he asks in a sexual tone.

REBECCA: I was in this two-year relationship, and I brought up so many stories from the past that I would just mention somebody's name, and he'd just think, "Did she sleep with him?" He wanted to know. Didn't mean he was jealous. He was just curious.

CEN: I think they want to know, but they really don't want to know.

CHORUS: Yeah.

ROBYN: Then they tell you a story about someone, and you ask if they slept with them, and they say, "Yes." Then you realize this is someone you haven't heard about before, so you have to top it by telling your story. Well, one time I went out with this guy and the same thing happened. You know the type—we'll just be friends. You have to compare histories, and then you are tricked.

VAN MORRISON'S ASTRAL WEEKS: There's no album more achingly romantic.

TYRA: I think it's a tough question. Because when you ask it, you have to be prepared to tell it. So they are going to ask how many people you've slept with, and you'd better be ready to 'fess up. Someone says, "Oh, three," and you're, like, "Ooops." [The women ask each other their numbers—four to six lovers seems to be the average.]

SHERI: Is a guy who's had a lot of partners a turnoff?

CHORUS: Yeah.

KARA: People go through active times, promiscuous times. I understand that.

ROBYN: You have to hear the whole story.

TYRA: Do you talk to your girlfriends about how a guy is in bed?

CHORUS: Yeah. All the time.

CEN: I used to. I don't anymore.

KARA: I think guys do it to boast, and girls do it to talk about the experience, to make everything detailed. Compare. Analyze. [laughter]

SHERI: Do you talk about it in real detail?

TYRA: To my best friends, yeah. I mean, only to my best friends.

ROBYN: The more serious the relationship, the less you'll talk about it.

REBECCA: I won't tell it to just anyone. Only to close friends. To Tyra, yes.

SHERI: Do you go as far as talking about penis size?

ROBYN: Penis size is very important.

CEN: Penis size is not important. It's a matter of what they do with it.

KARA: My friends and I have a new theory—we really think it has to do with a man's confidence. We can immediately tell if he is big or not.

GAYLE: We've talked about this, me and my roommate and Kara. We've decided that you can look at a guy, his demeanor, and tell. We look at the way he walks; the way he talks. And you just know if he's carrying the big gun. We've been right.

CEN: I think Tyra and I have both known some very confident men who were lousy lovers. I mean lousy, lazy lovers. I think sometimes size is less important than energy.

ROBYN: I knew a guy who was extremely confident, friendly, great personality, funny—everything, and he had the smallest penis I've ever seen in my life. I was like, "Wow." I was surprised. I didn't have sex with him.

REBECCA: Challenging that generalization, I think that some men try to make up for their size with confidence and by becoming real lovers who really please you.

CLEAN SHEETS:
Enough said.

TYRA: Absolutely.

CASSANDRA: The man who talks the most about how good he is is usually the lousiest lover. He is more concerned about his satisfaction.

KARA: I don't think size really matters.

ROBYN: Because too big is not good all the time. It's an aberration.

CEN: I don't like it too big. You don't want it painful.

SHERI: Of course a guy is always so intimidated by this issue. They don't know, actually, how they measure up.

GAYLE: They need an insecurity like this. Look at the things they have on us women, and we have only this one thing on them.

CASSANDRA: You know guys always think their penis is smaller than it is.

CEN: They look at porno movies and think that that is the size they should be. What guys are really like that?

CASSANDRA: I just talked to my boyfriend about this last night, and I was, like, "How do we know how big they are?" Guys don't look [at one another], you know. They see one another but really don't look.

ROBYN: They look when they are flaccid. So they really don't know.

CEN: I hate it when you ask a guy about another guy and you say, "Do you think he's handsome?" And he says, "I don't know if he's handsome."

REMI: They always do that.

REBECCA: You know how you look in the mirror because you compare yourself to the rest of women? We women look all the time. My guy and I appreciate women, and we appreciate men. I would just like to say that one of the reasons that my man is happy sexually is that we can watch beautiful women together. And I can say, "Do you think she's sexy?" And he says, "Yes, I do." And it is totally OK for him to watch her. We even look at the Playboy Channel together. I love watching with him because I get to reap the rewards. He's turned on. That's communicating. Getting that sexual energy with him is a real turn-on to me. That's really fine and healthy. He may feel that as long as I'm totally OK with that, he will never have to cheat because I'm not restricting him. He can look, appreciate, and get turned on by a woman in front of me, and that's totally OK. I love that.

KARA: Right. My ex-boyfriend and I still go to the strip bars.

CEN: Oh, men who like to bare their chests have no self-confidence. Especially if you have muscles and you feel you have to show them— you have no confidence.

ROBYN: Save the tank tops for the house only!

TYRA: What kind of underwear do you all like?

CHORUS: Boxers only!

TYRA: What's really bad in sex? And really good? Start with bad.

SHERI: Let me start. Some guys just don't know what to do. My boyfriend rubs me like he's starting a fire.

ROBYN: There are some guys who will touch your breasts and your clitoris and that's it.

CEN: They don't know that an arm, elbow, shoulder, and back are erotic zones. Legs, the back of the knee . . .

ROBYN: Why do guys think that your breasts can give you an orgasm?

TYRA: The more they rub, the more it gives *them* an orgasm.

REBECCA: I get turned on by my breasts being touched.

TYRA: I do, too.

CASSANDRA: I don't think it is just a matter of sensitivity. I think it is very important how they touch.

LIBA: But is it also about who's doing the touching?

TYRA: Totally.

CEN: This also comes down to whether you're just getting to know each other, because then he takes the time to look for those certain spots.

CASSANDRA: See, breast men know how to touch your breasts. Butt men know how to rub your butt.

REMI: You have to find a specialist for what you want.

KARA: Once you tell them what you want and how you want it, I think they are intimidated.

ROBYN: My guy turned out to be a good hand guy and not a good tongue guy, and then I just told him. Now he's good at both, so telling sometimes works.

KARA: It goes for women, too.

LIBA: I like to know what they want, and we should say what we like.

CEN: Every woman does not like to be spanked. OK?

ROBYN: Guys, tell your woman what you want because we don't want to be there all day. We'd rather be told and make it good, short, and sweet.

SHERI: Are you guys bold in bed? Do you like to talk dirty?

CHORUS: Yeah.

REBECCA: Who likes to tell fantasies?

CHORUS: We do.

ROBYN: A guy who can talk dirty is such a turn-on. Oh, my God!

REMI: Especially if he is not someone who talks dirty all the time.

BACK RUBS:
Give as good as you get.

REBECCA: Mine's a good Christian man who loves to talk dirty when we are in bed.

TYRA: Have you guys ever had phone sex?

ROBYN: You can't do a long-distance relationship without it.

TYRA: Yeah.

KARA: Of course it is really strange. You are talking and touching yourself and you open your eyes and spot your teddy bear looking at you from across the room and you think, "Nah. I can't do this."

CASSANDRA: As long as he doesn't expect it all the time, I'll do it.

CEN: If you are traveling and on the road all the time, sometimes you have to.

SHERI: What if they call you at work and talk dirty? I really start to squirm when they do that. I don't like it at all.

REBECCA: You know what my response is? "I can't get into this right now. Call me later."

SHERI: What's the biggest turnoff you've experienced?

TYRA: Too much talk in bed.

CEN: Kissing when the guy just rams his tongue down my throat.

ROBYN: A guy who can't kiss . . . a lot of saliva . . .

CASSANDRA: That is nasty.

GAYLE: Kissing gets better with time.

TYRA: Exactly, it's like everything else. You learn.

KARA: I feel that a lot of times if I'm mentally connected, our personalities click, and the chemistry is there from the beginning, and then, when we kiss, it is amazing. When the chemistry is not there, the kissing is always so-so.

REBECCA: I want to get something off my chest. My boyfriend is too concerned about breath all the time. Not mine, but his. He won't kiss me in the morning at all. I don't care about that. I've never smelled any bad breath. He doesn't have any body odor. But still he's so concerned about it.

CASSANDRA: Hey, that's good that he is concerned to give you only good smells.

REBECCA: He's going to kill me for this, but he'll get up first thing in the morning and go wash his mouth out.

SHERI: In Europe, where I lived for a while, it's almost like a ritual that most people just go to the bidet and wash before sex.

REBECCA: Well, while we're on hygiene . . . This is important to us, too. We always take a jacuzzi or a bath or shower together first.

KARA: I don't always clean first. You're in the mood and you're getting into it and you just got home from work—you took a shower

SINCERE COMPLIMENTS: Cool chicks can tell the difference.

that morning, and you're getting into it. How can you stop and shower?

REBECCA: If we know we are going to have a big night together, then we do. Sometimes the girl likes to make love, and sometimes it's nice to get nasty.

CEN: And to have your toes licked.

SHERI: Anything else unusual, not necessarily kinky, that you like? Such as strange positions or doing it outside?

REBECCA: We like watching . . .

TYRA: This is going into print, Rebecca.

REBECCA: . . . like, watching from afar, on TV or something.

ROBYN: It's a turn-on to do it in a place with a lot of mirrors.

TYRA: Watch out, you gals.

SHERI: How about sexual toys?

ROBYN: A vibrator? Maybe you'd get too used to it. I wouldn't want to get too used to it. Once in a while.

CEN: I like a man's anatomy. No toys. A man's anatomy and nothing else.

CASSANDRA: I like candles.

KARA: I like doing it in places where it is really risky and you might get caught. Not where little children are going to see it or anything like that . . . in the department store, in the dressing room. You are helping your boyfriend pick out shirts, trying them on, and you go in the dressing room and there's a knock on the door and . . .

ROBYN: I've always wanted to do it in an elevator. I've done it everywhere on my college campus—the library, the music practice rooms . . .

TYRA: I was going around with this guy in the sixth grade. We went to Disneyland, and we started fooling around, and over the loudspeakers they told us to stop.

SHERI: Is there such a thing as too much sex?

REMI: I don't think you should put rules on sex. Just go with the flow.

ROBYN: If a guy gets demanding and he wants it all the time, there is something wrong. You're not wanting to and he does. That means you're not sexually compatible. You have to be sexually compatible.

LIBA: Also, if you're doing it just to satisfy him, then that's wrong.

ROBYN: My boyfriend and I don't have sex too often because of our schedules. When we see each other and we do finally have sex, it is the best sex because we're so sexed up.

SHERI: Do you think that makes for better sex?

OPENING THE DOOR FOR HER: Chivalry is a lost art.

CHORUS: Oh, yeah.

SHERI: I think just the opposite—for me, anyway. When you really have a lot of sex, night and morning, you're very sexual. You want it more.

REBECCA: We go through phases where we just won't be that sexual, and it might be once a week or maybe every two weeks. Then all of a sudden, both of us start getting really turned on by something we're talking about or something we are doing. Or it starts on a vacation, and we just want to have sex three times a day. But it's not planned; it just happens. Over the last couple of weeks, we have just not been that sexual, either of us. We talk about it, too. "Are you feeling sexual?" Or, conversely, "Wow, I'm really turned on. Let's go."

SHERI: What are your favorite songs to make love to?

CASSANDRA: Just straight jazz for me.

ROBYN: I need to concentrate.

CEN: How about Sade?

ALL: That's very sexy.

TYRA: [joking] Barry Manilow.

REMI: "November Rain." That's a good song.

ROBYN: Channel 4 news.

KARA: I think something a guy should know is that a lot of women—probably the majority of women—don't have orgasms just from intercourse. It's surprising how many guys don't know that. I talk to my guy friends, and they say, "Really?" Most of them know the clitoris has some effect, but they think once they just touch it, it's stimulated and that's it.

SHERI: OK, I have a confession. I just don't like oral sex at all. I just feel like, "Don't waste my time."

CEN: I love oral sex, but I have to have regular sex afterwards.

ROBYN: My boyfriend—I've never been with a man like this before—can go three times in a row, just taking a little breather to clean up then go again. Sometimes, it's really sensitive, but he does it anyway because he knows I want to keep going. I have to say, "Stop, you don't have to go on doing that."

TYRA: Lucky girl. You get the last word.

SPONTANEITY:

Even the most rigid woman digs a surprise.

GIVING HER A TOOTHBRUSH:

Sometimes small things say it all.

CHAPTER 14

THE BIG "M"

Q: MY BUDDY ASKED ME TO BE HIS BEST MAN, AND I CAN BARELY AFFORD AIRFARE TO HIS WEDDING— WHAT'S MY MOVE?

In the old days the best man had two duties: (1) throw a bachelor party that ends with your friend and all his pals in a coma; and (2) come up with a five-minute speech that brings the wedding guests to tears. Now it means shelling out bucks for airfare, a tux, hotel stay, a gift, and, of course, the bachelor party. But remember: This is the guy who backed you up during that stupid bar brawl, helped you move your boxes of crap into the new place, and lets you hold the remote. You owe him. It's better to sell your own organs than let down your best friend on his big day.

Some will suggest talking to him about your cash problem ("he'll understand"). Wrong. Beg, borrow, or steal, but don't let him

AN ENGAGEMENT RING *SHE* LOVES: Remember—it ain't gonna sit on *your* finger for the rest of your life.

down or put him in an awkward situation where he feels like his buddy is bailing out on him when he needs you the most (he's clearly got enough problems as it is). Ask mutual friends to kick in, take on a temporary part-time job, or hock your goods—do whatever it takes to raise the dough you need.

If, on the other hand, the guy who asks you to be his best man isn't in fact such a close pal, tactfully decline. Tell him you don't have the money to plan what he deserves but that you'd be happy to help in other ways (assuming you are). Offer to be an usher, find entertainment for the bachelor party, drive relatives to the wedding, whatever. And then pull through. In *Miss Manners on (Painfully Proper) Weddings*, Judith Martin suggests that you tell him how "honored you were to have been chosen, how sorry you are that you cannot be in the wedding, and how much happiness you wish him." Piece o' cake.

No matter how you handle the situation, take solace in the fact that at least you don't have to buy a cotton-candy-inspired bridesmaid's dress for three hundred dollars.

BRING ON THE BACHELOR PARTY

Bachelor parties are powerful voodoo. Not just another drunken party, not a rite of passage, not a male-bonding experience. The mythical bachelor party is a talisman, meant to ward off a future of parent-teacher conferences and monogamy.

Since it never seems to work, the real-world bachelor party has evolved into a futile gesture to extend the free-spirited dominance of the single man into his next phase of life. That's a strong enough reason to allow the tradition to endure, even thrive, in the age of political correctness. Men are at their best, and their most fun, when making futile gestures.

The cardinal rule of bachelor parties: If a man has no trepidation about the institution into which he is entering, his bachelor party is going to suck. Regret, you see, is the key ingredient of a successful bash—regret on all levels by everyone involved. The bachelor regrets the chapter in his life that he is closing the door on. The best man regrets that his friend's social schedule will soon be littered with phrases like "I can't," "I'm busy," and "She won't let me." The single guests regret the loss of a comrade and fear for their own bachelor mortality. The married guests regret that they got married. All this regret generally leads to a great deal of drinking and commiserating, which is, of course, the point.

But booze alone does not a great bachelor party make. In fact, despite copious amounts of drinking, a large percentage of bachelor parties turn out to be pretty lame. Wine is fine, but it's actually proper planning, organization, and a healthy disrespect for societal values that will ensure a good time is had by all.

A great bachelor party starts with a great best man. Anyone contemplating marriage should remember this when choosing who will stand by his side at the altar. The best man should be selected based on his perceived ability to throw a bachelor party, not as a reward for past friendship or because he's a blood relative. It takes a friend, but it also takes a mix of smarts and sickness. Bart Simpson could throw a hell of a bachelor party. Charlie Brown could not. To be a great best man is to avoid the common pitfalls. For starters, do *not* . . .

1. INVITE RELATIVES.

This is probably the biggest rookie mistake made at bachelor parties. Hey, wake up and smell the stale beer! They won't be offended if they aren't invited. Hell, they don't even want to be there. But if asked, they will come because they feel obligated.

The bachelor will have plenty of time to pal around with dad and dad-in-law when he's married. Yeah, sure, his dad's really cool, but is he going to merengue with a hooker? Doubtful.

2. GO TO A STRIP BAR.

This is a special night. Do you really want to share it with the kind of people who frequent strip bars?

3. GO OUT TO A FANCY RESTAURANT.

Everyone's going to be drunk, and they won't be able to tell the difference between lobster thermidor and cold pizza. Besides, you're going to need all the cash you can get your hands on for girls, gambling and golf. You can eat anytime.

Too many bachelor parties go so far as to break all these rules in just one night. Thus, instead of feeling like bachelor parties, they sort of feel like, well, like going to dinner and a strip bar with dad. Except it's not your dad, and he doesn't pay.

A lot of best men go the opposite way, attempting to forge their place in history for the Most Original Bachelor Party Ever. They almost always fail.

This does not mean you should be afraid to try something new. Venturing away from home for a weekend-long fete is always a good idea, especially if you're heading for Vegas. Gambling and bachelor parties go together like gin and tonic water. International destinations like Mexico or the Caribbean are great, too, although you run the risk of ending up in a third-world prison. The language barrier can make negotiating with, say, a pimp difficult, and the next thing you know, you're being carted away by the *federales*. Resort hotels, rental homes, or even houseboats also make great bachelor party locales, as long as you remember the basics: broads, cigars, and free-flowing liquor. There's nothing wrong with spending the day golfing, skiing, going to a ball game, or off-roading in rental cars. Any of these activities will help you regain your sea legs for the next night of partying.

Many one-night variations on the bachelor party can be respectable, as long as libations and entertainment abound. Charter a bus, like the ones rock stars use, and take the party on the road, from bar to bar and town to town. Rent a hotel room or the private area of a particularly debauched haunt.

Regardless of format, bachelor party attendees have several traditions to uphold. If this means the crowd might nurse a few hangovers, so be it. Some of the crew probably quit their wild partying ways after college or high school. Remember: The bachelor party is a device that forces them to relive those days (and remind them why they chose to stop in the first place). Party on, Garth!

Sex is an important component as well, but it's more often implied than undertaken. Most bachelor parties opt for a stripper or two, providing the men with vicarious pleasure and creating the atmosphere and illusion of sin. (Usually, the audience is more embarrassed than the performers.) More ambitious party planners might arrange for a bit of a show, going beyond what you could see down at a nudie bar. But with discretion being the better part of valor, few parties today encourage the guests to partake of the wares.

There is a simple test to determine what makes a bachelor party special. Consider the itinerary, and ask yourself, "Would his fiancée let him do this if they were married?" She probably would let him go river rafting. She might even let him go to a strip bar. But would she

AN UNUSUAL PROPOSAL:

People will always ask how you got engaged; don't blow the chance for a great story.

let him fly to Reno with friends who had arranged in advance for a lesbian sex show in the bed of a hotel room? Now *that* sounds like a promising bachelor party.

When you are planning, size is probably the most important consideration. With a handful of close friends, you can consider a weekend at the beach, a junket to Caesar's Palace, or a golf trip. With forty people, you can't—you're better off with a hotel room, some bottles, and a stripper. Cost also matters: While you might be happy to lay out a few hundred bucks for your best friend, will the rest of the guests? Find out before you rent the bus.

Women, fortunately, do not understand bachelor parties. This is evidenced by their pathetic attempt at revenge: the bachelorette party. Let's face it—have you ever heard of a soon-to-be husband losing sleep because his fiancée is nursing an Amstel Light in front of the Chippendale dancers? The only reason women even have the damn thing is to try to get back at us. Have you ever heard of women going to Tijuana for a bachelorette party? Pictionary is more like it.

The bachelor party is a license to behave badly. Even the most prudish fiancée can't forbid her soon-to-be husband from attending his own bachelor party. Wives-to-be employ a "don't ask, don't tell" policy when confronted with the big night. The bachelor party is sacrosanct, off-limits, and, by nature, deviant. There is nothing you can't do. And therein lies the rub.

All this freedom is a big lie. Bachelor parties, like nuclear deterrence, operate on the principle of mutual assured destruction. In theory, the groom can do whatever he wants. In practice, if he comes home with a grin and announces, "Honey, the party didn't end until we ran out of rubbers," he immediately ceases to be a groom. There is a line that the groom should not cross, or else he should not be getting married.

So if it is his special night, what exactly does the prospective groom get out of all this? Something he probably never had before and certainly will not have after the wedding, and it has nothing to do with sex or booze, which, hopefully, he will continue to enjoy frequently. No, instead he spends a day or a weekend learning how the Sultan of Brunei lives. He wakes up in the morning and does whatever he pleases. Everyone with him does whatever he wants. He has handlers. He doesn't carry money. He doesn't carry a hotel key. He doesn't drive. Nothing is too good for him, nothing is too bad for him, and nobody says "no" to him. Whatever direction the party takes, whether the group is eating, drinking or sleeping, it's all about him.

PATIENCE:

No matter how much you think you have, planning the big day will push you to your limit.

That's the essence of the bachelor party. The wedding reception is for the mother-in-law. A week from now your pal will be working the room, shaking hands with relatives he did not even know he had. But not today. No matter how low his rung on the social ladder, he gets to be the king. That's really why the underlying theme of the party is regret. There are lots of things waiting in his new life that will bring him joy, and hopefully he'll never regret his choice to take a bride. But he will regret never again getting to be the king.

THE SAVVY WEDDING GIFTER

Consider this an official heads-up: Most married couples can cite at least one gump who gave them a really stupid wedding gift. Not every guest, of course. In fact, most people come through. The tragedy is that giving a great wedding gift is easy as long as you follow some basic rules.

♦ Don't think you're "boring" if you give the couple something they registered for. It's not cheating to give a couple something off their bridal registry. Registering is an engaged couple's version of a letter to Santa: these are the things they want, these are the things they need, these are the things you—unless you have a very good reason not to—should get them. (And spend a few extra bucks and have the gift delivered; it saves the couple the hassle of dealing with it at the reception.)

♦ Don't give something they'll only pull out when they have you for dinner. Taste is a funny thing—which is to say that you may not have any. Unless you know the couple and their likes and dislikes really well, resist the temptation to give something like a print, a sculpture, or a velvet painting of the NASCAR driver Jeff Gordon. And be wary of giving your own creative handiwork. Things like poems, paintings, and songs can be touching, but they can also be awful if the giver is not really talented. A compromise—write that poem, but wrap it around a good set of ice trays. Everybody needs ice trays.

◆ Give money. Money is a funny thing. To some people it's the *only* gift to give, while to others it's never given. Ask around.

How much to give? Unfortunately, there is no easy answer. One old rule of thumb says that you should give a gift worth roughly what the couple is spending on you—a hundred-dollar gift, for example, if the couple is spending fifty dollars a plate on you and your guest. In the end, however, it all really comes down to your conscience and your own financial situation. If you're broke, any couple will understand a smaller gift.

Cash is the Chinese food of wedding gifts. It's absolutely great—it'll pay for the Mexican honeymoon—but a few months down the line your friends may have to remind themselves that yes, you did actually give a gift. They just spent it on tequila.

◆ Be imaginative (but not too imaginative). Some of the best gifts are things they don't register for: a night at a bed and breakfast, a tent, a power drill. Be as creative as you want—tickets to the opera, a week of dog-sitting, really good gum—just be sure it's what the couple wants. Don't be afraid to ask in advance.

◆ Go in with somebody else. One frustration newlyweds sometimes find is that they get five $50 vases when what they really need is one $250 VCR. Call some friends and see if they want to go in a gift with you. Not only will it allow you to get something really nice, but if you play your cards right, you can get the other person to do the shopping. Few things are better than that.

OFFER TO PAY FOR SOMETHING: The band, the rehearsal dinner . . . the day of the dowry is done.

THE DEBEERS "HOW TO BUY A DIAMOND RING" BROCHURE: For when the untimely time comes.

KNOW YOUR CARATS FROM YOUR CARROTS

Getting engaged is one of the most momentous occasions in a guy's life, and not just for that "I've found the woman of my dreams" stuff: never again will you spend so much money on an object you know so little about.

Diamonds might be a girl's best friend, but buying one can be a guys worst nightmare—when it comes to rocks, most of us have them in our heads. Cars we can handle. Computers? Stereo systems? No problema. You're not alone, however, if you feel more qualified selecting nuclear weaponry for the Defense Department than buying your wife's engagement ring.

With a little homework and planning, however, buying a ring doesn't have to be such a terrifying proposition. Here are some suggestions to help you as you navigate through a sea of smiling bald men with magnifying glasses:

1. STICK TO YOUR BUDGET.

The ancient guideline, quoted gleefully by jewelers, is that the ring should cost two months' salary. Now here's a little secret: few people shell out that much. (Sorry, ladies.) There is no "right" amount of money to spend on an engagement ring. It's obviously going to cost, but you need to come up with a number that fits into your budget—then stick to it. If the salesman tries to guilt-whip you into spending more with canned lines like "You know, this is a once-in-a-lifetime purchase," beat him about the head with your shoe. You're the customer; you decide how much you're going to spend.

GET RID OF THE BLACK BOOK: Once the ring goes on, you don't need the number of that sure thing.

2. FIND OUT WHAT SHE LIKES.

Engagement rings come in more styles than Hillary Clinton's hair, so it's important that you choose a diamond shape and ring setting that your bride-to-be likes. The easiest way is to bring her with you when you go shopping. It may not be very romantic, but an estimated 75 percent of buyers do it. If you prefer that the proposal be a surprise, do some detective work—call her best friend; pay attention when she looks at other women's diamonds.

While you're at it, find out her ring size. Steal one of her favorite friendship rings for a day. Or if that's impossible, err on the large side. Nothing spoils the thrill of being engaged more than if your fiancée has to wear her new diamond on her pinkie (unless she looks like Joe Pesci, in which case you've got other problems).

3. BECOME A DIAMOND HEAD.

The more you know about diamonds, the better off you'll be. Carat weight counts for a lot, but as with other parts of your marriage, size is not everything. Equally important are factors that affect a diamond's brilliance. These include the following:

COLOR. This is measured on a scale from D to Z+. "D" diamonds have the least color and cost the most; "Z" diamonds are the most yellow and cost the least.

CLARITY. This is the degree to which the stone is free from internal and external marks. Diamonds receive one of eleven grades, ranging from F1 (flawless) to I3 (least perfect).

CUT. Diamonds with appealing proportions are worth more than those that are lopsided. A rule of thumb for round diamonds: the stone's depth should be between 55 percent and 65 percent of its width.

Most buyers try to split the difference, opting for a better diamond that's slightly smaller rather than a golf ball that looks like it's been run over by a car.

4. DON'T BUY FROM EDDIE, YOUR DENTIST'S BROTHER-IN-LAW WITH THE "DEAL."

The hardest part of buying a diamond is the fear that you may be spending five thousand dollars on a lovely piece of rock salt. To ensure that you're not being taken, deal with an established jeweler— preferably one where the salespeople are "diamond-certified" or, even better, qualified gemologists.

5. COMPARE APPLES TO APPLES.

No two diamonds are exactly alike, so comparing prices from store to store is not as easy as with mass-produced items like VCRs. Still, you can shop around if you measure stones of similar size and quality. If a jeweler is trying to sell you a one-carat diamond with a G color and VS1 clarity, for example, visit some other jewelers and ask how much they'd charge for a rock with those specifications. Shop around—then take the plunge.

DISPOSABLE CAMERA:
See what a good time your guests had while your new father-in-law was footing the bill.

CHAPTER 15

OTHER STUFF WE THINK YOU SHOULD KNOW

Q: HOW DO I KEEP MY CITY BIKE FROM BEING RIPPED OFF?

You just drained your savings account for that neon green Stump Jumper. Now your friends think you're crazy because you duck outside every fifteen minutes to check up on it. Relax. Here's how to keep your two-wheeled dream machine from becoming another statistic.

YOU'RE NOT PARANOID

While crime is declining around the country, more bikes than ever are getting ripped off. FBI records show a 13 percent increase in bike theft from 1991 to 1995. Always keep a copy of your serial number and receipt, since most police departments require both when reclaiming a bike.

ENTER, THE QUADRA

It weighs five pounds, costs about a hundred dollars, and if you lose your key, you'll need to find a locksmith with industrial equipment to get it off. New York City bike messengers have been using the St. Pierre QuadraChain, a massive square-link monster, since 1990. The hard-to-find Quadra can be ordered directly from St. Pierre Manufacturing (800-926-2342). To carry the weight evenly, messengers wear the chain around their waists, clipping it with a carabiner D-clip. Kryptonite now sells a similar product called the New York Chain (about $100), which has a different type of lock. Messengers will also use a second heavy-duty U-lock—the Kryptonite New York Lock ($75) or Specialized's Hard Lock ($45)—to secure the front wheel to the bike frame.

LOCK SMART

Always double-check that your chain or U-lock runs through the bike frame. Before locking up, shake a pole to make sure it's firmly anchored in concrete, and remember that thieves can unfasten street signs and lift your bike over in a New York minute.

TAKE IT WITH YOU

Take your seat and front wheel with you. If you can't, fit hose clamps or padlocks over quick-release levers, and lash down the seat by running an old chain or a cable through the seat rails. Solder down the stem bolt so nobody snatches the handlebar assembly. And disguise the bike by winding strips of old inner tubes tightly around the frame and securing the ends with tape.

FIND A "BEATER BIKE"

Even locked up like Fort Knox, bikes can be vandalized by frustrated thieves. If you can't live without the new bike, find yourself a second-rate machine to ride at night. Look for one in a thrift store, or put it together out of discarded parts. But never, ever buy a stolen bike, no matter how low the price.

Word
www.word.com
Ingenious. Elegant. Original. Enough superlatives for you? More than any other site, *Word* brings the best of the new-media gestalt to stories and art pieces on current issues and culture. Much emphasis placed on the site's look, as you'd expect—it's intuitive and atmospheric all at once—but also contains pieces written with care and intelligence by top writers. Go to the site with an open mind. Gaze at the future. What more could you want in a cyberspace zine for the next century?

Salon
www.salonmagazine.com
A simple fact: writing rules. And *Salon* was founded by writers and journalists who felt that the print medium left them wanting and were willing to try to create something literate for a medium founded on bells and whistles. Whether describing the "burnouts and mystics" of a Denis Johnson novel or reporting on the alterna-health craze surrounding blue-green algae, the writers at *Salon* pen pieces worthy of the best print pubs. In an age of aimless "interactivity" and "multimedia," *Salon* treats this new medium with respect—using its unique capabilities when warranted (as in a series of word games) and sticking more often than not with text (as in its book and movie reviews, travel pieces, and media commentary). If the Web ever produces a publication with the cachet of the *New Yorker, Salon* will be it.

Q: HOW DO I FIND A WINGMAN?

It's not hard to find a proud breast man. Or even an avowed leg man. But a wingman? That's a different story. After all, with the woman of your dreams draped over that bar stool, what kind of guy can you trust to bring along?

For the uninitiated, a wingman serves as the bridge between you and the night you'll never forget. He might be the guy who hooks up with her less savory friend. He might stand by your side and provide a well-timed quip during that excruciating first conversation. Or he may just provide company in case the field runs dry.

But picking such a person requires consideration of a few sensitive points, issues best guided by experience, history, and the ultimate font of wing wisdom, the 1986 film *Top Gun*. Follow these wing tips and you'll be flying high.

LIKE YOU, ONLY WORSE

Tom Cruise's Maverick offers the first vital tip: "What you want to get is a wingman who can stay up with you, who can match you move for move." In other words, a wingman is not a bumbling sidekick; he is not Dean Martin's Jerry Lewis or Don Quixote's Sancho Panza. He should not tell dirty jokes, pick his nose, or otherwise repulse. Remember, regardless of how good he might make you look in comparison, women judge men by the company they keep.

Still, make sure your wingman knows his place. If the woman starts shooting him vibes, will he try to step up to the helm? To prevent this common disaster, pick a pal who's garrulous but not overbearing; funny but neither more witty nor less obnoxious than you. Pick someone who's charming as hell but who has a girlfriend. But whatever you do, don't let your wingman outshine you.

A FRIEND IN NEED

If your wingman starts to act up, don't get caught up in the competition; i.e., start talking trash and you're going to lose the girl, your wingman and, most importantly, a buddy. He shouldn't look bad, merely lesser. Consider how you feel when talking to two women: by the laws of comparison, whoever you view as the more attractive probably wouldn't look quite as hot standing on her own. The same rule holds for women talking to you and your pal.

With that in mind, try to find a wingman whom you consider a good friend. It helps if he knows people and can facilitate introductions, or if he's familiar enough to drop your accomplishments into conversation, as in, "Hey, Bob, did you remember to dust off your Heisman Trophy last week?"

WOMEN AND GAYS ENCOURAGED TO APPLY

Recruiting a female to accompany you to a bar or party confers a number of benefits: It shows you're comfortable with women—it may even spark a jealous twinge. And presumably, your friend won't try to win the woman for herself. The obvious disadvantage is that other women may regard you as taken. That notion can be dispelled quickly enough, however, and few women deny the allure of an ambiguously single man.

Another way to minimize girl-theft is to select a gay man to serve as wing. But make sure he's not a covert bisexual and thus just as likely to woo her for himself. . . .

PRACTICE

By far the best way to hone your wing-seeking, however, is through firsthand second-stringing. See what kinds of wing behavior women respond to. Deconstruct the difference between Romeo and Tybalt, Han Solo and Luke Skywalker. Then look for the kind of guy who naturally possesses the traits you discover. With a little practice and solid communication, you might find someone worthy of the bold declaration made by Iceman, a *Top Gun* stud, to Maverick: "You can be my wingman anytime."

MASTERING MARCH MADNESS

There may be no more important document that crosses your desk than your NCAA Tournament office pool sheet. Winning the contest

PointCast Network
www.pointcast.com
Turn off your browser and tune into PointCast—and "push" technology, with news delivered (i.e. "pushed") to your PC, constantly running in the background as you do your work. In the PointCast version of infodelivery, your news fix arrives in the form of separate channels for health, sports, and weather, with the content coming from CNN, the *Boston Globe,* Wired News, and other sources. PointCast functions as a screensaver, but with headlines and stock quotes—rather than fish or stars—scrolling across your screen. It's quick and efficient, if not terribly electrifying. For news junkies, or those weary of surfing the Web, it's hassle-free infodelivery. Is this the future of cyberspace? Quite possibly.

means a year's worth of respect from colleagues and superiors—no matter how frequently you miss those deadlines—and a few Andrew Jacksons to boot. Ineptitude invites snickers and scoffs, the first step to office Siberia. Let us help you navigate your way through the confusing March maze—and perhaps right into the winner's circle.

1. DON'T LET THE SEEDINGS RULE YOU.

They don't call it March Madness for nothing. The NCAA tournament is largely devoid of logic and reason. That's why we love it. Don't pick *solely* according to the seeds. There are going to be upsets—lots of them. Tiny schools with cartoonlike nicknames and players about whom you know nothing are going to slay some giants. Instead, look for teams who enter the tournament on hot streaks.

2. KNOW THE FIRST-ROUND TRENDS.

The first round is where easy points are made (and lost). There are also ramifications throughout the tournament, since teams that you nix—then win anyway—cannot score you points in later rounds. Since you know there will be upsets, play it smart when figuring where they're going to occur.

Start at the top. Since 1985, when the tournament expanded to sixty-four teams, no number sixteen seed has ever toppled a number one. Ever. That's 48–0. So don't even think about bucking the trend. Pick all the second seeds as well. Only two of them (Syracuse in 1991 and Arizona in 1993) have dropped a first-round game.

Third and fourth seeds aren't as lucky in their openers—they're 39–9 and 40–8, respectively, in the sixty-four-team format. This is when an underdog hunch can pay off, but it must be very attractive. Fifth, sixth, and seventh seeds are 35–13, 29–19, and 35–13, respectively, versus the twelves, elevens, and tens. Caveat emptor.

Then there are those number-nine seeds, which have a healthy historical edge (28–20) over number eights. That's a big advantage for you, since most rookie pool pickers invariably lean toward the lower-ranked squad.

Still unsure about some of the first-round pairings? Sponge from the knowledge of those willing to put real money where they're mouths are—check out the Las Vegas line. If a number thirteen is only a three-point underdog versus a number four, maybe your hunch isn't so crazy after all.

3. MIX IT UP IN THE FINAL FOUR.

The bracket may be able to protect its top seeds for the first couple of rounds, but after that, anything goes. If your Final Four picks are too heavy with number ones, chances are you'll be out of contention. Parity rules in college basketball these days: the differences between the first three or four seeds in any bracket are often microscopic. Since 1985 there has been only one Final Four (1993) with more than two top seeds. Conversely, don't get *too* crazy: only five of the forty-eight teams that have qualified for the Final Four since the field was expanded to sixty-four have been lower than fourth seeds. And just two of those (Villanova in 1985 and Kansas in 1988) have won it all. Six of the last seven national champions have been top seeds.

4. PLAY THE COACHES.

Until he led Syracuse to the final game last year, everybody thought Jim Boeheim was the worst coach in America: great talent, no results. Now he's a genius. But not all of his peers have been able to rehabilitate their reputations. Arizona's Lute Olson and his 22–18 tourney record aren't bad, but the Wildcats have had some pretty good teams during his tenure, and there are some ugly losses (the fourteenth seed in 1992, East Tennessee State, and the fifteenth seed in 1993, Santa Clara). Georgia Tech's Bobby Cremins (15–11) isn't a sure bet come tournament time, either. And stay away from Louisiana State and coach Dale Brown (15–14). Anybody who can lose a first-round game with Shaquille O'Neal in the middle has to be considered a risk.

As for the good ones, remember that Iowa's Tom Davis has never lost a first-round game. Duke's Mike Krzyzewski, Indiana's Bobby Knight, and Louisville's Denny Crum are other tournament masters. And give special consideration to Temple's coach, John Chaney, whose maddening matchup zone defense causes significant problems for many first- and second-round rivals.

5. DON'T GET EMOTIONAL.

You may be a proud graduate of Alley-Oop State, but don't ruin your pool by selecting the Fighting Geldings to win it all when they are an eleventh seed. Don't choose schools that you like; pick those that you think will *win*. Play the percentages, and take reasonable risks. It may seem odd to try and forecast Madness with reason, but it can work.

And pay off.

AudioNet
www.audionet.com
Like having a radio (or even a television) on your PC. News, music, and talk served up with on-demand (or live) audio and video. Yep, the quality—and speed—depends on your connection, but AudioNet's selection rivals what you'll find on the television: concerts, interviews, sporting events, press conferences, and full-length CDs.

Newsworks
www.newsworks.com
The biggies in newspaper publishing—Advance Publications, Knight-Ridder, The New York Times Company, and several others—cull the best of their stories through the day (and night), and present them for your infostarved self in packages such as "What Comes After Welfare?" and "Stunning Statements from Big Tobacco." It's the ultimate paradise for news junkies, with stories from more than a hundred daily rags.

BUY WHOLESALE

It's the Holy Grail of every crusading shopper who has a friend who has an uncle in the business. *Wholesale.* Just saying it is pleasant and soothing, generating thoughts of 30-percent-plus savings simply by removing the cut from the middleman (a.k.a. every store you've ever visited). For those in the know, however, wholesale is more than a dream, and you don't even have to be a merchant or play one on television.

Simply start by picking up the bible of savvy consumerism, *Buy Wholesale By Mail 1999.* The latest in a series of publications by the Print Project of Brooklyn, New York, this weighty volume is a dog's breakfast of assorted goods from *A* to *Z*—more specifically, from what they dub "Amish specialties" (wool skeins and embroidery floss) to zippers (if you're in need of a 108-inch fly, stud, this is where to look)—and all at sharply reduced costs. In need of snake-proof boots, spare faucet parts, or any of the fine products from Accordion-O-Rama? Find them here. And it's not just ticky-tack yard-sale clutter, either; the good folks at *Buy Wholesale* traffic in appliances, automotive goods, clothing, antiques, computer equipment, home furnishings, athletic equipment . . . anything you can think of and quite a few things you probably can't.

You cannot, however, procure things directly from *Buy Wholesale* (for which, ironically, you'll have to pay retail at your local book-monger); instead, what you have is a metacatalog of catalogs, some free, most a couple of bucks. Here are some of our favorites:

◆ Business attire (suits, jackets, pants, shirts, ties): up to 30 percent off from Jos. A. Bank Clothiers, 800–285-BANK.

◆ Health and fitness gear (stationary bikes, stair climbers, blood-pressure testers): 30 percent off from Creative Health Products, 313–996–5900.

◆ Luggage (attaché cases, leather accessories): 30 percent off from Jobson's Luggage Warehouse, 212–355–6846.

◆ Mac and PC Equipment (hardware, software, accessories): Up to 60 percent off from Dartek Computer Supply, 630–355–3000.

◆ Stereo Speakers: 40 percent off from Audio Concepts, 608–784–4570.

◆ Teak Furniture (armchairs, couches, armless divans): 30 percent off from Genada Imports, 201–790–7522.

The world's other great source of premium wholesale info is Wholesale Central (www.sumcomm.com), a publisher of wholesale-goods books and magazines like the *Directory of Wholesalers, Importers, and Liquidators.* These publications are produced specifically for the larger merchants you're trying to avoid in the first place. With unusual candor, though, it doesn't matter. Odds are they won't ask for a company name. Don't ask, don't tell, and, goddammit, don't pay full price.

One final catch, though: many of the wholesalers have minimum-purchase requirements. Buying in bulk often defeats the purpose of individual wholesale, so check ahead and make sure you don't get stuck with a big *caveat* right up your *emptor.*

HOW TO SPEAK ESPN

You slice your car through rush-hour traffic; your passenger turns and declares you to be "en fuego." You miss the trash can with your wadded ball of paper; you mutter, "Guh." You watch a running back sprint down the sidelines; your girlfriend declares that he "could . . . go . . . all . . . the . . . way—*buthedoesn't.*"

Yes, thanks to the catchphrase, now every moment can be just like a *SportsCenter* highlight, as you go "rumblin', stumblin', bumblin'" through your life. Learn them, live them, love them—with our dictionary of the all-time greatest ESPN catchphrases.

BACK-BACK-BACK-BACK-BACK. (CHRIS BERMAN)
The (mildly irritating) home-run call that started the whole catchphrase craze.

CAN I GET A WITNESS FROM THE CONGREGATION? (STUART SCOTT)
Scott's homeboy schtick helps *SportsCenter* to market to African-American audiences. "I'm comfortable doing it," Scott says.

Firefly
www.firefly.com
An ambitious amalgam. On the one hand, it's a community connecting you with likeminded cyberfolk; on the other hand, it's an adviser, recommending movies and music based on your ratings of films and bands. (Let's say you like Joe Henry and the Replacements. If someone else likes those artists, plus another—Cake, say— then Firefly recommends Cake.) From a self-populating database, a fertile stomping ground has risen from the bytes of cyberspace.

EN FUEGO. (DAN PATRICK)

Patrick began by uttering *"el fuego"* ("the fire") before his high school Spanish teacher corrected him.

GUH! (KEITH OLBERMANN)

The shortest catchphrase ever—for dropped passes and the like—and also packs the most punch.

HE COULD . . . GO . . . ALL . . . THE . . . WAY. (BERMAN)

Boomer's nod to Howard Cosell. Has gotten old—then again, so has Berman.

HELLOOOO! (OLBERMANN)

Olbermann's silly falsetto call greeted anyone who got crunched on ice or gridiron.

I AM AMUSED BY THE SIMPLICITY OF THIS GAME. (KENNY MAYNE)

Former Seattle anchor custom-made this one for Ken Griffey, Jr. home runs.

I DON'T KNOW WHAT THAT PITCH WAS, BUT IT *TASTES LIKE CHICKEN!* (MAYNE)

We asked and Kenny said no, he did *not* steal this phrase from the Leading Off section of *P.O.V.*

MIGHT AS WELL FACE IT, HE'S ADDICTED TO GLOVE. (RECE DAVIS)

The only good thing to ever come from a Robert Palmer song.

NO SOUP FOR YOU! (DAVIS)

Seinfeld meets *SportsCenter.*

RI-COLA! (MAYNE)

Trifecta voice-over is not, as many suspect, "Three-cola."

THAT'S 6–4–3 IF YOU'RE SCORING AT HOME . . . OR EVEN IF YOU'RE ALONE. (OLBERMANN)

Olbermann left Bristol for New York in part to do more scoring himself.

THE WHIFFFFF. (PATRICK)

Patrick's subtly brilliant strikeout line was a product of childhood backyard Wiffle ball games with his brother.

YOU CAN'T STOP HIM, YOU CAN ONLY HOPE TO CONTAIN HIM. (PATRICK)

One of sports' all-time clichés . . . now thankfully reduced to irony.

YOU . . . YOU'RE NOT GOOD. (CHRIS MYERS)

All-time great *Caddyshack* reference—rent it if you don't believe us.

YOUR PUNY BALLPARKS ARE TOO SMALL TO CONTAIN MY GARGANTUAN BLASTS! BRING ME THE FINEST MEATS AND CHEESES FOR ALL MY TEAMMATES! (MAYNE)

The last—and longest.

RIVERSIDE SHAKESPEARE: Better proof you went to college than your diploma.

DAYLIGHT SAVINGS TIME: Because "fall-ing back" feels so relaxing.

FRIENDS: Priceless.

INDEX